Group Work
Building global connections to restore hope
in a fragmented world

Proceedings of the 41st and 42nd
International Symposia on Social Work with Groups
June 5-8, 2019
New York University, New York City, USA
June 17-20, 2020 by Virtual Platform

Group Work:
Building global connections to restore hope in a fragmented world

Edited by
Jennifer Currin-McCulloch and Greg Tully

w&b
MMXXIII

© Whiting & Birch Ltd 2023
Published by Whiting & Birch Ltd,
Forest Hill, London SE23 3HZ
ISBN 9781861776440

Contents

**Proceedings of the 41st and 42nd
International Symposia on Social Work with Groups
June 5-8, 2019, New York University, New York City, USA
June 17-20, 2020 by Virtual Platform**

Acknowledgements

Proceedings of the 41st and 42nd
International Symposia on Social Work with Groups
June 5-8, 2019, New York University, New York City, USA
June 17-20, 2020 by Virtual Platform

41st Symposium IASWG Honoree
Andrew Malekoff

42nd Symposium IASWG Honoree
Dominique Moyse Steinberg

41st and 42nd Symposia IASWG Planner
Emily Santonocito

The 2019 and 2020 Symposia each had their own flavor, with 2019 being held in-person at New York University, and 2020, as a result of the COVID-19 pandemic, being held virtually (2020 marked a new beginning for the organization in its launch of a virtual symposium); whether in-person or virtual, both events gave us the opportunity to connect with friends, old and new, bringing renewed energy and support in navigating life in a global environment.

Throughout the planning and implementation of both symposia, Emily Wilk (IASWG's Symposium Planner) created a seamless experience for participants whether in-person or virtually, helping to successfully envision each conference by balancing participants' needs for belonging, knowledge, and safety.

Tremendous gratitude to the Symposium Planning Committee members who crafted two symposia that addressed the needs of our global group work community, and offered opportunities to nurture knowledge and friendships, both old and new. Energy radiated throughout the symposia sessions, as well as hope for the role that social group work can play in supporting our global communities. Our sessions also would not have been possible or as fruitful without the help of our symposia volunteers, so thank you them for sharing their time and enthusiasm with us. We would like to acknowledge

Barb Muskat, President of IASWG, for her effective leadership of the organization and stellar oversight of both the 2019 and 2020 symposia.

Finally, a special thank you to the authors and the publisher of this volume. The authors documented their work by sharing with us their expertise in the social group work, and David Whiting, our publisher, tirelessly supported the publishing of this IASWG Proceedings with his expert eye, attention to detail, and collegiality.

About the Editors

Jennifer Currin-McCulloch, PhD, LSW, is an Assistant Professor at Colorado State University, Fort Collins, Colorado, USA. She teaches group work courses at the bachelor's and master's level. As an oncology and palliative care social worker, her group work practice is with individuals coping with a cancer diagnosis, and employs photovoice and solution-focused methods, art, cooking, journaling, and other forms of creative expression. Following her initial introduction to IASWG at the 2020 Symposium Jen has reveled in the opportunities to meet fellow group work educators and practitioners.
Email: jen.currin-mcculloch@colostate.edu

Greg Tully, PhD, MSW, is a Professor in Social Work at West Chester University, West Chester, Pennsylvania, USA. He also teaches courses for the Silver School of Social Work at New York University, has been a faculty member at both Iona College and Barry University, and has taught courses at the Hunter College Silberman School of Social Work. He has presented internationally, and published books and articles, including contributions to the Encyclopedia of Social Work with Groups, the Journal of Teaching in Social Work, Groupwork, and Social Work with Groups. He is Past President of the International Association for Social Work with Groups. Email: gtully@wcupa.edu

About the Contributors

Samuel R. Benbow, D.Ed., is an Associate Professor, Department of Social Work & Gerontology, Shippensburg University (Shippensburg, PA, USA). He has spent decades working in higher education focusing on student development, multicultural education, and building community. He serves on the IASWG Board as the leader of the IASWG Membership Committee, he has presented at numerous IASWG symposia, and he continues to work toward enhancing the overall awareness and importance of group work in social work practice.

Christina Chiarelli-Helminiak, PhD, MSW, is an Associate Professor at Westchester University (Westchester, PA, USA). Her areas of research focus on women's rights, immigrant civic engagement, and the integration of human rights into social work curricula, and organizational factors that affect job satisfaction and burnout.

Shelley L. Craig PhD, LCSW, is a Full Professor at the Factor-Inwentash Faculty of Social Work at the University of Toronto. She holds a Canada Research Chair in Sexual and Gender Minority Youth. Dr. Craig's program of research focuses on cultivating resilience in marginalized populations through innovative, community-based interventions. Dr. Craig has developed and tested the first evidence-informed interventions for sexual and gender minority youth mental health and has created INQYR, The International Partnership for Queer Youth Resilience, which consists of five regional research networks. She has an extensive practice history working with marginalized populations.

Catherine Dugas, erg. M.Sc., est ergothérapeute au sein du Service des toxicomanies et de médecine urbaine du CIUSSS Centre-Sud-de-l'île-de-Montréal, Québec, Canada. Elle collabore également à l'enseignement de l'ergothérapie à l'École de Réadaptation de l'Université de Montréal.

Michele Eggers, PhD, MSW, is an Assistant Professor and Director of the Bachelor of Social Work Program at California State University, (Chico, CA, USA). Her interests focus on human rights and justice related to Indigenous and women's rights, reproductive justice, environmental justice, globalization/Latin America, resistance, and critical social work.

Alkauthar Seun Enakele, PhD, is an avid researcher in the areas of domestic and intimate partner violence. He teaches social work and intimate partner violence content at Masaryk University, Brno, Czech Republic.

Éric Gascon, M.S.s., est spécialiste en activités cliniques au programme dépendance du CIUSSS Centre-Sud-de-l'Île-de-Montréal, Montréal, Québec, Canada. Il est aussi chargé de cours à l'École de travail social de l'Université du Québec à Montréal.

Elissa D. Giffords, DSW, LCSW, is a full Professor, and MSW Director at LIU Post (NY, USA). She enjoys teaching, advising students, producing scholarly research, and participating in service on and off campus. She serves on several community-based boards and committees including her role as Chair of the Nassau County Department of Social Services Advisory Council, and she is a member of the County Executive's Task Force on Family Violence.

Donna Guy, BSW MEd, is currently a Senior Lecturer in the four-year Bachelor of Social Work(BSW) program at Toi Ohomai Institute of Technology in Rotorua, Aotearoa, New Zealand. She teaches across both social work and group work, but social group work within an indigenous perspective is her specialist field and focus of her current research.

Gio Iacono, PhD, is an Assistant Professor at the University of Connecticut, School of Social Work (Hartford, CT, USA). His research focuses on LGBTQ+ youth mental health intervention development and evaluation, utilizing community-based participatory research approaches. He has a 16-year history of working in mental health.

John E. Imhof, PhD, LCSW-R, is former Commissioner of the Nassau County Department of Social Services. He is also the former Vice President of Behavioral Health Services for the Northwell Health System, and he is currently a member of the CN Guidance and Counseling Services Critical Incident Review Committee.

Teresa Kilbane, PhD, is an Emeritus Associate Professor from Loyola University Chicago, School of Social Work, where she retired in 2020 after 23 years on their faculty teaching research and policy to graduate students and doctoral students. She is an active member of IASWG where she currently serves on the Symposium Planning committee. She has presented at the IASWG Symposium for over ten years, most recently presenting an institute on the importance of research in evaluating group work practice.

Sangeun Lee, is a Ph.D. candidate at the Graduate School of Social Work and Social Research in Bryn Mawr College. Sangeun is a licensed social worker (LSW) and a certified case manager (CCM) who has been working with the Asian immigrant population since 2009. Sangeun's research is on bicultural and bilingual Asian human service workers, and their burnout with racially informed risk and protective factors, based on Asian critical race theory.

Kristina Lind, PhD, LICSW, is retired Associate Professor of social work at Plymouth State University, Plymouth, New Hampshire, USA. She now teaches group work as adjunct faculty at Loyola University, Chicago, Illinois, and St. Anselm College, New Hampshire. She continues her professional involvement with the International Association of Social Work with Groups and with the National Association of Social Workers.

Emily Loveland, is a Graduate Research Assistant and doctoral student at the University of Connecticut School of Social Work in Hartford, CT. She has over a decade of experience working in public service and administering state social services. Her research interests include using a human rights lens to explore food insecurity in the United States as well as LGBTQIA+ youth mental health.

Jaclyn McCarthy, LMHC, CASAC2, is the Division Director for Integrated and Mobile Treatment at CN Guidance & Counseling Services (Hicksville, NY, USA.) She has been in the mental health field for over 13 years, and she has been a key staff member involved in the growth of the agency and services provided to the community.

Rachael Pascoe, PhDc., MSW, RSW, is a SSHRC-funded PhD candidate at the Faculty of Social Work at the University of Toronto. She has worked as a facilitator of process groups for adults with concurrent disorders, and as the Clinical Evaluation Specialist for AFFIRM, an LGBTQ+ affirmative CBT group intervention for adolescents and adults developed by Dr. Shelley Craig and Dr. Ashley Austin. Her research focus and clinical practice concerns group therapy interventions for adolescent sexual abuse prevention.

Mamadou Mansor Seck, PhD, MSSA, is an Associate Professor at the Cleveland State University (CSU) School of Social Work (USA), and is currently the CSU Faculty Fellow for Civic Engagement. He has been teaching social work with groups in person as well as online for many years, and has published several articles on group work.

Elzahne Simeon, PhD, is a Senior Lecturer in the Department of Social Work in the School of Psychosocial Health, at North-West University, Potchefstroom, South Africa. Elzahne is teaching social work courses, including childcare legislation. Her field of expertise is children in need of care and protection (child protection), and she developed a program for street children.

Todd Tedrow, DSW, LCSW, is an Assistant Professor of social work at Barry University, Miami Shores, Florida, USA. Todd has been involved with the development of Narrative Therapy Group programs in various agencies as a method to build support and decrease social isolation.

Marie Ubbink, PhD, is an Associate Professor in the Department of Social Work in the School of Psychosocial Health, at North-West University, Potchefstroom, South Africa. Marie is teaching social work courses in social group work practice, and is instrumental in developing the Three Dimensional (3D) bullying group work program for students, parents, and teachers.

Ajwang' Warria, PhD, is an Associate Professor in the Faculty of Social Work, at the University of Calgary, Canada. Prior to joining academia, she worked in the counter-trafficking, migration, and child protection fields in sub-Saharan Africa. She continues to pursue intervention research interests on these and other emerging and intersecting themes.

Dedication

The editors would like to dedicate this volume to Dr. Ann Bergart. Ann began her professional education in social work in the School of Social Service Administration at the University of Chicago where she later returned to complete her doctoral degree. Ann has 20 years of practice experience in family service agencies where she trained and supervised students and staff in group work, as well as other modalities. She has edited two collective works and published numerous articles on group work in professional journals. She has been an elected IASWG Board Member, contributed greatly to various IASWG committees, and been an active member of the IASWG Illinois chapter.

Ann brings her creative spirit and passion to each group she encounters. An example of her visionary work is the development of the IASWG Social Work Group Camp, an event that celebrates an experiential approach to social group work. After COVID-19 halted in-person Group Camp activities, Ann worked alongside her fellow Group Camp partners to transform this offering to a virtual setting; thus, enabling people around the globe to participate and adapt to their regional group work customs. Colleagues cherish Ann's dedication, sense of excitement for everything she takes on, and her incredibly caring approach.

Of personal significance to the editors, Ann launched the virtual mutual aid groups during the 2020 Symposium. Her vision cultivated a network of global mutual aid groups to support group work educators and practitioners in navigating the teaching of group work in virtual formats. Ann's idea spurred a movement which has been invaluable in building virtual community, resources and friendships. These global virtual mutual aid groups have expanded over the past two years, and currently serve to enhance and extend social group work around the globe

Introduction

The title of this volume, *Group Work: Building Global Connections to Restore Hope in a Fragmented World*, suggests the potential for social group work to foster community healing across the globe in the midst of current social and environmental stressors facing all communities. The authors of the chapters in this volume represent the global presence of social group work educators, practitioners, and researchers.

This volume begins with a section of four chapters addressing global group work practice with youth as well as older adults, followed by a section of five chapters discussing group work in various global communities/environments. Next in this volume is a section with four chapters referencing effective group work interventions related to improving global academic and community environments, followed by a concluding section with a single chapter that focuses on evaluative practices in social group work contexts useful in any global setting. The following paragraphs in this introduction to the volume provide brief summaries of each of the chapters in the four sections of this volume.

The first section of this volume, with four chapters addressing group work practice with youth as well as older adults, opens with a chapter on group work by Gio Iacono, Emily Loveland and Shelley Craig, titled *Breaking down Barriers to Mental Health Supports for LGBTQ+ Youth through Group Work*, that shares content about the authors' intervention with lesbian, gay, bisexual, transgender, queer and questioning (LGBTQ+) youth. The authors used community-based participatory research methods to engage youth in discussions and activism surrounding their mental health needs, demonstrating strategies for integrating both micro and macro approaches to enhance a sense of belonging and well-being among youth who identify as LGBTQ+.

The second chapter in this volumes' first section, *Child Brides: Guidelines for a Norms-Based Group Work Intervention for Social Workers*, centers on the rights of young girls who are forced into child marriages. The author, Ajwang' Warria, guides the reader through the global literature on child marriage, incorporating social norm theory to elaborate on the processes that have led to an estimated annual rate of 15 million girls under 18 years being forced into marriage. The author portrays the harmful impact on the girls' physical and emotional health, as well as on their rights within their communities, concluding with a vision for how to design, recruit and facilitate a group for girls in forced child marriages with the goals of increasing coping skills, enhancing social support, and discovering new ways to express themselves.

In the third chapter in this section, *Uniting in Treatment and Refining Our Lives: Group Therapy Practice for Adolescents Who Sexually Harmed,* Rachael Pascoe and S.L. Craig describe their intervention with LGBTQ+ adolescents that reduced their risk for reengaging in sexual offending, identifying factors youth cite as reasons for their sexual offending, as well as the role of social group work in fostering psychoeducation about healthy sexual relationships and consent. The authors explain the Uniting and Refining Group Therapy Intervention, describe the activities used during each stage of the group work with the adolescents, and provide findings on their intervention that highlight group members' reduction in shame and increased feelings of hope.

The fourth and final chapter in this volumes' first section, *Using Narrative Group Therapy to Eradicate Social Isolation,* is written by Todd Tedrow, and it explores the experiences of older adults participating in a group intervention to reduce social isolation while living within a skilled nursing facility. The author describes a research study with a sample of older adults living in a skilled nursing facility prior to the pandemic in which an 8-week group intervention elicited narratives on their experiences that led to finding a sense of commonality, community, and hope.

In the second section of this volume, the five chapters discuss group work in a specific global community/environment, beginning with an informative chapter shared in French. Dans le chapitre, *Inclure des Exclus: le Récit d'un Groupe de Soutien Improbable Surune unité hospitalière de Toxicomanie et de Santé urbaine,* Catherine Dugas partage une intervention de groupe dans un hôpital pour patients hospitalisés à Montréal. Voici les mots de Catherine pour décrire l'objet du chapitre. Certaines personnes ayant un trouble d'utilisation de substances sont orientées vers le STMU afin d'encadrer de façon sécuritaire leur sevrage ou d'adapter les soins à leur réalité de consommation. Un des moyens préconisés par l'équipe psychosociale pour accompagner les usagers dans les changements souhaités est la mise en place de groupes de soutien bihebdomadaires co-animés par un des travailleurs sociaux et l'ergothérapeute. L'objectif de ce récit de pratique est de vous partager cette expérience de groupe que nous jugeons improbable et pourtant réelle afin d'encourager d'autres intervenants à surpasser les obstacles apparents et créer des espaces de soutien pour des personnes qui autrement seraient exclues des interventions de groupe.

The second of five chapters in this volumes' second section, written by Christina Chiarelli-Helminiak and Michelle Eggers, and titled *A Human Rights Praxis Approach to Group Work*, issues a call to action to social group workers to embrace their social work values and to fight for social justice and the rights of all individuals. The authors apply Wiseman's human rights praxis approach to group work to encourage the use of group work principles of conscious use of self, relationships, and participatory democracy. They situate the increased presence of police violence and murders, racial and transgender hate crimes, and human trafficking, amidst the global health crisis of the COVID-19 pandemic, strategically positioning group workers' interpersonal skills and use of self as instrumental in raising critical consciousness and creating social change.

The third of five chapters in this volumes' second section, *Identifying and Preventing Burnouts among Asian Identifying Social Workers* by Sangeun Lee, proposes that burnout among social workers has increased during COVID-19, placing our profession at risk for losing our treasured workforce. Lee introduces a culturally specific framework to fully illustrate the problem of Asian Americans experiencing increased discrimination, hate crimes, as well as health and mental health disparities since the start of COVID-19. The author explains that these factors, coupled with a small workforce, have placed bilingual Asian social workers at increased risk for burnout. The chapter concludes with suggested opportunities for bilingual Asian social workers to enhance the well-being of their communities and their own careers.

The fourth of five chapters in this volumes' second section, *Domestic Violence against Men in Africa* written by Alkauthar Seun, encourages group workers to consider the complexity of the role of group work in working with men in abusive relationships, presenting findings from an interpretive phenomenology study that explores the experience of men in Ondo-state Nigeria who live within an abusive relationship with a female partner. The study reveals how factors such as culture, socialized gender roles, and the patriarchal structure influence men's experiences and ability to seek social support. The author suggests that three key essences of the men's experience include unemployment, power and control, and perceived infidelity, and concluding with a cultural/clinical call to action.

The fifth and final chapter in this volumes' second section, *Applying the Collectivism-Individualism Framework for the Data Analysis of a Rapid Rural Participatory Research Methodology,* is written by Mamadou Seck, and it focuses on African communities, describing a rapid rural participatory research methodology used to examine the needs of women from several villages in rural Africa. Citing the study's framework and the relationship between the individual and the community, the author reveals how social workers from several African schools of social work led focus groups with Senegalese women within four villages in the region of Thies to discover the women's perspectives of what their communities needed to survive. The study's findings expose unique and overlapping needs within the villages that are influenced by gaps in systems of education, occupation, healthcare, and water, power and traffic infrastructure, concluding that collective orientations may influence the desire to promote the well-being of the community.

The third section of this volume, with four chapters referencing effective group work interventions related to improving academic and community environments, begins with a chapter titled *A Community-Academic Partnership: A Successful Inter-Organizational Group Effort to Improve the Delivery of Government Social Services.* The chapter's author, Elissa Giffords, portrays the strength of social group work in building community-academic partnerships to support the well-being of community members who receive services at their local Department of Social Services. In the chapter, Giffords portrays the roles, skills, and connections of each member of the partnership, including the community organization and the academic partner, to illustrate how they were able to solicit funding to create a research design that enabled recipients of services at the local Department of Social Services to share their concerns and unmet needs. The author suggests that the model presented in the chapter can be incorporated by other communities to foster the well-being of their residents.

The second chapter in this volumes' third section, by Donna Guy, titled *Working with a Māori Model of Social Work Practice: An Experiential Lens to Support Knowledge Transfer for Students,* demonstrates the extensive knowledge base that Guy brings to experiential learning within the group work classroom. She summarizes the literature in experiential learning theory while applying it to the classroom context with a step-by-step description of classroom activity, including the roles and responsibilities of the instructor and students. The application of theory to practice fosters the students' ability to further understand a model of health and wellbeing among the Māori peoples of New Zealand. Guy suggests that group work educators can apply this method within their communities through the integration of their culture's model of health and well-being.

In the third chapter in this volumes' third section, written by Elzahne Simeon and Marie Ubbink, and titled *Group Work Practicum Education: A Community-based Anti-bullying 3D Group Work Programme to Create Hopeful Outcomes in Primary Schools*, the two authors share an example of how their social work program created a student internship program in their school system that supported anti-bullying in elementary schools in South Africa. The authors provide context about their university's social work program, group work education models, and student internships. Their 3D Anti-Bullying Programme brings together children, parents, and teachers through a collaboration with the social work program, a social welfare organization, and the local community schools to reduce bullying. The authors supply readers with precise details about the program, including the topics for all of the group sessions and the final group session's content on termination and evaluation.

In the fourth and final chapter in this volumes' third section, the author, Samuel Benbow, provides insight on how individuals with intellectual and developmental disabilities (IDD) face discrimination and stigma that creates longstanding emotional and social harm, pointing out that social isolation is common for members of the IDD community. Benbow describes a successful academic and community partnership endeavor focused on community members with IDD called the Inclusive Basketball Club, a community/group endeavor that used a fun basketball group work intervention to bring together local university persons, individuals with IDD, IDD families, as well as various community members. Case examples, recruitment guidance, and group rules are described within the chapter to enable the reader to gather ideas implementing a similar community program.

The fourth and final section of this volume includes one chapter, penned by Terri Kilbane and Kristina Lind, titled *Evaluation of Group Work Practice: Status, Need, and Recommendation*. The chapter focuses on evaluative practices in social group work to provide supportive content to social group work instructors and practitioners that may enhance their group work evaluative processes. The authors guide the reader through the history, theory, and methods of group work evaluation, including specific examples of how to integrate different evaluative research designs into group work practice, Their chapter provides concrete methods for group workers to integrate evaluative strategies into their practice, highlighting the value of discovering the influence of our group work interventions on clients' well-being.

Breaking Down Barriers to Mental Health Supports for LGBTQ+ Youth through Group Work

Gio Iacono, Emily K. Loveland, Shelley L. Craig

Introduction

Lesbian, gay, bisexual, transgender, queer and questioning (LGBTQ+) youth continue to face significant health and mental health disparities (e.g., depression and suicidality) compared to non-LGBTQ+ youth, despite some recent systemic and legal progress. Moreover, LGBTQ+ youth are underserved in social work practice. There is also a dearth of literature focused on LGBTQ+ youth mental health and group work. This chapter aims to provide a critical self-reflective narrative describing group work with LGBTQ+ youth through community-based participatory research (CBPR). We explore how we may break down barriers to mental health supports for LGBTQ+ youth through group work, and ways it may foster greater global connectedness with others engaged in LGBTQ+ mental health activism. CBPR is an approach that links group work practice, research, and social justice advocacy by lifting and centering LGBTQ+ youth voices. This approach may not only help improve LGBTQ+ youth mental health, but it may also serve as a vehicle to generate collective consciousness to better address LGBTQ+ youth issues at the community and policy levels. We conclude with a case illustration of how an LGBTQ+ youth group member participated and engaged in micro-level group work and macro-level social advocacy. The case illustration highlights how social justice-oriented group work practice and research with LGBTQ+ youth can lead to individual mental health improvements, as well as the promotion of LGBTQ+ activism.

LGBTQ+ Youth and Minority Stress

Despite some systemic and legal progress related to LGBTQ+ rights, LGBTQ+ youth continue to experience significant challenges. LGBTQ+ youth experience mental health disparities, such as depression, anxiety, and suicidality, compared to their non-LGBTQ+ youth counterparts (Hatzenbuehler et al., 2012; Institute of Medicine, 2011; Mustanski et al., 2010; 2011; Paley, 2020; Russell & Fish, 2016; United Nations General Assembly, 2011). A recent national survey by The Trevor Project (Paley, 2020) found that nearly half of LGBTQ+ youth, and alarmingly, more than half of transgender youth in the United States have seriously considered suicide in the past year. LGBTQ+ youth may also experience exacerbated and compounding forms of oppression (e.g., racism, sexism, ableism, classism) because of their intersectional identities (Crenshaw, 1989; Logie et al., 2011). What is more, they are often overlooked and underserved in health and mental health research and practice (Dysart-Gale, 2010). A major gap also exists in the study of empirical group interventions for LGBTQ+ youth (Craig & Austin, 2016; Iacono et al., 2022).

LGBTQ+ youth also report experiencing more stress compared to non-LGBTQ+ youth, partly due to anti-LGBTQ discrimination (Russell & Fish, 2016). LGBTQ+ populations experience this type of stress, commonly referred to as minority stress (Meyer, 2003), in large part as a result of specific anti-LGBTQ+ bias and discrimination found within societal systems and institutions (Fredriksen-Goldsen et al., 2014). Robust evidence supports the significant link between LGBTQ+ minority stressors and the mental health problems LGBTQ+ youth face (e.g., Centers for Disease Control and Prevention: CDC, 2019; Cochran et al., 2006; Institute of Medicine, 2011; Russell & Fish, 2016). LGBTQ+ youth are also vulnerable to minority stress because of their internal identity competing with the dominant ideology of a cis/heteronormative society (Craig et al., 2021b; Meyer, 2003). LGBTQ+ youth may also have limited opportunities to develop coping strategies related to these identity-specific stressors (Austin & Craig, 2015; Higa et al., 2014). Given these inequities, together with broader organized legal and policy work from advocacy groups around the world, LGBTQ+ youth require early intervention efforts to ameliorate many of the documented mental health disparities they face.

As social workers and group workers, we have also observed that LGBTQ+ youth are particularly underserved in social work research and practice (Craig et al., 2021b; Iacono, 2019). We possess a deep passion to continue to develop more LGBTQ+ affirming ways of doing social work practice with LGBTQ+ youth that can lead to effective social change and global connection. Group work practice is a key approach to change for both individual lives as well as societies. We believe that the social support, shared experience, and group process components of group work are highly valuable to LGBTQ+ populations. We also deeply appreciate the way mutual aid transpires when individuals come together to support one another. As social workers, we knew that group work would be a fundamental component of our social work practice and social advocacy approach.

Group Work With LGBTQ+ Youth

The co-authors have worked with LGBTQ+ youth in groups for many years. Our group work efforts are international and aim to enhance a sense of global interconnectedness with others engaged in LGBTQ+ rights activism. Our work involves regularly collaborating with LGBTQ+ youth in conducting CBPR to build the evidence base for LGBTQ+ youth group interventions (Austin & Craig, 2015; Craig & Austin, 2016; Craig et al., 2021a; 2021b; Iacono et al., 2022). Building and sustaining the capacity to support the mental health of LGBTQ+ youth through group work is an important social justice endeavour that is being directly addressed through our ongoing group work research. Through much advocacy and systematically building an evidence base, this important work involves setting a foundation for placing the needs of LGBTQ+ youth on the national agenda in the United States and Canada.

Our research with LGBTQ+ youth in groups (specifically AFFIRM, a manualized affirmative cognitive behavioral intervention) has yielded significant improvements among LGBTQ+ youth in terms of depression, coping and overall mental health (Craig et al., 2021a; 2021b). We have also witnessed LGBTQ+ youth group members come to life within these groups, as they learn and discover practical approaches to addressing intersectional anti-LGBTQ+ stigma and discrimination in their personal lives, in their communities, and more broadly across their country. For instance, a fundamental component of our AFFIRM group curricula involves learning about and building skills to combat oppression from the micro level (e.g., coming out, important conversations with family) to more macro level (e.g., starting a Gay–Straight Alliance/Genders & Sexualities Alliance within schools, political advocacy, lobbying, coalition building). We have also witnessed numerous positive reports from LGBTQ+ youth who have completed AFFIRM groups, such as transitioning, increased political advocacy, changing their name to match their gender identity, coming out to family and peers, addressing victimization and bullying at school and work, forging new connections and community through an empowered state, and connecting to important community resources. It is truly remarkable to witness LGBTQ+ youth thriving and expressing their power and effectiveness in creating positive social change!

In our research work with LGBTQ+ youth, we have found that group work is an excellent modality to facilitate CBPR and social action. CBPR is a collaborative research and social action approach which we have found engages LGBTQ+ youth well (Craig, 2011). CBPR can help identify LGBTQ+ youth perspectives so that social workers and other professionals (e.g., teachers, parents, youth leaders, etc.) can better meet their needs and work towards social justice. CBPR may also help uncover and explore mental health barriers for LGBTQ+ youth. One of the ways this is achieved is by sharing power with youth as co-researchers (Olshansky & Zender, 2015). This ensures that the voices of the youth, who are often marginalized by being both LGBTQ+ and young, are lifted and incorporated into every aspect of the research process (Israel et al., 2010.). This approach helps contribute to a major goal of CBPR, which is to support empowerment among participants and contribute to the elimination of oppressive structures in society in alignment with a social justice perspective (Olshanksy & Zender, 2015). Ultimately, we have found that CBPR is an approach to research that is in alignment with social justice-oriented group work. In using group work and CBPR approaches, we have been able to collaboratively develop culturally responsive approaches to mental health group interventions (Austin & Craig, 2015; Iacono, 2022), which have supported macro-level efforts to support LGBTQ+ youth. The following sections will provide narratives of our approach to engaging with LGBTQ+ youth through group work.

LGBTQ+ Youth Group Members and Group Workers Unite in Solidarity

One of the most striking things we have witnessed as group workers conducting community-based group work research with LGBTQ+ youth are the rich and meaningful interactions among group participants. No matter what city, organization, or agency in which we have facilitated LGBTQ+ mental health groups, the crucial interactions among group members, the desire to participate in research to help make group work interventions more LGBTQ+ affirming and culturally responsive, the group process, and the exchanges of ideas and support are always remarkable to witness. While there are issues of oppression within LGBTQ+ communities, it is especially moving to see LGBTQ+ youth with diverse intersecting social identities come together to support each other.

We have come to realize that these interactions among diverse group members disrupt the old and re-imagine new ways in which LGBTQ+ youth want to exist and move through the world. For example, many LGBTQ+ youth link their challenges with mental health to larger sociopolitical issues and intersectional minority stressors. The level of articulation and understanding among these young group members of how larger systemic and structural oppressive forces negatively impact their personal lives is truly extraordinary. Many of the LGBTQ+ youth that come to our groups have endured great challenges, from familial and peer rejection, to racism, homelessness, severe abuse, complex trauma, hostile school environments, and significant acts of violence in their communities. In the group environment, we sit and actively resist pervasive discrimination and oppressive narratives that readily appear in our lives. Group members speak about how addressing and improving their mental health is a political act — an act of resistance, in that they refuse to let oppressive forces get the better of them.

Often group members speak from a place of deep pain and trauma; they often fundamentally understand that improving their mental health will support them in engaging more fully in social justice work. One group member spoke about the efforts they were making to improve their health and mental health (e.g., reducing alcohol use, spending more time with supportive friends, getting more sleep) and how their improvements in mental well-being provided them the energy to engage in community activism related to LGBTQ+

human rights. Once they were starting to feel a bit better and were stabilized, they began to participate in many protests, engaged more with politicians, and conducted online social activism. This particular youth reported that support and solidarity among group members were instrumental in their ability to take actions that lead to improved health and well-being. Although some youth that participate in groups engage in social activism, it is important to note that it may not be important for all LGBTQ+ youth.

Social Justice-Oriented Group Work

As discussed above, many LGBTQ+ youth who participate in our community-based group work research are engaged in and adopt a social justice framework to improve their own mental health and advocate for greater mental health supports for LGBTQ+ populations more generally. Segal and Wagaman (2017) call social justice both an ideology and a practice approach. Working in groups is an opportunity for members to engage in a critical consciousness and collaboratively explore how issues of oppression affect individuals and their common struggles. Group members can make and share space to critically examine how current macro structures and institutions may align with the unmet needs of LGBTQ+ youth. Thus, group work can be a space where social justice and macro-level change can move from principle to practice.

Hays et al. (2010) call for not only exploring critical consciousness within group work, which LGBTQ+ youth certainly have, but also having group leaders trained in community organizing skills so that individuals who are marginalized, such as LGBTQ+ youth, have the space within groups to develop necessary skills and wisdom for exercising power to effectively engage in social action. This is in alignment with the "social justice advocacy" dimension of the Social Justice Model to group work by Ratts et al. (2010). The Social Justice Model exists among a continuum, with five dimensions: naivete, multicultural integration, liberatory critical consciousness, empowerment, and social justice advocacy. Recognizing cultural diversity, and with the recognition of the sociopolitical roots of injustice, group members are empowered to engage in social advocacy on behalf of a common cause or issue identified by the group. The LGBTQ+ youth in our groups exemplified this by focusing on their well-being and self-care while simultaneously exploring ways to become more engaged in social advocacy in their communities. Indeed, the group setting acted as a holding place for these various processes to emerge and flourish. By seeking opportunities to engage in social advocacy, this process reflects the International Association for Social Work with Groups (IASWG) (2015) standards that group members, as well as the group as a whole, can seek changes to the external social environment.

We are present and engaged with LGBTQ+ youth in our groups, committed to the process of utilizing group work for broader social advocacy. Our group work with LGBTQ+ youth aims to collectively engage in the healing journey that blossoms into empowerment, critical consciousness and the capacity to effect change in society. In our groups, we have discussed that LGBTQ+ youth who cultivate mental health and well-being, and who hold the tools to engage in political work can flourish into adulthood and contribute to social change and social justice aims.

IASWG (2015) refers to *mutual aid*, the group dynamic consisting of multiple helping relationships that help group members achieve individual and group goals. Inherent to this is an intentional presence and a commitment to accompany group members on their journey to achieve their goals. While supporting the mental health of LGBTQ+ youth, our community-based group work research aims to leverage social action, which oftentimes resembles a modified version of the traditional Alinsky-style organizing (Wilkinson & D'Angelo, 2019). Alinsky-style community organizing is grounded in collective power, local leadership, and direct, at times adversarial, political action (Post, 2018). We have aimed to prioritize relationships, acknowledge institutional and structural oppression, engage in mutual learning and capacity building, while also utilizing traditional Alinsky-style social action (i.e., critically analyzing social problems, strategies to shift power). Aligned with group work principles (IAWSG, 2015), this process facilitates reflexive praxis that emphasizes partnership and collaboration, and leverages privilege to build social movements that address oppressive and structural social problems (Wilkinson & D'Angelo, 2019).

Group Work as a Bridge to Macro Social Work Practice

The nature of conducting community-based group work research with LGBTQ+ youth, in alignment with social justice aims, naturally lends itself to macro social work practice. Since the inception of social work as a profession, level of intervention has been siloed into "micro", "mezzo" and "macro", generating a tension that undermines the true integration of these methods (Austin et al., 2005). Knight and Gitterman (2018) indicate that instead of putting micro and macro social work practice into silos, group work in communities can naturally be merged into an integrated intervention of social work practice with groups that can lead to empowerment and change at both the individual and community levels. Social work education is designed to train social workers to cultivate skills that integrate macro or micro social work practice. Austin and colleagues (2005) call these "common skills" which can include relationship building, assessment, promoting the helping process and change strategies, fostering empowerment, and use of empathy.

Staples (2012) states that social justice is deeply connected to both community organizing and group work. For instance, using task-oriented groups, communities can organize and generate change through collective empowerment and self-advocacy. Knight and Gitterman (2018) indicate that groups formed to promote community change must engage in six tasks: recruiting members for collective action, acknowledging questions about the group worker's ability to be helpful, enhance members' critical consciousness, help identify strategies for community change, enhance the likelihood that members will be successful, and sustain the group's efforts over time. Each of these tasks requires both micro and macro social work skills to implement. While our group work with LGBTQ+ youth, on the surface, appears to be micro-level focused, as group workers we ground our work in facilitating empowerment and maintaining the goal of shifting mental health systems and policies to center the needs of LGBTQ+ youth. We work on meeting these goals with LGBTQ+ youth, through our ongoing collaborative development of group mental health programs, and by joining with LGBTQ+ youth in challenging oppressive systems (e.g., within their schools and communities) to support improved access to mental health care.

Furthermore, as LGBTQ+ youth congregate within groups and build supportive networks, they are better able to strategize and organize around collective social action within their communities and society at large. Staller (2010) states that different stakeholders define social problems which will directly impact how policy solutions are proposed. From a macro lens, conducting LGBTQ+ youth group work with social justice aims can help set the stage for agenda setting and problem definition *by* LGBTQ+ youth to inform macro social work policy practice, and to facilitate greater global interconnectedness for communities engaged in this political work. Thus, LGBTQ+ youth group work can lend to not only community-level interventions, but macro- level work by building policy agendas and advocating for change (Jansson, 2014).

Encounters Among LGBTQ+ Youth Group Members and Group Worker

The following is an illustration of how micro (i.e., focus on an individual group member's needs) and macro-level processes (i.e., supporting political advocacy) have simultaneously emerged in our community-based group work research with LGBTQ+ youth. This case illustration was chosen with the express permission from "James" (a research participant in one of our community-based intervention groups) and we disguised information to protect their privacy and confidentiality. As a group worker, I (first author G.I.) had a particularly moving experience with James, which directly speaks to a social justice practice perspective. I worked with James recently in one of our groups. James is 16 years old, biracial, identifies as transgender, and uses they/them pronouns. They have recently begun transitioning and are undergoing hormone therapy. James has also experienced significant family challenges, as their parents have been quite disapproving of their transition from female to male. We spoke several times about their father's antagonism towards them and the deeply painful impact of their experience of parental rejection. I witnessed such deep pain and suffering within James and my heart broke often when we talked. There would also be many moments in group where I would see a glimmer of hope in their eyes, once we had processed some of what they were experiencing (e.g., shouting matches with their dad, extreme isolation, feeling ganged up against by their mother, father and sibling, panic attacks) and had devised a plan of action.

During one group session, James appeared quiet and anxious. I will never forget the pain on their face that day, as they disclosed to me after the group that they were being kicked out of their family home and sent away to live with a relative in a rural region outside of the city. The devastation and fear that James held in their eyes was alarming. They reported that they would no longer have access to continued hormone treatment and trans-affirming healthcare. Frozen and despairing, they asked for my help in obtaining continued access to hormone therapy after moving. I remember feeling extremely empathetic as I experienced flashbacks of a 16-year-old version of myself with a similar look on my face. I wanted to offer support while also wanting them to feel that they had the strength and courage to address their needs, as well as the constant barrage of transphobia and racism in their life. I thought to myself: "How might I support their sense of empowerment and agency in this moment?" I made it clear that reaching out and asking for support was brave and an important step to help address their problems. We thoroughly explored several options and I created space for them to see the possibilities in their new circumstances. They were open to living with their relatives, but worried about their transition (e.g., hormone therapy) and the lack of social support outside of the city. Importantly, they were quite politically active and they worried that their work would be stifled while living outside of the city and being disconnected from their community. I was aware of a few affirming health clinics that they could connect to near their new home and was able to find an LGBTQ+ youth group accessible to them at a local school; we also explored the possibility of connecting to an affirming counsellor at a local hospital. In terms of their continued LGBTQ+ advocacy, we brainstormed ways to continue their work by joining a province-wide advocacy group for LGBTQ+ rights and connecting with those group members through online platforms. This plan was quite acceptable to James.

While working together, I felt that something had shifted in James — I sensed that they appeared more courageous. I knew that there would be many challenges ahead for them, but I could also see the way they demonstrated resilience, agency, and their ability to self-advocate. In those moments, I was reminded of the potency and importance of always bringing a social justice framework to group work and individual therapeutic work. As we link broader structural and systemic issues to a group member's life, we may be able to facilitate a sense of critical consciousness, empowerment and ultimately social change. In James's case, they connected with the appropriate health and mental health supports in their new community, and continued doing critical province-level advocacy work related to LGBTQ+ rights. It was deeply heartening and meaningful to accompany James through this process, to know that they will continue to be a strong advocate for the rights of LGBTQ+ communities, and will be a part of a global and intergenerational process of working towards social justice for all.

What I learned through these group work experiences, in a very embodied and compelling manner, was that addressing the immediate needs of marginalized communities is deeply political and can create a powerful ripple effect towards enhancing social justice work that builds directly from within the community. I also believe that transparency with LGBTQ+ youth and stakeholders is crucial. In our work, we routinely consider the input and feedback from LGBTQ+ youth and communities within a larger sociopolitical context. I strive to determine who we may not be serving in our group work due to accessibility issues, stigma and/or other unjust factors. I am constantly reflecting on ways in which we may be more flexible in our endeavors (without compromising efficacy) and modify activities to enhance accessibility and equity.

Concluding Remarks

The purpose of this chapter was to explore group work that aims to break down barriers to mental health supports for LGBTQ+ youth, and foster greater global connectedness with others engaged in this important political work (i.e., LGBTQ+ youth mental health). LGBTQ+ youth experience disparate mental health outcomes and group work (particularly the AFFIRM group intervention; Craig & Austin, 2016; Craig et al., 2021a; 2021b) has been found to help LGBTQ+ youth improve mental health outcomes. We have argued that CBPR is an important method in linking group work research, practice, and advocacy towards LGBTQ+ youth mental health supports, as well as broader related social justice aims. Group work that is embedded in a social justice context is inherently a bridge and vehicle for macro-level social work practice.

Our hope in community-based group work research and practice with LGBTQ+ youth is to achieve a ripple effect as we build community capacity to offer effective mental health supports for LGBTQ+ youth across various cities, towns, states/provinces and countries. The presence of these LGBTQ+ supports also sends a strong message to communities that LGBTQ+ people matter, and that their health and well-being matter. We see this approach as contributing to social reform and social justice aims — slowly and steadily unfolding over time and building momentum for these important group-based mental health initiatives. We engage and are passionate about this group work and research because it is very focused on meeting the *immediate* needs of LGBTQ+ youth who are suffering. It is also extremely political in that we strive to place LGBTQ+ youth issues on the national agenda, shed light on glaring disparities they may experience, and advocate for funding and resources to support this vulnerable youth population.

Ultimately, we are inspired by the LGBTQ+ youth that we work with and feel immense gratitude for the work we do within various communities. We are inspired and persistent because we do believe that positive change can occur. We have seen this change among the LGBTQ+ youth we serve through our group work practice and research (e.g., AFFIRM; Craig et al., 2021a), as they exhibit reductions in sexual health risk and depression, improvements in coping and well-being, and are better able to address stigma, discrimination, and oppression in their lives and in the broader sociopolitical sphere. Our reflections come from our collective perspectives as social workers, group workers, researchers, clinicians, learners, as well as trainers and clinical supervisors who support other practitioners and community stakeholders, locally and globally, to implement group work with LGBTQ+ youth in their communities.

References

Austin, M. J., Coombs, M., & Barr, B. (2005). Community-centered clinical practice: Is the integration of micro and macro social work practice possible? *Journal of Community Practice, 13*(4), 9–30. https://doi.org/10.1300/J125v13n04_02

Austin, A., & Craig, S. L. (2015). Empirically supported interventions for sexual and gender minority youth. *Journal of Evidence-Informed Social Work, 12*(6), 567-568. https://doi.org/10.1080/15433714.2014.884958

Centers for Disease Control and Prevention (CDC). (2019). Health disparities among LGBTQ youth. https://www.cdc.gov/healthyyouth/disparities/health-disparities-among-lgbtq- youth.htm.

Cochran, S. D., Sullivan, J. G., & Mays, V. M. (2006). Prevalence of mental disorders, psychological distress, and mental health services use among lesbian, gay, and bisexual adults in the United States. *Journal of Consulting and Clinical Psychology, 71*, 53–61. https://doi.org/10.1037/0022-006X.71.1.53

Craig, S. L. (2011). Precarious partnerships: Designing a community needs assessment to develop a system of care for gay, lesbian, bisexual, transgender and questioning (GLBTQ) youth. *Journal of Community Practice, 19*, 1–18. https://doi.org/10.1080/10705422.2011.595301

Craig, S. L., & Austin, A. (2016). The AFFIRM open pilot feasibility study: A brief affirmative cognitive behavioral coping skills group intervention for sexual and gender minority youth. *Children and Youth Services Review, 64*, 136-144. https://doi.org/10.1016/j.childyouth.2016.02.022

Craig, S. L., Eaton, A. D., Leung, V. W., Iacono, G., Pang, N., Dillon, F., Austin, A., Pascoe, R., & Dobinson, C. (2021a). Efficacy of affirmative cognitive behavioural group therapy for sexual and gender minority adolescents and young adults in community settings in Ontario, Canada. *BMC Psychology, 9*(1), 1-15. https://doi.org/10.1186/s40359-021-00595-6

Craig, S.L., Leung, V.W.Y., Pascoe, R., Pang, N., Iacono, G., Austin, A., & Dillon, F. (2021b). AFFIRM online: Utilising an affirmative cognitive-behavioral digital intervention to improve mental health, access, and engagement among LGBTQA+ youth and adults. *International Journal of Environmental Health Research and Public Health, 18*,(4), 1-17. https://doi.org/10.3390/ijerph18041541

Crenshaw, K. (1989). Demarginalizing the intersection of race and sex: A black feminist critique of antidiscrimination doctrine, feminist theory and antiracist politics. *University of Chicago Legal Forum: 1*(8), 139- 167.

Dysart-Gale D. (2010). Social justice and social determinants of health:

Lesbian, gay, bisexual, transgendered, intersexed, and queer youth in Canada. *Journal of Child and Adolescent Psychiatric Nursing, 23*(1), 23-28. https://doi.org/10.1111/j.1744-6171.2009.00213.x

Fredriksen-Goldsen, K. I., Simoni, J. M., Kim, H., Lehavot, K., Walters, K., L., Yang, J. & Hoy- Ellis, C. P. (2014). The health equity promotion model: Reconceptualization of lesbian, gay, bisexual, and transgender (LGBT) health disparities. *American Journal of Orthopsychiatry, 84*(6), 653 – 663. https://doi.org/10.1037/ort0000030

Hatzenbuehler, M. L., McLaughlin, K. A., & Xuan, Z. (2012). Social networks and risk for depressive symptoms in a national sample of sexual minority youth. *Social Science & Medicine, 75*(7), 1184-1191. https://doi.org/10.1016/j.socscimed.2012.05.030

Hays, D. G., Arrendondo, P., Gladding, S. T., & Toporek, R. L. (2010). Integrating social justice into group work: The next decade. *The Journal for Specialists in Group Work, 35*(2), 177 – 206. https://doi.org/10.1080/01933921003706022

Higa, D., Hoppe, M., Lindhorst, T., Mincer, S., Beadnell, B., Morrison, D., Wells, E.A., Todd, A. & Mountz, S. (2014). Negative and positive factors associated with the well-being of lesbian, gay, bisexual, transgender, queer, and questioning (LGBTQ) youth. *Youth & Society, 46*(5), 663-687.

Iacono, G. (2019). An affirmative mindfulness approach for lesbian, gay, bisexual, transgender, and queer youth mental health. *Clinical Social Work Journal, 47*(2), 156- 166. https://doi.org/10.1007/s10615-018-0656-7

Iacono, G., Craig, S. L., Crowder, R., Brennan, D. J., & Loveland, E. K. (2022). A qualitative study of the LGBTQ+ Youth Affirmative Mindfulness Program for sexual and gender minority youth. *Mindfulness, 13*(1), 222-237.

Institute of Medicine. (2011). *The health of lesbian, gay, bisexual, and transgender people: Building a foundation for better understanding.* The National Academies Press.

International Association for Social Work with Groups, Inc. (IASWG) (2015). *Standards for social work practice with groups, 2nd edition.* https://www.iaswg.org/assets/docs/Resources/2015_IASWG_STANDARDS_FOR_SOCI AL_WORK_PRACTICE_WITH_GROUPS.pdf

Israel, B. A., Coombe, C. M., Cheezum, R. R., Schulz, A. J., McGranaghan, R. J., Lichenstein, R., Reyes, A. G., Clement, J., & Burris, A. (2010). Community-based participatory research: A capacity-building approach for policy advocacy aimed at eliminating health disparities. *American Journal of Public Health, 100*(11), 2094 – 2102. https://doi.org/10.2105/AJPH.2009.170506

Jansson, B. (2014). *Becoming an effective policy advocate: From policy practice to social justice. 7th Edition.* Cengage Learning.

Knight, C. & Gitterman, A. (2018). Merging micro and macro intervention: Social work practice with groups in the community. *Journal of Social Work Education, 54*(1), 3 – 17. https://doi.org/10.1080/10437797.2017.1404521

Logie, C. H., James, L., Tharao, W., & Loutfy, M. R. (2011). HIV, gender, race, sexual orientation, and sex work: a qualitative study of intersectional stigma experienced by HIV-positive women in Ontario, Canada. *PLoS Medicine, 8*(11), 1-12.

Meyer, I. (2003). *Minority stress and mental health in gay men (2nd ed.).* Columbia University Press. https://doi.org/10.1371/journal.pmed.1001124

Mustanski, B. S., Garofalo, R., & Emerson, E. M. (2010). Mental health disorders, psychological distress, and suicidality in a diverse sample of lesbian, gay, bisexual and transgender youths. *American Journal of Public Health, 100*(12), 2426 – 2432. https://doi.org/10.2105/AJPH.2009.178319

Mustanski, B., Newcomb, M. & Garofalo, R. (2011). Mental health of lesbian, gay, and bisexual youth: A developmental resiliency perspective. *Journal of Gay & Lesbian Social Services, 23*(2), 204-225. https://doi.org/10.1080/10538720.2011.561474

Olshansky, E. & Zender, R. (2015). The use of community-based participatory research to understand and work with vulnerable populations. In B. Anderson & M. de Chesnay (Eds.) *Caring for the vulnerable: Perspectives in nursing theory, practice and research.* Jones & Bartlett Learning.

Paley, A. (2020). *National survey on LGBTQ youth mental health 2020.* The Trevor Project. https://www.thetrevorproject.org/survey-2020/

Post, M. (2018). Alinsky style organizing. In R. A. Cnaan & C. Milofsky (Eds.), *Handbook of Community Movements and Local Organizations in the 21st Century* (pp. 299 – 308). https://doi.org/10.1007/978-3-319-77416-9_18

Ratts, M. J., Anthony, L., & Santos, K. N. T. (2010). The dimensions of social justice model: Transforming traditional group work into a socially just framework. *The Journal for Specialists in Group Work, 35*(2), 160 – 168. https://doi.org/10.1080/01933921003705974

Russell, S. T., & Fish, J. N. (2016). Mental health in lesbian, gay, bisexual, and transgender (LGBT) youth. *Annual Review of Clinical Psychology, 12*(1), 465–487. http://doi.org/10.1146/annurev-clinpsy-021815-093153

Segal, E. A. & Wagaman, M. A. (2017). Social empathy as a framework for teaching social justice. *Journal of Social Work Education, 53*(2), 201 - 211. https://doi.org/10.1080/10437797.2016.1266980

Staples, L. (2012). Community organizing for social justice: Grassroots groups for power. *Social Work with Groups, 35*(3), 287 – 296. https://doi.org/10.1080/01609513.2012.656233

Staller, K. (2010). Social problem construction and its impact on policy and program responses. In. S. B. Kamerman, S. Phipps, & A. Ben-Arieh (Eds.). *From child welfare to child well- being: An international perspective to knowledge in the service of policy-making.* Springer.

United Nations General Assembly. (2011). *Discriminatory laws and practices and acts of violence against individuals based on their sexual orientation and gender identity.* https://www.ohchr.org/documents/issues/discrimination/a.hrc.19.41_english.pdf

Wilkinson, M. T. & D'Angelo, K. (2019). Community-based accompaniment and social work - A complementary approach to social action. *Journal of Community Practice, 27*(2), 151 – 167. https://doi.org/10.1080/10705422.2019.1616641

Child Brides: Guidelines for a Norms-Based Group Work Intervention for Social Workers

Ajwang Warria

Introduction

Child marriages have negative consequences for a child's education, health and psychosocial functioning and development. It robs girls of their childhood, rights and dignity. Furthermore, it is a gender-based violation, a human rights violation and a practice that undermines strategies to promote and achieve sustainable development. The enmeshment between culture and community influences lifestyles and being married young can indeed be a norm and a way of life in some societies. Child brides have their status elevated and they are glorified and celebrated. With this in mind, it becomes challenging for the majority of young girls in these marriages to simply walk away or leave the relationship. Based on a review of literature, this paper identifies key social norms-based guidelines for successful group work with this population group. This is because group-based interventions can be an efficient and cost-effective way to address the needs of children in marriages – by providing opportunity for empowerment, receipt of affirmation and reduced isolation Child marriage is a global phenomenon that cuts across cultures, ethnicities, race and religions. Child marriages have been described as both a cause and effect of violence against children (Chaudhuri, 2015; Mehra, Sarkar, Sreenath, Behera & Mehra, 2018). According to a recent report by United Nations Children's' Fund (UNICEF) (2021), globally, approximately 650 million girls and women alive today were married before the age of 18. This is approximately 10% of the world's population. Future projections by Girls not Brides (2016) indicate that "if there is no reduction in the future, the total number of women married as children will grow to 1.2

billion by 2050" (p. 6). In light of this, it is crucial to support married girls to fulfil their potential as we identify other promising strategies to end this practice.

Girls not Brides (2016) describes child marriage as a "formal marriage or an informal union in which at least one of the parties is a child" (p. 5). The terms child marriage and early marriage are often used interchangeably. However, early marriage refers to a marriage involving persons who are 18 years or older, but other factors such as level of development, disability and lacking information about life options make them immature to consent to marriage. On the other hand, forced marriage "occurs without the full or free consent of one or both of the parties and/or where one or both of the parties is unable to end or leave the marriage, including as a result of duress or intense social or family pressure" (Girls not Brides, 2016, p. 5). It is worth noting that boys also marry when under 18 (Warria, 2017a; 2019), although girls are much more greatly affected – i.e., almost seven times more than boys (Girls not Brides, 2016; Kohno et al., 2020). In South Asia, the family helps in choosing a partner, whereas it has been noted that in some parts of Africa, girls have autonomy in partner choice selection (Mehra et al., 2018; Petroni et al., 2017, n.p). However, choice selection does not mean much if there are other elements of coercion when the marriage is entered into and if the girl is underage and immature developmentally.

Forced child marriage is a harmful traditional practice which causes immediate and long-term psychological and physical pain and has serious consequences for girls' development (Girls not Brides, 2016). According to Nour (2009), "child marriage truncates girls' childhood, stops their education, and impacts their health and the health of their infants" (p. 54). These views have been echoed in several studies around the world (Kohno et al., 2020; Mehra et al., 2018; Nasrullah et al., 2014). Child brides are an invisible yet emerging category of population that social workers work with due to their vulnerability, social isolation and marginalization that they face. According to Girls not Brides (2016), policies and investments in programmes to support married girls are lacking in many countries. Indeed, there is a need to tackle the unique needs of married children (Nasrullah et al., 2014; United States Agency for International Development (USAID), 2012), both in policy and practice. Services should be available for those who want to leave or annul such marriages, and those at risk of forced marriages. In cases of child brides who choose to remain in the marriage, interventions should ensure that they are offered the necessary protection, opportunities and resources to thrive in these environments, and caution taken not to put or expose them to additional risk(s) (Schlecht, 2016; Warria, 2019). Special protection measures should be extended to children at risk of violence in child marriage (Chaudhiri, 2015).

Group work can be one way to support children who remain in marriages. Similar to the study by Kenny, Helpingstine, Harrington and McEachern (2018) on group work with exploited girls, a key aspect of group work application with child brides is to address the social isolation that happens when the girl is married off from her family. Kenny et al. (2018) further indicate that groups can "provide opportunities to share experiences, provide mutual support and validation, and members learning from one another" (p. 378). Groups can also allow for the creation of alternative stories, management and reduction of distressing symptoms, and restoration of trust and hope for the future.

Thus, although there is much information on the causes and consequences of child marriages, we know very little about the needs of children trapped in marriages and how to support them. This is a critical area for policy, advocacy and practice. There is a dearth of research on group work interventions with child brides, but there is literature on trauma that we can draw upon to assist in the group interventions. What this paper additionally offers is a close look at guidelines that can be used towards meaningful group engagement as a component of holistic programming for child brides. The purpose of engaging the girls in groups is to empower them to find strengths as they adjust to their marital situations. This paper starts by briefly highlighting the methodology applied. Next, the causes and consequences of child marriages are linked to development. The nexus between children's rights, the law and child marriages are outlined, followed by a discussion on social norms. Finally, the guidelines for a norms-based group intervention are presented.

Method

A review of the literature was undertaken to understand the nature of child marriages. The initial search for material used the key words such as "child marriages", "child marriages Africa", "child marriages", "child marriage interventions", and child marriages AND group work." Some of the databases that were used for the search included ScienceDirect, GoogleScholar and PubMed. In addition, news reports and reports commissioned by various organizations such as UNICEF and Girls not Brides were reviewed. Grey literature search was also conducted and additional publications were identified from the list provided in the reviewed manuscripts.

This was not a systematic review or a scoping review although some search elements from both types of reviews were applied in identifying publications that were included. This, in itself, is a limitation of this study as the criteria for selecting the literature that was reviewed was limited. Another limitation was that only publications written from 2014 and in English were included in the study. This means pertinent studies written prior to 2014 and in other languages were excluded. An exception was considered for the inclusion of Nour (2009) as it is referenced in numerous manuscripts reviewed and it supported several arguments presented in this paper.

Applying Social Norms Theory in the Context of Child Marriages

Social norms exist in a variety of contexts. According to Cislaghi and Heise (2018), social norms are "informal rules of behaviour that dictate what is acceptable within a given social context" (p. 1). Social norms significantly influence individuals' choices and behaviours. Thus, social norms theory takes into account local contexts in understanding and intervening with challenges. Considering this, Schlecht (2016) notes that "research on child marriages is firmly rooted in major global processes and standards" (p. 6) and it is crucial to present a global perspective. Studies on effectiveness of social norms interventions for increasing wellbeing are sparse but growing (Cislaghi & Heise, 2018). A multi-pronged intervention programme in Senegal to fight female genital mutilation (FGM) as described by Cislaghi and Heise (2018) integrated a social norms element and addressed "the community's individual attitudes and knowledge, local institutional policies and political accountability, and community members' economic conditions" (p. 2). Thus, it is clear that social norms are addressed in their interplay with other significant factors influencing wellbeing, stigma, and social standing in the community.

The two distinct types of social norms reported in the study by Cislaghi and Heise (2018) are descriptive norms (i.e., "beliefs about what others do") and injunctive norms (i.e., "beliefs about what others approve or disapprove"). Compliance with both sets of norms or with either of them is impacted by a variety of factors (Chadambuka & Warria, 2019). For example, child marriages are often considered private family matters yet influenced by religion and culture with varying causes. In relation to child marriages, for example, initiation ceremonies occurring earlier leave children thinking and feeling that they are adults and that they are old enough to get married. Furthermore, there is also decision to get married if they fall pregnant to avoid the stigma and shame of having a child out of wedlock (Lilian et al., 2015). Other examples include admiration of child brides' families, glorification of child brides and the marriage ceremonies depicting a celebratory mood full of joy (Nour, 2009). Schlecht (2016) reports further that the "stigma associated with being unmarried or being unable to marry was pervasive … and viewed negatively by both adolescents and adults alike, and believed to be linked to mental illness or social deficiency" (p. 22). The consequence of this is the socio-cultural pressure to ensure a girl does not lose her opportunity for marriage by waiting too long. According to UNICEF and Religions of Peace (2010 as cited in Greene et al. 2015), child marriage is a long held traditional practice that is perpetuated "without a primary intention of violence, but reflects deeply rooted discrimination against women and girls" (p. 15). In light of this, USAID (2012) therefore recommends that interventions must be sensitive to cultural contexts and engage a variety of stakeholders in identifying locally effective strategies.

The application of social norms theory to interventions requires caution (Chadambuka & Warria, 2019; Warria, 2018). Cislaghi and Heise (2018) reiterated that "using social norms theory without appreciating the place that norms occupy among other drivers of behaviour, might position interventions for failure, ultimately discrediting promising strategies simply because, in isolation, they are inadequate to improve health" (p. 1) and wellbeing. This supports Karam's (2015) argument that "the extent of the connectedness and cohesion among that community will determine, to some extent, the rate of success in mobilization towards achievement of that objective i.e. in eradicating a harmful practice" (p. 60). Conducive contexts influence child marriages (Chantler & McCarry, 2020). In relation to child marriages, Karam (2015) further emphasizes that it is crucial to use parental and community engagement as a strategy, given that the girls' family is instrumental in decision-making processes and the broader community administers sanctions when the traditions are not followed and societal expectations are not met. In light of this, practitioners need to forge more supportive and less punitive environments, which then helps in mitigating the unintended consequences of the child bride's participation in the group work and other intervention programmes.

Child Marriages: Overview of Causes, Consequences and Development

Approximately 15 million girls are married every year before they turn 18 years old. This translates into 41,000 girls every day and one in four girls globally (UNICEF, 2014). This has a significant impact on development and on the achievement of Sustainable Development Goals (SDGs). SDG Target 5.3, which aims to end child marriage by 2030, sets out to eliminate "all harmful practices, such as child, early and forced marriage and FGM". The multi-faceted nature of child marriage links to related SDGs on poverty, economic growth, reduction of inequalities (especially gender) and nutrition. Child marriages undermine the fight against Human Immunodeficiency Virus (HIV) and Acquired Immunodeficiency Syndrome (AIDS), children's rights and protection, national economic progress and progress towards education goals (Mehra et al., 2018). In addition, it ironically preserves and negatively maintains the cycle of poverty, while stalling progress towards the achievement of the SDGs.

The three main drivers of child marriage as identified by Nour (2009) are: (i) marriage as security and to offer protection, (ii) poverty, and (iii) tradition and the need to reinforce social ties. Other dual drivers include impoverished communities and parents who marry off their daughters with complete disregard of existing legislation (Lilian et al., 2015). Petroni et al. (2017) further add that child marriages are entrenched in inequitable gender norms that prioritize and "interact closely with poverty and a lack of employment opportunities for girls and young women [to] perpetuate marriages as a seemingly viable alternative" (p. 781). This is linked to a previous observation made by

Girls not Brides (2016) on why child marriages continue to happen - gender inequality and low value accorded to girls, tied to weak legal and policy reforms.

Fragility and conflict have been closely linked to child marriage practices. Many countries with particular vulnerability to natural disasters are among the highest in terms of child marriage prevalence (Kohno et al., 2020; Mourtada et al., 2017). The current COVID-19 pandemic has also been reported to be a contributory risk factor for child marriages. UNICEF (2021) "warns that school closures, economic stress, service disruptions, pregnancy, and parental deaths due to the pandemic are putting the most vulnerable girls at increased risk of child marriage" (np) This has also been highlighted in other reports by Girls Not Brides (2020), Cousins (2020) and Ontiveros (2021).

Forced, arranged and early marriage increases vulnerabilities for young girls. According to Lilian et al. (2015) these marriages often "overburdens, dehumanizes and traumatizes girls into servitude who often relapse into hopelessness ... *it* is traumatizing, taxing ... and *girls'* future remains bleak" (p. 73). Furthermore, according to Schlecht (2016) "marriage isolates adolescent girls from friends and programs that would help them overcome the challenges of marriage" (np). The needs of child brides might vary depending on factors such as age of marriage, participation in choosing partner, support from family of origin and husband's family, opportunities to pursue life goals and other contextual factors, but there are also certain needs and challenges that present themselves in most child marriage situations. According to Wodon et al. (2017), "child brides may be disempowered in ways that deprive them of their basic rights to health, education and safety" (p. 1). A report by Santhya and Erulkar (2011) highlighted the following characteristics common to married girls: less social mobility in comparison to unmarried girls the same age as them or to adult married women, increased risk of intimate partner violence, limited autonomy and say in the home, and less access to ICT and sources of information.

Adverse health outcomes in child brides can be attributed to concerns related to limited access to health information and services, lack of access to contraceptives, poor to non-existent communication between couples, gender power imbalances and financial dependence (Mehra et al., 2018). Once married, marital and domestic demands and responsibilities increase, and, while many of the girls would like to continue schooling, they may be practically and legally excluded from doing so (Girls not Brides, 2016). These young married girls will have expected responsibilities as wives, mothers, in-laws and other roles with little support, resources and life experience to manage these challenges. These could lead to other psychological disorders such as depression (Mehra et al., 2018).

According to a study by Schlecht (2016), children in these marriages rarely have someone to talk to when they are uncertain and have questions to ask or when they need advice. They tend to be typically at home caring for children. In addition, they do not engage with others or they are not involved in programmes that would enable them to overcome their life challenges. Furthermore, it has been noted that they have few opportunities to connect with others or peers or have access to much-needed livelihoods or education. Support from family and church is crucial as noted by community members, parents and programme implementers in a study conducted by Schlecht (2016).

From a socio-ecological perspective, these factors affect more than the girls only, and include medium- and long-term consequences for their children, household, communities and societies. Given that the consequences of child marriages and the needs of child brides vary, these are best addressed using a multi-disciplinary approach for the solutions to be effective and sustainable.

Child Marriages, Child Rights and Legislation

Child marriage is connected to child rights and protection. The Convention on the Elimination of All Forms of Discrimination against Women, the International Covenant on Civil and Political Rights, the International Covenant on Economic, Social and Cultural Rights, the Convention on the Consent to Marriage, the Convention on the Rights of the Child, the Minimum Age for Marriage and Registration of Marriages and the Slavery Convention and the Protocol to the Convention on the Sale of Children, Child Prostitution and Child Pornography all indicate that child marriages harm children's rights. The regional instruments such as the African Charter on the Rights and Welfare of the Child tackled issues related to communal childcare and protection and the socio-cultural and economic realities found in Africa. According to Warria (2017b), counter trafficking conventions and policies aimed at children must reflect a child-rights approach. Furthermore, a study by Maswika, Richter, Kaufman and Nandi (2015) reported that in order for girls to be protected from exploitation, it is necessary to have consistent minimum marriage age laws. Recently, Melnikas et al. (2021) recommended that minimum marriage laws be complemented with other contextual interventions that directly address drivers of child marriage.

According to Karam (2015), "once girls are married, their status infringes upon a range of their rights" (p. 60). This is further supported by Chaudhuri's (2015) argument that child brides are not viewed either as children or adults i.e.

They are denied children's rights because they are viewed as adults and lack the decision-making power and agency of adults because they are effectively children. As marriage distorts their identity and illegitimately projects them as adults, their life is stranded in a no-man's land where they are no longer girls and not yet women (p. 5)

The marriages lead to conditions that undermine child protection and rights such as neglect, marginalization, stigmatization, exploitative domestic labour and destitution. The respectability accorded to marriage influences the violence that these adolescent brides endure, yet the abuse remains invisible, unrecognized and mostly not addressed in policy, practice or research. Hence the importance of exploring child marriages and related issues through a continuum of harm and rights violations.

The rights affected when children are forcefully married off include the free expression of individual views, protection from abuse, traditional practices, child labour and hazardous environments prohibiting participation in education/learning (Lilian et al., 2015). When children are married young, evidence points to violation of interconnected rights such as the right to equality on grounds of sex and age, the right to marry and create a family, the right to life, and the right to education, development and the highest attainable standard of health.

Reports in several studies is that despite national laws being important, they are usually not sufficient in ending child marriages (Warria, 2019; Wodon et al., 2017). Therefore, to mitigate this, Girls not Brides (2016) advocates that "international legal instruments also go beyond age and consent in calling for political, economic, social, cultural and civil environments that protect women and girls, and supports them in the enjoyment of their human rights and fundamental freedoms" (p. 10). There should be a willingness to create enabling environments where girls' and women's rights can be realized. This then opens the way for a discussion of social norms as part of creating an enabling environment.

Results

Guidelines for Social Norms-Influenced Group Work Intervention with Child Brides

The multi-faceted nature of child marriages requires a continuum of care, rights and protection with long-term response(s) to tackle the inter-woven and intersecting determinants. From a socio-ecological perspective, the complexities around and within child marriages require effective programmatic measures to be identified, considered and implemented at all levels. Aligned to this is the theory of change, which indicates there is no "one size fits all" solution in ending child marriages. This means that everyone has a role to play and that, ultimately, interventions addressing child marriages must respond to local contexts. According to Cislaghi and Heise (2018), integrating social norms perspective within psychosocial interventions can be valuable and can generate results intersectionally. It is worth noting that the guidelines suggested below will take different forms depending on the context.

Group-based interventions can be an efficient and cost-effective way to address the needs of children in marriages, as they can provide an opportunity for empowerment, receipt of affirmation and reduced isolation (Olson-McBride & Page as cited in Hickle & Roe-Sepowitz, 2014). The child brides have an opportunity to develop solidarity through the peer group and collective action-power of groups. In order for the groups to be successful and for sustainable goals to be achieved, the following guidelines for establishing group purpose and goals, member recruitment, identifying group facilitators, formatting group structure, designing group programming, activities and evaluation are recommended and will be discussed in that order.

Group Purpose and Goals

Group leaders should tailor the programme to participants' needs and make the group and the activities practical. Based on the needs identified in a variety of studies on child marriages, the goals of the group can be aligned to increasing coping skills and relaxation, enhancing support networks, and exposing the girls to new opportunities and experiences through life skills training. Therefore, doing a needs assessment is crucial in identifying the core needs as relates to the group. For example, legal and other support services are geared towards the girls escaping these marriages. However, there are other brides who, despite receiving the support to leave these marriages, choose to stay. Therefore, the intervention will not have a focus on primary prevention but secondary or tertiary prevention – i.e., that of their own children in future. This builds on the notion that prevention is not reactive but long-term. Another example is that many of the child marriages are conducted outside of formal legal structures and the girls might want to formalize them. This can be empowering in its own way.

Member Recruitment

The group facilitator ought to ascertain who the traditional leaders are and seek their permission. This promotes buy-in, helps in building trust with the community and creates supportive allies. It also shows respect, tolerance and a willingness to embrace the community's norms and ways of living. According to Greene et al. (2015), "as custodians of culture and tradition, these leaders are held in high regard by their communities, and can be influential advocates for change in their communities" (p. 14).

In most communities, the marriages are also concluded in front of a traditional leader and they are expected to keep records in some settings. Therefore, they can be instrumental in assisting the facilitator identify and/or refer potential group members. Self-referrals might also be common. The eligibility criteria should be that they were married early and that they are still in that marriage.

Engaging with the husbands of the young brides can lead to positive outcomes for the group members. Child brides are socially excluded. As a practitioner, when you engage the girls without considering their husbands' influence on the girls' socio-economic capital, health and psychosocial wellbeing, the intervention might not yield long-term outcomes (Greene et al., 2015). This is because the dynamics of power within marriages are shaped by social norms that set the roles for men and women. Thus, engaging the husbands in or out of a group work session can help to mitigate the negative effects on child wives and increase access to health, economic and education support. If we exclude men and husbands, the group work programme will fail to create a setting where change, especially on sensitive issues related to child marriages, can be nurtured. For example, from a community-based participatory approach, other stakeholders such as in-laws and parents can be approached to help identify barriers to accessing services but also as an attempt to understand needs, interests and challenges (Mehra et al., 2018). This approach increases the girls' commitment and the group work momentum, impact and the sustainability gained.

Group Facilitator(s)

The facilitator should be skilled in running groups, especially with vulnerable populations. If not, they should have received training on working with abused, exploited and/or trafficked children and adolescents. Where possible, a co-facilitator who was a child bride from the community where the group training is happening should be recruited and trained. This can help provide authenticity, and the co-facilitator can be a role model for the other group members. This will help not only in building trust, but also in having local supportive social networks through the sharing of experiences and vulnerabilities, and also strengths, when the formal group sessions come to an end. The co-facilitator has played the role of a mentor and can run the support group thereafter on an ad hoc basis.

Group Structure

Running an open group is recommended to fit with other roles that the child bride group members might have and to allow for members to join at any time. The facilitator should strive as much as possible to schedule group work sessions for 1 to 1.5 hours and when the girls are most likely to have finished chores around the house – e.g., in the afternoon around 2.30pm - 4pm. One does not want unintended consequences where the group members are put at further risk and/ or are totally prevented from external activities because it is alleged that they are neglecting their core responsibilities in the home. In addition, the sessions should be kept open and permit for flexibility to allow for that reflective space based on group members' own/personal realities even though they might belong to the same community, ethnic group or even village. These safe reflective spaces nurture growth of self-confidence and self-esteem. According to Kenny et al. (2018), "each group members' modes of coping and progress become valuable agents for change for all participants" (p. 378).

Group Programming and Activities

The group could be a psychoeducational group with a focus on (secondary) prevention and personal development. The group can offer the girls opportunities to acquire new skills and also develop hidden talents towards reshaping and redefining how they view themselves (Kenny et al., 2018). Some select activities and discussions include:

a) art work, using different mediums as a form of expression, to learn new skills or to enhance old ones also indirectly learn to express themselves in a variety of ways;
b) life skills training to help them manage the demands of being a young bride such as interpersonal relationships, problem solving, entrepreneurship and coping with stress and anxiety;
c) recreation and relaxation activities as a way to learn to ground and centre themselves and release stress through dancing, poetry and singing; and
d) community norms discussion on role expectations, which can incorporate cooking, child care, sexual and reproductive health, menu budgeting and planning.

A light healthy meal or snack should also be provided during the session to nourish the group members and as a way of incorporating their culture and bonding. The incorporation of non-formal education/ learning techniques can lead to greater participation by the group members. The group facilitator could also tap into and incorporate cultural activities and elements such as dance, storytelling and songs. This can ensure that lessons can be better absorbed and sustained. In addition, by discussing new ideas and practices within an open and familiar environment the girls might tend to feel more comfortable with you as the facilitator and with each other.

Groups do not exist in a vacuum. Using a multi-levelled systematic approach, the facilitator can mobilize community members. For norm-change interventions to be effective, the entire community must be involved to create an enabling environment (Greene et al., 2015). If this is not there, the young brides in one's group will be swimming upstream against the tide, which is rather unsafe and risky for them. Instead, they should be swimming downstream with it. The facilitator could start by engaging with the community leaders in dialogues about changes they would like to see in the community and how to make them happen (Green et al., 2015). The themes of these conversations can also be generated within the group but applied in a manner that does not jeopardize the group members, individually or collectively.

Given the complexity of group practice and social norms, dilemmas unique to group work with children in marriages will arise. For example, despite all the mitigating efforts put in place, it is important to anticipate challenges – e.g., time, husband's resistance (even if initially agreed), and limited mobility. The programme should also be adapted for young mothers by allowing them to bring their children and have a child minder and include activities with them. Other potential problems include cultural issues such as season-related activities, safety issues and girls not being permitted to interact with other people when menstruating.

Group Evaluation

Group monitoring and evaluation are crucial aspects of group work. According to Kenny et al. (2018), group interventions should seek to "consistently involve the client in a collaborative relationship which seeks to develop and evaluate services" (p. 388). Thus, on-going feedback from the group members, at the end of each group session and at the conclusion of the group intervention should be encouraged. This information can be used to improve future group work interventions with a similar population or clients. The facilitator/s should also evaluate the group, the group members, and the setting on an on-going basis and be able to put in place balancing and safeguarding acts. For example, the group work intervention might be seen as a way to access resources and opportunities, and thus the incidence of child marriage might increase. Precautions should thus be taken to avoid negative unintended consequences and a suggestion could perhaps be to run different groups of those vulnerable and at-risk in that community as well.

Conclusion

Children with a sense of agency choosing to remain in forced marriages are indeed a complex population group and providing interventions that address their unique needs is crucial to their empowerment and the creation of a meaningful future. The voices of child brides have been silent for a very long time. Researchers, policymakers and practitioners must engage with them and allow them to tell us how we can better facilitate their successful future(s), and extend their involvement and participation. Only then can programmes and services meet their specific needs and allow them to fulfil their potential. Finally, if group intervention is not feasible for the child bride, other culturally sensitive interventions should be identified and pursued in collaboration with the child.

Critics might say that this study is contradictory and conflicts with legislation/policy – i.e., not allowing child marriage but supporting child brides. I am not condoning the practice of child, early, arranged or forced marriages. Integrating advocacy as part of social justice poses both practical and ethical challenges. I am merely advocating for the provision of adequate safeguards – i.e., the crucial focus on early intervention and legal measures – but also responding to the needs of married girls due to marginalization, exclusion and stigma that they face.

References

Chadambuka, C. & Warria, A. (2019). Hurt or help? Understanding intimate partner violence in the context of social norms as practised in the rural areas. *Social Work, 55*(3), 301-310. https://doi.org/10.15270/55-3-741

Chantler, K. & McCarry, M. (2020). Forced marriage, coercive control and conducive contexts: The experiences of women in Scotland. *Violence against Women, 26*(1), 89-109. https://journals.sagepub.com/doi/pdf/10.1177/1077801219830234

Chaudhuri, E.R. (2015). *Thematic report: Unrecognised sexual abuse and exploitation of children in child, early and forced marriage.* ECPAT-Plan International, Bangkok. https://www.girlsnotbrides.org/learning-resources/resource-centre/unrecognised-sexual-abuse-and-exploitation-of-children-in-child-early-and-forced-marriage/

Cislaghi, B. & Heise, L. (2018). Using social norms theory for health promotion in low-income countries. *Health Promotion International*, 1-8. doi: 10.1093/heapro/day017

Cousins, S. (2020). 2.5 million more child marriages due to COVID-19 pandemic. https://www.thelancet.com/journals/lancet/article/PIIS0140-6736(20)32112-7/fulltext

Girls not Brides. (2016). *The role of parliamentarians in ending child marriage: A toolkit* (2nd ed.). London: Girls not Brides. https://www.girlsnotbrides.org/learning-resources/resource-centre/the-role-of-parliamentarians-in-ending-child-marriage/

Green, M.E., Perlson, S., Taylor, A. & Lauro, G. (2015). *Engaging men and boys to end the practice of child marriage.* Washington, D.C: GreeneWorks/Promundo. https://promundoglobal.org/resources/engaging-men-and-boys-to-end-the-practice-of-child-marriage/

Hickle, K.E. & Roe-Sepowitz, D. (2014). Putting the pieces back together: A group intervention for sexually exploited adolescent girls. *Social Work with Groups, 37*(2), 99-113. DOI: 10.1080/01609513.2013.823838

Karam, A. (2015). Faith-inspired initiatives to tackle the social determinants of child marriage. *The Review of Faith & International Affairs, 13*(3), 59-68. https://doi.org/10.1080/15570274.2015.1075754

Kenny, M.C., Helpingstine, C.E., Harrington, M.C. & McEachern, A.G. (2018). A comprehensive group approach for commercially sexually exploited girls. *The Journal for Specialists in Group Work, 43*(4), 376-398. https://doi.org/10.1080/01933922.2018.1484540

Kohno, A., Techasrivichien, T., Sugulmoto, A.P., Dahlui, M., Farid, N.D.N. & Nakayama, T. (2020). Investigation of the key factors that influence the girls to enter into child marriage: Meta-synthesis of qualitative evidence. *PLoS ONE, 15*(7):e0235959. https://doi.org/10.1371/journal. pone.0235959.

Lilian, G.K., Nancy, I.A., Odundo, P.A., Akondo, J.O & Ngaruiya, B. (2015). Early and forced child marriage on girls' education in Migori County, Kenya: Constraints, prospects and policy. *World Journal of Education, 5*(4), 72-80. http://dx.doi.org/10.5430/wje.v5n4p72

Maswikwa, B., Richter, L., Kaufman, J. & Nandi, A. (2015). Minimum marriage age laws and the prevalence of child marriage and adolescent birth: Evidence from sub-Saharan Africa. *International Perspectives on Sexual and Reproductive Health, 41*(2), 58-68. doi: 10.1363/4105815

Mehra, D., Sarkar, A, Sreenath, P., Behera, J. & Mehra, S. (2018). Effectiveness of a community based intervention to delay early marriage, early pregnancy and improve school retention among adolescents in India. *BMC Public Health, 18*, 732. https://doi.org/10.1186/s12889-018-5586-3

Melnikas, A.J., Mulauzi, N., Mkandawire, J. & Amin, S. (2021). Perceptions of minimum age at marriage laws and their enforcement: qualitative evidence from Malawi. *BMC Public Health,* 21: 1350. doi: 10.1186/ s12889-021-11434-z

Mourtada, R., Schlecht, J. & DeJong, J. (2015). A qualitative study exploring child marriage practices among Syrian conflict-affected populations in Lebanon. *Conflict Health, 11*(1). https://www.ncbi.nlm.nih.gov/pmc/ articles/PMC5688503/

Nasrullah, M., Zakar, R., & Zakar, M. Z. (2014). Child marriage and its associations with controlling behaviors and spousal violence against adolescent and young women in Pakistan. *Journal of Adolescent Health, 55*(6), 804-809

Nour, N. (2009). Child marriage: A silent health and human rights issue. *Reviews in Obstetrics and Gynaecology, 2*(1), 51-56. https://www.ncbi. nlm.nih.gov/pmc/articles/PMC2672998/

Ontiveros, E. (2021). Covid child brides: 'My family told me to marry at 14'. https://www.bbc.com/news/world-56292247

Petroni, A, Steinhaus, M, Stevanovic, N., Stobenau, K. & Gregowaki, A. (2017). New findings on child marriage in sub-Saharan Africa. *Annals of Global Health, 83*(5-6), 781-790. DOI: 10.1016/j.aogh.2017.09.001

Santhya, K.G. & Erulkar, A. (2011). *Supporting married girls: Calling attention to a neglected group.* Transitions to Adulthood. Brief No. 3. Population Council. DOI: 10.31899/pgy12.1014

Schlecht, J. (2016). *A girl no more: The changing norms of child marriage in conflict.* Women's Refugee Commission. New York.

UNICEF. (2014). *Ending child marriage: Progress and Prospects.* UNICEF.

https://www.unicef.org/media/files/Child_Marriage_Report_7_17_LR..pdf

UNICEF. (2021). 10 million additional girls at risk of child marriage due to COVID-19. https://www.unicef.org/press-releases/10-million-additional-girls-risk-child-marriage-due-covid-19

USAID. (2012). *Ending child marriage and meeting the needs of married children: The USAID vision for action.* Washington, DC. https://www.usaid.gov/sites/default/files/documents/2155/Child_Marriage_Vision_Factsheet.pdf

Warria, A. (2019). Child marriages, child protection and sustainable development in Kenya: Is legislation sufficient? *African Journal of Reproductive Health, 23*(2), 121-133. http://www.bioline.org.br/pdf?rh19028

Warria, A. (2018). Girl's innocence and futures stolen: The cultural practice of sexual cleansing in Malawi. *Children and Youth Services Review, 91,* 298-303. https://doi.org/10.1016/j.childyouth.2018.06.011

Warria, A. (2017a). Forced child marriages as a form of child trafficking. *Children and Youth Services Review, 79,* 274-279. https://doi.org/10.1016/j.childyouth.2017.06.024

Warria, A. (2017b). International and African regional instruments to protect rights of child victims of transnational trafficking. *Victims & Offenders: International Journal of Evidence-based Research, Policy, and Practice, 12*(5), 682-699. http://www.tandfonline.com/doi/abs/10.1080/15564886.2016.1238859

Wodon, Q., Tavares, P., Fiala, O., Nestour, A. & Wise, L. (2017). *Ending child marriage: Child marriage laws and their limitations.* Children's Investment Fund Foundation, Global Partnership for Education, Save the Children and The World Bank. https://thedocs.worldbank.org/en/doc/134161519943385981-0050022017/original/WBL2017ChildMarriageLaws.pdf

Uniting in Treatment and Redefining Our Lives: Group Therapy Practice for Adolescents Who Have Sexually Offended

Rachael Pascoe & Shelley Craig

Through specialized assessment and treatment, adolescents who sexually offend can take responsibility for the impact of their abuse behaviours and go on to live fulfilling and productive lives. Group therapy can be an important addition to the therapeutic repertoire offered to this population. This paper seeks to provide a brief overview of adolescent sexual offending literature and describe a group treatment approach, the Unite and Redefine Group, offered in Southern Ontario, Canada. The stages of the group and activities of the program are described here.

Adolescents who have sexually offended are a clinical population distinct from other adolescents. They are often referred for treatment to address their sexual offending behaviours. They are different from adolescents with mental health concerns or youth who have engaged in general delinquency. They require specialized assessment to identify their risks to reengage in sexual offending and to determine the strengths that will support them in treatment. Adolescents who have sexually offended often present in treatment with a number of issues, including social isolation and low self-esteem and are more likely to have a personal history of physical abuse, familial domestic violence, and early exposure to sexual media than are adolescents engaged in general delinquency (Seto & Lalumiére, 2010). When compared to children without significant abuse histories, adults with a history of abuse were more likely to be arrested for sexual offending (Widom & Massey, 2015). Specifically, childhood histories of physical abuse and neglect (not necessarily sexual abuse) were the greatest predictors of future sexual offending in adolescence and adulthood (Widom & Massey, 2015). Emotional abuse and neglect are also significant contributors to later sexual offending behaviours (Zakireh et al., 2008). While quantitative evidence points to these adverse childhood experiences as possible predeterminants, no single experience predicts later sexual offending in adolescents.

Youth generally cite the following reasons for their sexual offending: curiosity about sex, access to children or another victim, and an opportunity to offend (Seto & Pullman, 2014; Worling, 2012). Contrary to commonly-held misconceptions, a minority (25-36%) of adolescents who sexually offend do so because they hold deviant sexual interests, such as sexual interest in children, nonconsensual, or violent sexual encounters (Seto et al., 2000; Seto et al., 2003; Seto & Lalumière, 2010; Worling, 2004; Worling, 2013). Although many adults who sexually abuse children reportedly start as teenagers, research has demonstrated that youth who sexually offend generally do not go on to recidivate and sexually abuse as adults (Caldwell, 2016), while approximately 90% of youth who receive specialized treatment do not engage in future sexual offending (Worling et al., 2012).

Adolescent Sexual Offending Treatment

Adolescent sexual offending specialized treatment leads to decreases in recidivism, as well as addressing important psychosocial needs (Borduin & Schaeffer, 2001; Borduin et al., 2009; Bourgon et al., 2005). Best practice guidelines have been developed for this population, which emphasize nonjudgemental, objective, and holistic services centered around mutually agreed upon assessment treatment goals (ATSA, 2017). Historically, treatment for adolescents who have sexually offended have mimicked adult models of sexual offending treatment. However, more recently, a developmental perspective that incorporates the unique factors which contribute to adolescent sexual offending has shaped specialized treatment. A number of modalities and treatment approaches have been applied to work with this population including behaviour modification and cognitive behavioural therapies (DiCataldo, 2009). As unique factors exist for sexual abuse that occurs within families (Costin et al., 2009), holistic treatment approaches can address familial sexual abuse by removing the secrecy of the event; allowing victims to heal on their own timeline; illuminating the impact of the sexually offending harm; and appropriately engaging in restorative practices for the whole family. Another holistic rehabilitation framework, The Good Lives Model, shifts the client's focus from shame and guilt, to highlighting strengths and reducing recidivism risk, while also assisting in the development of personally meaningful and fulfilling lives (Fortune et al., 2012). A social work lens, that focuses on the tenants of rehabilitation and holistic support, may be especially critical for work this population.

Group Therapy and Adolescents who Sexually Offend

Group therapy has been the predominant modality for North American treatment in the sexual offending field since the 1950's. Group cohesion and fostering an environment in which members feel able to express themselves are essential preconditions to enhance positive change in the adult sexual offending population (Marshall et al., 2013). Group therapy is considered a helpful modality for adults who have sexually offended given their high levels of isolation, loneliness, and interpersonal and intimacy skill deficits (Marshall et al., 1999). Group therapy is considered an effective environment to address the societal stigmatization experienced by adults who have sexually offended (Frost & Connolly, 2004). Adolescents in sexual offending treatment have stated that group therapy was the most beneficial component of their care (Halse, et al., 2012). While practitioners have praised groups for its low cost and efficiency (Jennings & Deming, 2017), researchers have criticized group therapy as a sole modality because of its inability to apply to all levels of developmental difference, sexual functioning (Bukowski et al., 1993), and cognitive processing, instead recommending individualized approaches (Worling, 2013). However, the clinical literature agrees that group therapy is generally advantageous for adolescents, given group's emphasis on life skills, its space to practice behaviours in a safe environment, and because groups are a natural way for youth to relate to each other (Malekoff, 2015; Schechtman et al., 1997). As well, groups are a modality to deal with major life changes (Deck & Saddler, 1983) and increase self-esteem, and self-control (Omizo & Omizo, 1988). Adolescents who sexually offend can likely benefit from groups for similar reasons.

In Canada, approximately 40% of community sexual offending treatment programs offer group therapy programming, compared to 60% in the United States (McGrath et al., 2009). Group therapy models for adolescents who have sexually offended have demonstrated improvements in knowledge regarding sexual consent, education, laws, and healthy relationships, as well as attitudes less supportive of sexual offending (Fanniff & Becker, 2006). Holistic group treatment modalities that have demonstrated efficacy with this population include multisystemic treatment, which incorporates family and community interventions into individual counselling (Borduin & Schaeffer, 2001; Letourneau, et al., 2009). Adolescents in sexually offending treatment ranked the top five most meaningful therapeutic factors (Yalom & Leszcz, 2005) as: catharsis, group cohesion, self-understanding, interpersonal learning, instillation of hope, and family re-enactment (Sribney & Reddon, 2008). Further research on group process is required to fully understand the effects and benefits of group therapy for adolescents who sexually offend (Marshall & Burton, 2010).

The Unite and Redefine Group Therapy Intervention

The Unite and Redefine group, named by its clients, was developed at Radius Child and Youth Services, to provide additional support, complementary to individual therapy for adolescents who have sexually offended clients (Pascoe & Nicholls, 2019). The group program runs once a week during the high school academic year (approximately September until June, or 30 sessions), and group members receive regular individual sessions in addition to the weekly two-hour group sessions. Since its formation in February 2017, the group curriculum has evolved by incorporating processing strategies for emotions and cognitions, and through a deeper understanding of client needs and processes. Group members are referred to the program by their individual therapists, with most clients participating in two rounds of group therapy (i.e., fall- winter and winter-spring, or 15 sessions ofeach round). The group is conceptualized as a mandatory component of community treatment at Radius Child and Youth Services, unless a therapist determines that a client will not benefit from the group modality (such as if they are actively in crisis, or unable to relate to other members of the group). This intervention is informed by trauma-informed and anti-oppressive principles (Pascoe & Nicholls, 2019), as well as invitational practice approaches (Jenkins, 2009; Seto & Lalumiére, 2010). Invitational practice was developed for work with men and adolescents who have engaged in violence and sexual abuse and seeks to encourage clients to uncover and understand their potential (Jenkins, 2009). Invitational theory emphasizes human behaviour and thinking, thereby increasing the chances of positive treatment outcomes (Shaw & Siegel, 2010), such as engagement within the group, a reduction in loneliness, and an increase in hope for the future. Invitational practice summons clients to seek and realize their boundless and worthwhile potential (Jenkins, 2009).

The specific content of the group is determined by the needs of the members presenting in each iteration. Like most clinical groups, the beginning sessions are used to establish norms, decrease awkwardness and tension by having members get to know each other, and to develop a general list of goals that the group members wish to get out of the program. Group content has three distinct phases which are intended to be offered nonconsecutively, depending on the needs of the group. Some iterations of the program may never reach later stages, while others may vacillate between these stages. Group activities and discussions with members are directed by the identified needs of the group members. Flexibility and adaptability are especially important when working with this population. These three distinct phases are:

1. Addressing shame- with sessions such as myths and facts about adolescent sexual offending, feelings, and cognitive distortions about sexual offending
2. Expanding masculinity- with sessions including masculinity, male role-models, the man box, defining your own man box, men and the media, and
3. Becoming the man you want to be- including sessions on victim empathy, apologizing, accountability, and planning the future

Group therapy sessions last two hours, with a break in the middle. The session begins with a facilitator-led mindfulness activity, before leading into a discussion that may pick up on themes from the previous week's sessions. After the break, group members engage in a participatory activity based on the theme of the week. A brief description of the theoretical rationale and some activities developed for each of these sessions will be discussed below.

Beginnings

As with other group therapy programs with adolescents, the initial stage involves the setting of group norms and priming the group for the vulnerable and important discussions to follow. As young men enter the therapy room to begin the group, they are greeted by their facilitators, who ask them to complete a paper and pencil survey for group evaluation purposes. This individual activity allows the youth to focus on a task, while their fellow group members filter into the session. Once all have arrived, the group begins with a welcome from the facilitators involving an emphatic expression of love for groups and their belief that the group therapy program at Radius Child and Youth Services offers a wonderful complement to treatment, as demonstrated through experiential wisdom. The group members are then asked to introduce themselves to each other through the sharing of information unrelated to their offending histories. Their ages, schools, and interests are often shared in an effort to humanize members. Once introductions have been made, norms are discussed. At this point, between 25-50% of the way through the session, the first mention of sexual offending is made by one of the facilitators. This topic is introduced through the casual mention of the group's purpose, before leading to a discussion of the group norms.

The norms of the Unite and Redefine group therapy program are generally standard to other group therapy programs: confidentiality and respect remain paramount. However, specialized group norms relevant to this population often include no overt or disrespectful sexualized humour and no mandatory disclosure of their sexual offending. Protocols for managing traumatic responses is also an important consideration for the group as approximately 45% of adolescents in treatment for sexual offending have experiences of interpersonal abuse and trauma (Worling & Curwen, 2000). The first sessions always include a gamification component, in the form of cooperative activities, trivia games with prizes, or team building exercises, in which group cohesion and rapport begin to develop.

Examples of activities done in the first group session have included the group deciding what items they would like to have on a desert island or the development of a strategy to approach various survival situations. By the end of the first group, it is the experience of facilitators that rapport and comfortability are built very quickly in time for the second group, when content (determined in a group discussion) is introduced.

Stage I- Addressing Shame

Violent offending has been long associated with a decreased ability to demonstrate empathy (Geer et al., 2000; Joliffe & Farringdon, 2004). Shame, described as a global negative feeling about the self in response to a shortcoming (Tangney & Dearing, 2002), is a commonly described experience of adolescents in sexually offending treatment (Halse, et al., 2012; Owen & Fox, 2011; Sandvik et al., 2017). Shame has been demonstrated to increase one's inability to adequately express anger and lower self-esteem. Thus, increasing one's risk for psychological issues and impairing one's ability to feel or express empathy (Tangney & Dearing, 2002). For those who have offended, the emotions of shame can lead to evading responsibility for their behaviour by denying or minimizing their offending or blaming their victims (Bumby et al., 1999).

Group therapy can address shame for adolescents who sexually harm by identifying misinformation about adolescent sexual offending, enhacing acceptance by members, and opportunities to demonstrate accountability (Brown, 2004). The processes of expressing vulnerability and sharing feelings in the group to decrease shame (Tangney & Dearing, 2002) often must be first modeled by the group facilitators, before being taken up by group members. Although a clinically significant treatment target, additional research must be done to demonstrate effective clinical practices for addressing this powerful and behaviourally suppressive emotion (Owen & Fox, 2011).

Myths and Facts about Adolescent Sexual Offending

Once the group has established the task of norming and is beginning to develop a sense of cohesion, discussions and activities are introduced that centre around the identification and reduction of the emotion of shame. A key activity concerns the sharing of myths and facts about sexual offending. This activity serves the purpose of identifying common shaming myths about adolescent sexual offending (Worling, 2013) that are based on commonly held stigmatizing beliefs. During the activity, many of the group participants express common myths that they have heard or believe themselves, such as the fact that they will not be able to travel across any borders for fear of being flagged by customs, or that they will never be able to hold a job in the future that involves work with children or vulnerable individuals. The myth of the enduring nature of sexual abusive behaviour is addressed during this activity, with many youth feeling relief upon learning that a majority of youth who sexually offend do not go on to reoffend as adults (Caldwell, 2016). The myths and facts discussion is often framed through a game, which in the past has taken the form of jeopardy, holding up myth/ fact paddles while seated, or the scaling of responses along a myth-fact line on the floor of the group room. This game allows members to dispute commonly held myths and to hear facts about adolescent sexual offending based on nearly three decades of research in the field. This means group members can begin to distinguish between their offending behaviours and their self-worth, individual responsibility, and the right to be respected as individuals.

The Weight in My Backpack and Obstacle Course

Another activity with the aim of literally demonstrating the weight of societal stigma and shame involves providing participants with backpacks (or using their own) and labeling heavy objects (usually stacks of printer paper) that are then placed in the backpack. The participants take turns identifying labels of consequences of sexual offending that they feel weigh them down. Such examples include their girlfriends or boyfriends breaking up with them as a result, the feeling of shame, and self-judgement. These labels are discussed as a group with an emphasis on developing emotional vocabulary and expressing vulnerability. Youth will demonstrate the weight of their backpacks by putting them on and walking around a room in one session. In future sessions, name tags are used to identify particular labels they hold as a result of the weight of their backpacks. The group will briefly walk around the room carrying their backpacks (if able), and introduce themselves to each other using the stigmatizing label.

At the end of the session, the youth develop a sort of obstacle course in the room using chairs and boxes that are on hand. They then label the objects with various pitfalls they may experience, such as "being mean", "toxic people", "not liking other people", "self-isolating", and "peer pressure". Group members either physically or symbolically guide each other through the obstacle course and discuss various strategies to overcome barriers instead of being weighed down by their backpacks. After each obstacle has been successfully navigated, the group member removes a weight from their backpack. At the end of the activity, the group members choose a new label they wish to be identified by ("independent", "smart", "brave", "insightful", "good listener", "kind", "athletic"), and wear that for the remainder of the session.

Stage II- Expanding Masculinity

All adolescents are affected by hegemonic understandings of gender and masculinity, (Pascoe & Hollander, 2015). Sexual violence has been conceptualized as a tool to assert masculinity as the dominant gender, resulting in the internalization of these beliefs by adolescents and eventual behavioural externalization (Cowburn, 2005). Adolescents who have sexually offended often hold hegemonically masculine beliefs, such as callous sexual or adversarial attitudes, towards females and sexual minorities, when compared to nonoffending adolescents (Farr, et al., 2004). Beliefs pertaining to hypermasculinity may be a particular reinforcer of sexual abuse as a means of enforcing gender norms, however, offending and nonoffending males did not significantly differ in regards to their hypermasculinity inventory scores (Farr et al., 2004). Therefore, all adolescents may benefit from cognitively dismantling and deconstructing hegemonically masculine ideals (Connell, 2002), and group therapy may be an effective modality to discuss masculine ideals, and for group members to begin recreating their preferred masculinity performances.

Male Role Models and Creating Your Own Man Box

When discussing masculinity with adolescents, it can be helpful to rely on prominent examples of what it means to be a man in media.

When the Unite and Redefine group is asked about what men they look up to for their manliness, typical responses generally include muscular actors cast to play superheroes or athletes. Responses have appeared to shift overtime to examples of men from the media who are famous not just for looking and being strong, but also for being a "nice guy". For instance, The Rock or John Cena, who are known for their sense of humour, kindness, and even demonstrations of their respect towards women (Google "The Rock's Daughters" for a salient example). These examples of tough and tender men are forging a new normal of Connell's hegemonic masculinity (2002) that leave space for discussions of respect and accountability-taking, while simultaneously ensuring gender-based violence becomes more subtle and innocuous (Duncanson, 2015). By setting the stage with prominent examples of men in the group therapy context, future discussions can be directed to describe how factors such as race, sexual orientation, sexual or dating prowess, wealth, and academic or athletic ability play in determining whether an individual is deemed "manly" or not.

Building on these discussions, activities based on Tony Porter's conceptualization of "The Man Box" (Porter, 2016) are presented, with hegemonically masculine character traits written or attached with sticky notes onto a cardboard box. Descriptors such as athletic, strong, funny, good looking, straight, and serial daters are added. This activity serves as a visual demonstration of what has been communicated to the participants as important in their gender presentation. The implications and sources of this conceptualization of masculinity are processed as a group. Leading from this discussion, the group then works together to construct a man box that they wish to emulate. Their new definitions of masculinity have included being honest, funny, a loyal friend, a good son or brother, and a respectful boyfriend. Strategies to enact these concepts are shared and discussed in an effort to enhance mutual aid amongst members.

Stage III- Becoming the Man You Want to Be

Adolescents who sexually offend often experience disproportionate levels of low self-esteem and social isolation (Miner, et al., 2010; Seto & Lalumiére, 2010). Compared to their nonsexually offending peers, this population frequently demonstrates deficits in social skills, an important component of the adolescent developmental stage

(Righthand & Welch, 2001). Feelings of low self-worth and experiences of social rejection or failure, combined with feelings of shame inherent to sexual offending, can be internalized by youth to result in a loss of hope for living productive and meaningful futures. As a result, one of the stages integral to the Unite and Redefine group therapy intervention is the facilitation of hope for the future and plans for lifelong meaning-making.

Victim Empathy, Apologizing, and Taking Accountability

One of the important components of sexual offending treatment is the consideration of the emotions and experiences of the victims who have been sexually offended. This topic is approached at such a time when shame has been effectively addressed and dealt with in the group context, and if the group has been deemed, by the facilitators and through the introduction of the subject with the members, able to approach the subject with honesty and vulnerability. Generally, it is best supported with a number of group members, who may be further along in their treatment, and who are able to lead the other members by modeling accountability and empathy. This topic is approached through the use of case studies and video demonstrations. Video clips demonstrating restorative justice and apology practices are chosen based on their relevance to ensure the materials are up to date and concerning recent issues that the group members can relate to. Examples include relevant scenes from adolescent or young adult television shows, or documentaries about restorative justice. At times, these sessions may require a return to discussing shame and how to overcome feelings of shame and low self-worth to honour the voices and experiences of their victims. The #metoo movement has allowed for a variety of responses to allegations of sexual abuse, ranging from a few examples of appropriate demonstrations of accountability to outright denial (Alexander, 2020). Youth are presented with apology letters that have beenvpublished in the media and are asked to share their thoughts and critiques. Often, the group participants find notable examples of responsibility deferral or minimization in the writing, and work together to improve the accountability-taking and apology component of the letters. Individual responsibility letters to their victims are often introduced in individual counselling, however the opportunity to hear from others and receive feedback based on an external source can build their self-esteem through practice knowledge and set the stage for the enactment of restorative apology work in their own relationships.

Planning the Future

One of the final activities carried out in the Unite and Redefine group includes the creation of a large road or path using postal board paper that expands the room. The road has designated stations with "Before", "Now", and "The Future" clearly labeled. The youth are invited to creatively contribute through writing, drawing, stickers, or roleplay who they thought of themselves in the past, how they think of themselves now, and who they wish to be in the future. Youth have written that in the past they have felt ashamed, alone, and in a cage. For the present time, they have explained that they feel less closed off or secretive about their identity, less alone, and guilty instead of ashamed for the sexual offending. When considering the future, the participants have shared that they want to feel like they are an ideal man, though the sharing of emotion, not taking advantage of women, and being more empathetic. At the end of this activity, a large piece of paper circles the group therapy room, externalizing and demonstrating how far the group members have come and where they wish to go.

Conclusion

Group therapy is an important treatment modality for adolescents who sexually offend. Group offers an opportunity for clients to learn prosocial attitudes through sharing and supportive challenging from other members and a decrease in feelings of loneliness and isolation. The Unite and Redefine group continues to evolve and grow with every iteration, as the needs of members change. For instance, the #Metoo Movement and the COVID-19 pandemic have brought new issues and concerns for this population, such as increased isolation, greater access to online offending opportunities or sexual media, and increased access to potential victims. These concerns can be addressed in the supportive environment of group therapy. Anecdotally, the group facilitators have noticed substantial changes in the lives of its group members, specifically in the realms of shame reduction, definitions of masculinity, and increased feelings hope as a result of participating in group therapy. Future research should investigate the effects of the Unite and Redefine group intervention on group members' sense of shame and guilt, adherence to masculinity ideologies, hope, and self compassion.

References

Alexander, C. S. (2020). Sorry (Not Sorry): Decoding# MeToo Defenses. *Texas Law Review, 99*, 341-388.

ATSA. (2017). *ATSA practice guidelines for assessment, treatment, and intervention with adolescents who have engaged in sexually abusive behavior.* Association for the Treatment of Sexual Abusers.

Borduin, C. M., & Schaeffer, C. M. (2001). Multisystemic treatment of juvenile sexual offenders: A progress report. *Journal of Psychology and Human Sexuality, 13*(3/4), 25-42. https://doi.org/10.1300/J056v13n03_03

Borduin, C. M., Schaeffer, C. M., & Heiblum, N. (2009). A randomized clinical trail of multisystemic therapy with juvenile sexual offenders: Effects on youth social ecology and criminal activity. *Journal of Consulting and Clinical Psychology, 77*(1), 26-37. https://doi.org/10.1037/a0013035

Bourgon, G., Morton-Bourgon, K. E., & Madrigano, G. (2005). Multisite investigation of treatment for sexually abusive juveniles. In B. K. Schwartz (Ed.), *The sex offender: Issues in assessment, treatment, and supervision of adult and juvenile populations: Volume V.* (pp. 15.1-15.17). Civic Research Institute.

Brown, J. (2004). Shame and domestic violence: Treatment perspectives for perpetrators from self psychology and affect theory. *Sexual and Relationship Therapy, 19*(1), 39-56. https://doi.org/10.1080/146819904 10001640826

Bukowski, W. M., Sippola, L., & Brender, W. (1993). Where does sexuality come from?: Normative sexuality from a developmental perspective. In H. Barbaree, W. L. Marshall, & S. Hudson (Eds.), *The juvenile sex offender* (pp. 84-103). Guilford Press.

Bumby, K. M., Marshall, W. L., & Langton, C. M. (1999). A theoretical model of the influences of shame and guilt on sexual offending. In B. Schwartz, & H. Cellini, *The sex offender* (pp. 5.1-5.12). Civic Research Institute.

Caldwell, M. F. (2016). Quantifying the decline in juvenile sexual recidivism rates. *Psychology, Public Policy, and Law, 22*(4), 414-426. https://doi.org/10.1037/law0000094

Connell, R. W. (2002). On hegemonic masculinity and violence: Response to Jefferson and Hall. *Theoretical Criminology, 6*(1), 89-99. https://doi.org/10.1177/136248060200600104

Costin, D., Schuler, S. A., & Curwen, T. (2009). *Responding to adolescent sexual offending recommendations for a regional protocol.* Halton Trauma Centre.

Cowburn, M. (2005). Hegemony and discourse: Reconstrucing the male sex offender and sexual coercion by men. *Sexualities, Evolution, & Gender, 7*(3), 215-231. https://doi.org/10.1080/14616660500231665

Deck, M., & Saddler, D. (1983). Freshmen awareness groups: A viable option for high school counselors. *The School Counselor, 30*(5), 392-397.

DiCataldo, F. C. (2009). *The perversion of youth controversies in the assessment and treatment of juvenile offenders.* NYU Press.

Duncanson, C. (2015). Hegemonic masculinity and the possibility of change in gender relations. *Men and Masculinities, 18*(2), 231-248. https://doi.org/10.1177/1097184X15584912

Fanniff, A. M., & Becker, J. V. (2006). Specialized assessment and treatment of adolescent sex offenders. *Aggression and Violent Behavior, 11*, 265-282. https://doi.org/10.1016/j.avb.2005.08.003

Farr, C., Brown, J., & Beckett, R. (2004). Ability to empathise and masculinity levels: Comparing male adoelscent sex offenders with a normative sample of non-offending adolescents. *Psychology, Crime & Law, 10*(2), 155-167. https://doi.org/10.1080/10683160310001597153

Fortune, C. A., Ward, T., & Willis, G. M. (2012). The rehabilitation of offenders: Reducing risk and promoting better lives. *Psychiatry, Psychology and Law, 19*(5), 646-661. https://doi.org/10.1080/13218719.2011.615809

Frost, A., & Connolly, M. (2004). Reflexcivity, reflection, and the change process in offender work. *Sexual Abuse, 16*(4), 365-380. https://doi.org/10.1177/107906320401600408

Geer, J. H., Estupinan, L. A., & Manguno-Mire, G. M. (2000). Empathy, social skills, and other relevant cognitive processes in rapists and child molesters. *Aggression and Violent Behaviour, 5*, 99-126. https://doi.org/10.1016/S1359-1789(98)00011-1

Halse, A., Grant, J., Thornton, J., Indermaur, D., Stevens, G., & Chamarette, C. (2012). Intrafamilial adoelscent sex offenders' response to psychological

treatment. *Psychiatry, Psychology and Law, 19*(2), 221-235. https://doi.or
g/10.1080/13218719.2011.561763

Jenkins, A. (2009). *Becoming ethical a parallel, political journey with men
who have abused* . Russell House Publishing.

Jennings, J. L., & Deming, A. (2017). Review of the empirical and clinical
support for group therapy specific to sexual abusers. *Sexual Abuse, 39*(8),
731-764. https://doi.org/10.1177/1079063215618376

Joliffe, D., & Farringdon, D. P. (2004). Empathy and offending: A systematic
review and meta-analysis. *Aggression and Violent Behaviour, 9,* 441-476.
https://doi.org/10.1016/j.avb.2003.03.001

Letourneau, E. J., Henggeler, S. W., Borduin, C. M., Schewe, P. A., McCart,
M. R., Chapman, J. E., & Saldana, L. (2009). Multisystemic therapy for
juvenile sexual offenders: 1-year results from a randomized effectiveness
trial. *Journal of Family Psychology, 23*(1), 89-102. https://doi.org/10.1037/
a0014352

Malekoff, A. (2015). *Group work with adolescents 3rd Edition.* The Guilford
Press.

Marshall, W. L., & Burton, D. L. (2010). The importance of group processes in
offender treatment. *Aggression and Violent Behavior, 15,* 141-149. https://
doi.org/10.1016/j.avb.2009.08.008

Marshall, W. L., Marshall, L., & Burton, D. L. (2013). Features of treatment
delivery and group processes that maximize the effects of offender
programs. In J. L. Wood, & T. A. Gannon (Eds.), *Crime and crime
reduction: The importance of group processes* (pp. 159-176). Routledge/
Taylor & Francis Group.

Marshall, W., Anderson, D., & Fernanyez, Y. (1999). *Cognitive behavioural
treatment of sexual offenders.* Wiley.

McGrath, R. J., Cumming, G. F., Burchard, B. L., Zeoli, S., & Ellerby, L. (2009).
Current practices and emerging trends in sexual abuser management.
The Safer Society.

Miner, M. H., Robinson, B. E., Knight, R. A., Berg, D., Swinburne Romine,
R., & Netland, J. (2010). Understanding sexual perpetration against
children: Effects of attachment style, interpersonal involvement, and
hypersexuality. *Sexual Abuse, 22*(1), 58-77.

Omizo, M., & Omizo, S. (1988). The effects of participation in group counseling
sessions on self-esteem and locus of control among adolescents from
divorced families. *The School Counselor, 36*(1), 54-60.

Owen, T., & Fox, S. (2011). Experiences of shame and empathy in violent and
non-violent young offenders. *Journal of Forensic Psychiatry & Psychology,
22*(4), 551-563.

Pascoe, C. J., & Hollander, J. A. (2016). Good guys don't rape: Gender, domination, and mobilizing rape. *Gender & Society, 30*(1), 67-79.

Pascoe, R. V., & Nicholls, R. L. (2019). A narrative of hope in group therapy with adolescents who have sexually harmed. *Social Work with Groups, 43*(1-2), 92-98. https://doi.org/10.1080/01609513.2019.1639015

Porter, T. (2016). *Breaking out of the "man box": The next generation of manhood.* New York: Simon and Schuster.

Righthand, S., & Welch, C. (2001). *Youths who have sexually offended: A review of the professional literature.* Office of Juvenile Justice and Delinquency Prevention.

Sandvik, M., Nesset, M. B., Berg, A., Søndenaa, E., (2017). The voices of young sexual offenders in Norway: A qualitative study. Open Journal of Social Sciences, 5, 82-95. https://doi.org/10.4236/jss.2017.52009

Schechtman, Z., Bar-el, O., & Hadar, E. (1997). Therapeutic factors and psycho educational groups for adolescents: A comparison. *Journal for Specialists in Group Work, 22*(3), 203-213. https://doi.org/10.1080/01933929708414381

Seto, M. C., & Lalumiére, M. L. (2010). What is so special about male adolescent sexual offending? A review and test of explanations through meta-analysis. *Psychological Bulletin, 136*(4), 526-575. https://doi.org/10.1037/a0019700

Seto, M. C., & Pullman, L. (2014). Risk factors for adolescent sexual offending. In G. Bruinsma, & D. Weisburd (Eds.), *Encyclopedia of criminology and criminal justice* (pp. 4466-4475). Springer.

Seto, M. C., Lalumiére, M. L., & Blanchard, R. (2000). The discriminative validity of a phallometric test for pedophilic interests among adolescent sex offenders against children. *Psychological Assessment, 12*(3), 319. https://doi.org/10.1037/1040-3590.12.3.319

Seto, M. C., Murphy, W. D., Page, J., & Ennis, L. (2003). Detecting anomalous sexual interests in juvenile sex offenders. *Annals of the New York Academy of Sciences, 989*(1), 118-130. https://doi.org/10.1111/j.1749-6632.2003.tb07298.x

Shaw, D. E., & Siegel, B. L. (2010). Re-Adjusting the kaleidoscope: The basic tenants of invitational theory and practice. Journal of Invitational Theory and Practice, 16, 106-113.

Sribney, C. L., & Reddon, J. R. (2008). Adolescent sex offenders' rankings of therapeutic factors using the yalom card sort. Journal of Offender Rehabilitation, 47(1-2), 24-40. https://doi.org/10.1080/10509670801940367

Tangney, J. P., & Dearing, R. L. (2002). Shame and Guilt. The Guilford Press.

Widom, C., & Massey, C. (2015). A propsective examination of whether sexual abuse predicts subsequent offending. JAMA Pediatrics, 169(1), e143357-e143357. https://doi.org/10.1001/jamapediatrics.2014.3357

Worling, J. (2004). Essentials of a good intervention programme for sexually abusive juveniles. In G. O'Reilly, W. L. Marshall, A. Carr, & R. C. Beckett (Eds.), The handbook of clinical intervention with young people who sexually abuse (pp. 275-296). Brunner-Routledge.

Worling, J. (2013). What were we thinking? Five erroneous assumptions that have fueled specialized interventions for adolescents who have sexually offended. International Journal of Behavioral Consultation and Therapy, 8(3-4), 80-88. https://doi.org/10.1037/h0100988

Worling, J. R., & Curwen, T. (2000). Adolescent sexual offender recidivism: Success of specialized treatmenet and implications for risk prediction. Child Abuse & Neglect, 24(7), 965-982. https://doi.org/10.1016/S0145-2134(00)00147-2

Worling, J. R., Bookalam, D., & Litteljohn, A. (2012). Prospective validity of the estimate of risk of adolescent sexual offense recidivism (ERASOR). Sexual Abuse, 24(3), 203-223. https://doi.org/10.1177/1079063211407080

Yalom, I., & Leszcz, M. (2005). The theory and practice of group psychotherapy (5th edition). Basic Books.

Zakireh, B., Ronis, S. T., & Knight, R. A. (2008). Individual beliefs, attitudes, and victimization histories of male juvenile sexual offenders. Sexual Abuse: A Journal of Research and Treatment, 20, 323-351. https://doi.org/10.1177/1079063208322424

Using Narrative Group Therapy to Eradicate Social Isolation

Todd Tedrow

The American Academy of Social Work and Social Welfare, through the Grand Challenges of Social Work initiative, has identified Social Isolation as one of the Grand Challenges for Social Work and Society. In the Academy's concept paper on this topic, social isolation is described as a "potent killer". The negative impact of social isolation on multiple life domains, is fully explored (Fong et al., n.d.). This submission for the International Association for Social Work with Groups (IASWG), illustrates the components of a session presented for IASWG at their annual symposium in 2019 at New York University where the theme was, *Group Work in Communities: Breaking Down Barriers, Building Global Connection.* The presentation that is the subject of this chapter, *A Toolkit for Social Engagement: Using Narrative Therapy to Eradicate Social Isolation*, was developed to provide an overview of how narrative therapy group work could be considered as a pathway to social connection, and therefore, potentially mitigate the host of negative outcomes that come from social isolation. This paper explores how a narrative therapy group process may offer paths to social re-emergence, positive social experiences, and improved relationships for participants. This chapter, and the original presentation was informed by a study completed at a skilled-nursing facility in 2016 as a requirement for the completion of a doctorate in social work.

Social Support

The availability of social and emotional support has been shown to be a correlate, as well as a factor related to the nature and course of depression. The CDC Behavioral Risk Factor Surveillance and Indicators Data demonstrate that adequate social support is associated with a reduced risk of several negative outcomes. The support functions identified include instrumental support (direct services), informational support, and emotional support (Centers for Disease Control and Prevention [CDC], n.d.). A model developed by Sadavoy (2009), considers depression within a "complex cascade" that considers not only the complexity, but also chronicity, comorbidity, continuity, and context. Each of these factors informed the study as many of the participants exhibited multiple challenges in each of these areas.

All participants suffered from chronic diseases that led to the need for placement in a skilled-nursing facility. Comorbidity was observed as a constant, with participants experiencing multiple medical illnesses during the 8-week group intervention. The idea of continuity involves patterns of involvement in life vs. withdrawal, support, self-esteem, reactions to loss, and other patterns that inform the development of depression. Many of these factors were observed in the sample. Finally, context involves social support and other factors that define an elder person's current experience. The context of the participants' experience in this study was complex, and several themes emerged related to the context of the group. Reker (1997) considers declining social contacts owing to health limitations and a decreased range of coping options as factors to consider with late-life depression. Finally, Krause (2007) considers social support and meaning in life, and discusses enacted support, anticipated support, and negative interaction as factors to consider. The impact of the quality and type of social support is a critical factor to consider when exploring mental health in later life.

Mental Health in Later Life

Depression with the aging population is a public health issue in need of additional research. Society is aging, and depression is the most prevalent mental health issue with older adults. Institutionalized adults have rates of depression as high as 35% (Thakur & Blazer, 2008). The rate of depression for those with Alzheimer's Disease is estimated to be between 20% and 50% (Sadavoy, 2009). There are numerous negative outcomes associated with depression and the elderly, including a decreased quality of life, increased morbidity (Berkman et al., 1986), poor adjustment, increased risk of suicide, disability, increased mortality and poorer outcomes from physical illnesses (Rodda, 2011).

Mental distress has an impact on major life activities as well as physical health (Centers for Disease Control and Prevention [CDC], n.d.).

The treatment of depression presents a particular challenge when working with older adults (Snowden et al., 2008). In a review of 97 studies, considering 24 different treatment modalities, the authors determined that only two types of treatment, depression care management (both home-based and clinic-based), and cognitive behavioral therapy, were recommended. Other approaches were noted to have mixed effectiveness, were ineffective, or were not sufficiently studied. Pharmacotherapy, primarily with anti-depressant medication, has demonstrated mixed effectiveness and carries certain risks with the elderly (Thakur & Blazer, 2008). In addition, pharmacotherapy may not always be as effective with the elderly as with younger populations (Knochel, et al., 2015). Finally, older adults may be reluctant to consider pharmacotherapy (Chand, 2013). These factors demonstrate a need for additional research, and a strong consideration of alternative treatment strategies.

The larger picture of mental health is illustrated in the data collected by the CDC through the Behavioral Risk Factor Surveillance System and Indicators (Centers for Disease Control and Prevention [CDC], n.d.). All 50 of the United States collection information on life satisfaction, the number of mentally unhealthy days, and the availability of social and emotional support. Thirty-eight states additionally collected information relating to anxiety and depression. Measures collected represented social and emotional support, life satisfaction, and whether the subject was currently depressed, or had a lifetime of depression. Adequate social support was associated with reduced risk of several negative outcomes including reduced mortality, reduced rates of mental illness and reduced risk of physical illness. The major support functions identified included instrumental support (direct services), informational support, and emotional support such as venting emotions and sharing problems.

Reker (1997) considered precipitating factors to late-life depression, which he described as distinct from early-age onset depression. These included psychosocial factors, genetic factors, situational factors and biological factors including illness. He stressed the greater importance of environmental events in late-life depression such as "the loss of self-esteem (helplessness, powerlessness, alienation), loss of meaningful roles (work productivity), loss of significant others, declining social contacts owing to health limitations and reduced functional status, dwindling financial resources, and a decreasing range of coping options" (p. 709) as factors that may contribute to late-life depression.

These factors coalesce around a few significant domains that include environmental risks, inadequate social support, illness and other biological factors, negative life events, financial stressors, personality vulnerabilities, and a lost sense of purpose and meaning in life. These identified factors are expected to have a negative impact on mental health outcomes described by Sadavoy (2009) as demoralization, hopelessness, anxiety, withdrawal, and loneliness. Reker (1997) offered additional negative outcomes such as loss of self-esteem, loss of meaningful roles (and identity), and loss of meaning in life.

Method

Study Sample

The study involved a group of participants residing in a long-term care facility. The sample of subjects who chose to participate, received an 8-week group intervention using narrative approaches. Participants ranged in age from 58 to 99 and were noted to have significant functional and medical deficits.

Intervention Design

The group met weekly at the skilled-nursing facility for 8 weeks. Each session lasted 90 minutes. Participants were instrumental in guiding the topics, with a shared understanding of the purpose and structure of a narrative therapy group. The group was facilitated by the lead author and an activity aide with extensive experience in working with older adults. At the start of each session, participants were provided with a container of narrative prompts. A participant would draw a question from the bowl and direct the question to another participant, and each participant would eventually answer the question; answers that were often accompanied by rich descriptions of participants' lived experience. The facilitation process involved curious inquiry and carefully considered responses to magnify positive characteristics of the story, the individual, and similarities in their experiences. Participants were noted to adopt this facilitation style as the group progressed, mirroring the style of the facilitators.

Data Collection

The mixed-methods study measured three variables before and after an 8-week narrative therapy group. The variables considered included depression, meaning-in-life, and self-esteem. In addition, group members participated in focused individual interviews to explore the impact of the narrative group after the group was completed. While there were not any significant quantitative findings, strong themes emerged in the qualitative data which appear in the following section.

Results

The study findings demonstrated several thematic elements that inform social support and the group factors that inform that support including: *Learning about Others, Emerging Socially, Comparing Ourselves to Others, and Transforming Relationships.* These major thematic elements were comprised of several sub-categories that allowed for a fuller description of the data and ultimately the therapeutic process that was experienced by the participants.

Learning About Others and Ourselves

The first major theme to emerge from the data, *learning about others and ourselves*, appeared in multiple sections of the interviews. The responses were organized into two sub-categories. The first category, *learning about others*, had 17 different responses by seven (100%) of the participants, indicating a value was placed on learning about others' experiences. In contrast, there were four responses by two participants (29%) that indicated that they valued *learning about ourselves*-still identified as important, but not mentioned nearly as often, nor by nearly as many participants, as *learning about others.*

Within the sub-theme of *learning about others*, there were several examples shared where participants indicated they were able to experience one another in ways that may not have been experienced outside of the group. On theme presented as *a developing social interest* in others. These comments involved quotes such as, "I learned a lot of things about other people, things I didn't know before, I'm sure, very interesting". One participant stated, "I thought *what* the sessions were for, were meaningful, and I got to learn from each session, because each of the participants who spoke, on any of the essential questions, I learned from what each of them had to say". An additional participant stated, "…[the group] was interesting because everybody tell story, I [was] just so happy [to] find out what people [were] going through".

An additional sub-theme involved the idea that new exposure to other participants prompted an *acceptance and appreciation* of the other participant's lived experience. A participant captured the concept of appreciation in stating:

> *I think it has more helped, especially for me, in learning what other people's life was like, because they all grew up differently than me, and very much differently than each other, but they were happy to talk about what that difference is, and we were all happy to listen to it" (interview, 2016).*

Another example that illustrates *acceptance and appreciation* included a comment from a participant who stated, "I got a picture of just about everybody that was there and talked…even (identifies another participant), I listened to him, which is unheard of, because him and I don't get along". Another illustration of the idea of acceptance was when a participant indicated that one of the aspects she liked best involved, "accepting what they did, and accepting where they were going".

Participants also expressed the experience of *learning about themselves*. One participant stated, "I learning things in my life that I thought were dead". Yet another, enjoyed, "telling them everything that I did".

Emerging Socially

The second theme involved the theme of *emerging socially* and these responses appeared in answers to multiple questions. The sub-categories included, *positive social experience, wanting more social interaction, sharing,* and *emergence.* These experiences were reflected in comments about their participation and indicated they found participation enjoyable, and found "just being" with other people as beneficial. Sixteen responses by seven participants (100%), indicated having a *positive social experience* in the group. An important, but less prevalent set of responses, with nine responses from four participants (57%), indicated that they wanted *more social interaction.* This included wanting others to contribute more, as well as wishing they had contributed more. In addition, a related component involved identifying the desire for the group to meet more often, and for the group to continue after the completion of the study. This category seems to represent an expression of *social longing*-a desire to have more quality interaction. Eleven responses by seven participants (100%) identified the experience of *sharing* as a positive outcome of the group. Finally, a sub-category appeared that involved the identification of a type of *emergence.* This category was conceptualized through the consideration that something "new" was either experienced or learned by participation in the group. A few examples of emerging socially through the group process included "waking up", "getting out of my shell", "I learned things in my life that I thought were dead" and a process of "opening up". There were 24 responses from six participants (86%) that indicated a type of *emergence.* One participant stated (with an accent):

> *I liked most about group, get[ting] together and open[ing] up, people get together and talk about whatever problem they have and I think that is very helpful for people (interview, 2016).*

Comparing Ourselves to Others

A third theme or category identified involved *comparing ourselves to others.* Sub-categories within this domain include the identification of the experience of developing a sense of *relatedness* with four responses by three participants (43%). Participants also engaged in a process of *direct comparison* of themselves to others in the group. Fourteen responses, by five participants (71%) reflected a *direct comparison.* Two participants, in four different statements, made *upward appraisals*-

meaning others in the group were "better off" than they were. In the case of one respondent, she felt as though seeing other people relate "happy" life experiences was of benefit. She stated, "I like the happiness… maybe [they] have a better life than my life". Two participants did direct comparisons that were neutral. Eight responses indicated a *downward comparison*; they indicated that a benefit of the group was that they learned they were "better off" than other participants. This idea was expressed by four of the seven participants or 57%. One statement that represented this concept was, "well you didn't have it so hard as some of them did. It made me stronger, and I felt I wasn't so bad off myself" (interview, May 10, 2016).

Transforming Relationships

The fourth and final theme involved *transforming relationships*. This concept involves the sub-categories of *improved relationships* and *helping others*. The quality and type of the relationships appeared to have changed throughout the group process. Improved relationships were noted in 10 of the responses by five participants (71%). Some of the responses involved an improvement in a current relationship with another group member. For example, prior to group, a negative relationship was experienced, but after participation in group, the relationship improved. Other responses indicated that the process of learning and knowing about others lead to opportunities for better relationships. Nine of the responses in this category by three respondents (43%) indicated that participation in group allowed an opportunity to *help others*; this was viewed as beneficial by the respondents.

Discussion

Several of Yalom's (2005) therapeutic factors provide a structure for consideration of the results of this study. In particular, universality, altruism, interpersonal learning, and group cohesiveness will be considered.

Universality involves people having a sense of "extreme social isolation" and a heightened sense of uniqueness. When concerns are shared, a sense of universality develops. This "we are all in the same boat" experience helps to reduce a sense of isolation, according to Yalom. The idea of Universality was clearly demonstrated in this study. First, participants did experience *social longing*; one aspect involved isolation, a second component involved poor quality relationships. An additional component involves *comparison to others*. Many of the participants went through a process of making a direct comparison to others. In this comparison, either downward (I am not as bad off as others), upward (I like to hear about their happiness because I had a hard life), or neutral; participants gravitated toward comparisons, and in many comments, this was viewed as beneficial. This allowed for additional opportunities for relatedness.

Altruism is described by Yalom (2005) as a process where helping others helps us feel better about ourselves. This involves providing support, reassurance, suggestion, insight, and the sharing of similar problems. The process prevents "morbid self-absorption" and allows participants to become absorbed in something external to themselves. This concept was demonstrated in the study in the observation of the theme of *transforming relationships*, with a specific sub-theme of *helping others*, where several of the group members described the process of helping others as a benefit of participation. The shift from sharing one's life experience to helping others is likely a process that would have continued, had the group extended beyond the 8-week intervention.

Interpersonal learning, is an additional, and relevant factor described by Yalom. Here, Yalom expanded upon this concept by describing the importance of interpersonal relationships, the experiencing of a corrective emotional experience, and the group as a social microcosm. For the purpose of this study, the importance of interpersonal relationships and the corrective emotional experience are considered. Interpersonal learning was experienced throughout this group process. In fact, learning about others was a highly valued aspect of the group with every participant identifying this as something they valued in the group. Learning about others appears to have been of much higher value than learning about themselves. The desire for social engagement was matched by a keen desire to learn about others. Relationship quality was expressed in several stages of the model as *improved relationships*. *Learning about others* helped improve their relationships by developing a sense of relatedness through *sharing*. There also appears to be a corrective emotional experience where participants described troubled relationships transforming into positive relationships.

The final of Yalom's therapeutic factors considered was group cohesiveness. Yalom described group cohesion as analogous to the idea of therapist-client relationship in individual therapy. The relationship with the group determines clinical outcome. One of the factors Yalom considered was how the participant's attraction to the group could be impacted by a sense of belonging. Also considered is Yalom's description of how cohesiveness develops. He described this process as an "affective sharing of one's inner world and then acceptance by others" (p. 56). Although the degree of cohesion appeared to vary among participants in this study, several of the themes identified indicate that cohesion was sought, experienced, and then helped produce a positive outcome.

Narrative Considerations

The design of this study involved the use of narrative approaches toward existential ends in order to have an impact on well-being. In general, in this group, stories were not necessarily presented for the purpose of change. The stories shared were quite entrenched. However, the group appeared to work toward the creation of *new experiences* and relationships by actually *experiencing* others in a novel context. Something *new* developed in their relationships.

Another way to consider this idea is to consider the group process itself as a story. The stories prior to group were sometimes explicit, and other times, submerged. An example of a submerged narrative would be the illumination of some of the conflictual relationships described at the end of the group. These were captured in the expressions of transformed relationships.

> *[She] was kind of, you know, everybody said she's kind of mean to people. I was sitting by the table a couple of times (in group)... and she was nice to me, it's nice to talk to her and since then we are very good friends. No problem. It's like everybody says like, 'are you all right with her?', and I said, 'yes, no problem with me', and we make friends just like that (interview May 10, 2016).*

In this quote, the participant identified a transformed relationship, but also we see a narrative transforming, following these steps:

1. Everybody said she's mean.
2. I had a nice experience with her in group.

3. Now we are very good friends.
4. I have developed a new source of social support.

There is an important distinction in this group that warrants restatement. The participants were less engaged with transforming past stories, but rather, were focused on creating new experiences, new relationships, and new stories, most with a more positive view of others than prior to group. The narrative approach provided a *path* to learn about others, have positive social experiences, emerge socially, share with others-all leading to improved relationships and improved narratives. Their individual stories may not have changed, but their stories about experiencing one another *did* change.

The narrative approach, and the use of narrative techniques in group work are an area for further research. Telling life stories, sharing life experience, and hearing the experiences of others appeared to create a comfortable and dynamic format for group participants to learn about others and to reconsider their own life experiences. It also allowed the participants to create new experiences with new meaning. In this particular group of participants, this narrative experiencing with others seemed to have a benefit toward *social emergence, new learning, and improved relationships.*

Implications for Social Work

Social work values are reflected in six core principles that include service, social justice, the dignity and worth of the person, the importance of human relationships, integrity and competence (NASW, 2016). The institutionalized elderly are highly vulnerable and are an oppressed population, plagued with poor outcomes in multiple domains (Thakur & Blazer, 2008) and often caught in a "complex cascade" of events that lead to poor mental health outcomes (Sadavoy, 2009). Many of the problems experienced stem from social factors, relating to social policy, social isolation, and impaired relationships. An integrated treatment model, such as social work, is well suited to address the complex needs of this population.

This study informs direct practice in several ways, both at the micro and mezzo level of practice. In working with the institutionalized elderly, this study seemed to indicate that while many basic needs may be met, especially as it relates to medical care, housing, food, and others; emotional needs and the need for social support are areas for improvement. Of interest, many nursing home residents are often in a more social environment than they were prior to placement. Why then, in an environment that should allow for more opportunities for socialization (more people, more activity, interaction with staff, interaction with volunteers, and others) do people experience a *social longing* or sense of isolation? One answer may be related to the quality of the social experience. While there may be many diversional activities or group events, many of which may promote a positive social experience, they may not provide the type of environment that allows for *learning about others, sharing, social emergence* and *improved relationships* with a level of thoughtfulness that helps formally develop strong social support networks. Nursing homes often appear to be "resource poor". The formal development of a resident social support network might be a path toward better outcomes that requires very little time from direct care providers. From the perspective of the social worker at the facility, formal processes to develop support networks within the nursing home may be an area of consideration. This idea relates directly to the social work value of the importance of human relationships.

At the macro practice level, there are considerations related to the findings in this study. Social work is unique in the mental health profession in its focus on the person-in-environment (NASW, 2016). The National Association of Social Workers provides guidance on the practice of social work in long-term care settings (2003) which indicates that the function of social work in these settings is multi-faceted, but should focus on the preservation and enhancement of social functioning through strengthening communication, creating and enhancing a therapeutic environment and promoting interaction. This study illustrates one approach that may assist with these social work functions.

Social justice is a social work value that underscores the very purpose of this study. The institutionalized elderly are a vulnerable and oppressed population who are subject to an array of negative outcomes at every level of human functioning and every level of society-yet our ability to effectively support and treat these individuals is woefully inadequate. The aging of our population supports the need to develop better interventions and options for a better quality of life for the elderly population. Narrative group therapy is an area to consider for improving that quality of life.

References

Berkman, L. F., Berkman, C. S., Kasl, S., Freeman, D. H., Leo, L., Ostfeld, A. M., Cornoni-Huntley, J., & Brody, J. A. (1986). Depressive symptoms in relation to physical health and functioning in the elderly. *American Journal of Epidemiology, 124*(3), 372–388. https://doi.org/10.1093/oxfordjournals.aje.a114408

Chand, S. P., & Grossberg, G. T. (2022). Adapting cognitive behavioral therapy for older adults with anxiety disorders and depression. In *Evidence-based treatment for anxiety disorders and depression* (pp. 599–619). Cambridge University Press. https://doi.org/10.1017/9781108355605.034

Knochel, C., Alves, G., Friedrichs, B., Schneider, B., Schmidt-Rechau, A., Wenzler, S., Schneider, A., Prvulovic, D., F. Carvalho, A., & Oertel-Knochel, V. (2015). Treatment-resistant late-life depression: Challenges and perspectives. *Current Neuropharmacology, 13*(5), 577–591. https://doi.org/10.2174/1570159x1305151013200032

Krause, N. (2007). Longitudinal study of social support and meaning in life. *Psychology and Aging, 22*(3), 456–469. https://doi.org/10.1037/0882-7974.22.3.456

NASW. (2016). National association of social workers. https://www.socialworkers.org

Reker, G. T. (1997). Personal meaning, optimism, and choice: Existential predictors of depression in community and institutional elderly. *The Gerontologist, 37*(6), 709–716. https://doi.org/10.1093/geront/37.6.709

Reker, G. T. (2001). Prospective predictors of successful aging in community-residing and institutionalized canadian elderly. *Ageing International, 27*(1), 42–64. https://doi.org/10.1007/s12126-001-1015-4

Rodda, J., Walker, Z., & Carter, J. (2011). Depression in older adults. *BMJ, 343*(sep28 1), d5219–d5219. https://doi.org/10.1136/bmj.d5219

Sadavoy, J. (2009). An integrated model for defining the scope of geriatrics: the 5 Cs. *International Psychogeriatrics, 21*(5), 805–812. https://doi.org/10.1017/S104161020999010X

Thakur, M., & Blazer, D. G. (2008). Depression in long-term care. *Journal of the American Medical Directors Association, 9*(2), 82–87. https://doi.org/10.1016/j.jamda.2007.09.007

Yalom, I. D., & Leszcz, M. (2008). *The theory and practice of group psychotherapy* (5th ed.). Basic Books.

Inclure des exclus : le récit d'un groupe de soutien improbable sur une unité hospitalière de toxicomanie et de santé urbaine

Catherine Dugas et Éric Gascon

En 2017 démarrait le service de toxicomanie et de médecine urbaine (STMU) à l'hôpital Notre-Dame de Montréal, situé en plein cœur d'un centre-ville marqué par une diversité ethnique, sexuelle et socio-économique, dont une partie significative de la population est touchée par des problèmes d'utilisation de substances psychoactives ou d'itinérance. Certaines personnes ayant un trouble d'utilisation de substances sont orientées vers le STMU afin d'encadrer de façon sécuritaire leur sevrage ou d'adapter les soins hospitaliers à leur réalité de consommation. L'approche s'y veut holistique, humaine, accessible, favorisant la réaffiliation et l'autonomisation. Dans l'offre de services de cette nouvelle unité d'hospitalisation, l'équipe psychosociale – composée de travailleurs sociaux, d'une ergothérapeute et d'une neuropsychologue – s'est vu donné le mandat d'accompagner les personnes hospitalisées dans un processus de changement favorable à la réduction des méfaits liés à l'utilisation de substances. La réduction des méfaits englobe une pluralité d'objectifs allant de l'abstinence à la minimisation d'une conséquence spécifique d'un usage actif de substances.

Un des moyens préconisés par l'équipe psychosociale pour accompagner les usagers dans les changements souhaités est la mise en place de groupes de soutien bihebdomadaires co-animés par un des travailleurs sociaux et l'ergothérapeute. Rapidement, de multiples obstacles cliniques, organisationnels et professionnels sont venus complexifier l'implantation des groupes et freiner l'inclusion de certaines personnes déjà fortement marginalisées. Malgré ceci, l'équipe psychosociale persévère et les groupes en viennent à s'inscrire de façon durable dans l'offre de services, avec des bénéfices évidents pour les participants.

L'objectif de ce récit de pratique est de vous partager cette expérience de groupe que nous jugeons improbable et pourtant réelle afin d'encourager d'autres intervenants à surpasser les obstacles apparents et créer des espaces de soutien pour des personnes qui autrement seraient exclues des interventions de groupe. D'abord, nous présenterons les obstacles auxquels nous avons été confrontés ; ensuite, nous discuterons des actions posées pour surpasser ces barrières, en s'appuyant de la littérature qui nous a inspirés; enfin, nous élaborerons sur les bénéfices observés chez les membres du groupe.

Des groupes improbables

Le dictionnaire Robert énonce qu'est improbable ce « qui a peu de chance de se produire » ou « qui étonne par son caractère peu ordinaire ». Nous avons l'habitude de qualifier d'improbables les rencontres de groupe que nous réalisons au STMU car autant les caractéristiques des usagers que du contexte organisationnel nous ont initialement fait douter de la faisabilité de tels groupes et peut étonner encore aujourd'hui. Dans cette section, nous souhaitons identifier ces facteurs qui auraient pu nous décourager à déployer cette intervention de groupe et ainsi amorcer une réflexion sur ce qui peut faire obstacle au déploiement des interventions de groupes dans les milieux de soins et de services.

Des participants aux caractéristiques improbables

Ces groupes réunissent des exclus, des personnes dont on encourage peu la participation sociale et qu'on invite par conséquent trop rarement dans des groupes de développement. Lors de ces rencontres, se côtoient autant des personnes identifiées comme toxicomanes, itinérantes, autochtones, trans, autistes, handicapées, démentes, schizophrènes... Ce sont autour de ces étiquettes, de ces stigmates, que se sont développé leur isolement et leur désaffiliation. Ce n'est pas par hasard que ces populations marginalisées sont surreprésentées dans nos services, car cette exclusion participe grandement à la gravité de leur dépendance. Certaines de ces caractéristiques sociales sont par ailleurs considérées comme des critères d'exclusion dans de nombreux groupes.

En effet, ces caractéristiques donnent lieu à des états ou des comportements qui peuvent faire obstacle à leur participation et inquiéter les intervenants : certains sont psychotiques ou confus, d'autres sont intoxiqués ou en sevrage, d'autres encore sont agités, endormis, agressifs, désinhibés ou inattentifs. Ce sont les symptômes des troubles qui les affligent, des traumas qu'ils ont vécus, de la dureté de leur mode de vie, de leur place dans les rapports sociaux. C'est sur la base de ces comportements ou sur la crainte de ceux-ci que des usagers sont souvent exclus lors de la composition des groupes. Pourtant, nous ne pouvons demander à ces personnes de guérir de leurs troubles et de leur vie avant de participer au traitement.

Comme le mentionne Eaton (2017) lorsqu'elle relate son expérience de groupe de réduction des méfaits auprès d'une population marginale, dire que la composition de nos groupes est diverse serait un euphémisme. Au STMU, nous avons pris le pari d'accueillir tous ceux et celles qui souhaitent participer aux groupes et d'embrasser cette diversité plutôt que de la concevoir d'emblée comme un obstacle.

Un contexte improbable

Nos groupes peuvent aussi être considérés improbables en raison du contexte organisationnel dans lequel ils se sont développés. Les centres hospitaliers sont des univers principalement axés sur les soins médicaux. Il peut être plus difficile pour des services psychosociaux d'y trouver leur place. Nous soulèverons ici quelques enjeux liés au contexte hospitalier, tel que les horaires de soins, la durée des hospitalisations, la diversité des objectifs et la collaboration interprofessionnelle.

Cette priorité aux soins médicaux peut, en effet, nuire à la disponibilité des participants car les horaires d'examens, de soins, de traitements peuvent être incompatibles avec l'horaire du groupe. Par exemples, est-ce qu'un examen par résonance magnétique, un prélèvement sanguin, la tournée du médecin doivent avoir préséance sur la participation à un groupe de soutien ? C'est avec cette réalité que nous avons composé.

De plus, la plupart des durées d'hospitalisation sur notre unité sont brèves et ne dépassent souvent pas une semaine. Les usagers sont parfois, en début de séjour, dans une condition physique les rendant peu disponibles pour leur participation au groupe. La fenêtre de participation est donc réduite tout comme la possibilité de s'engager dans plus d'une rencontre.

Aussi, les participants sont, en majorité, hospitalisés sur notre unité dans le contexte d'une urgence médicale. Ils n'avaient donc pas prévu, ni initialement souhaité, être invités dans un groupe de soutien. Leur état de santé évoluant rapidement, la date exacte du congé n'est que rarement prévue à l'avance; les participants ne peuvent généralement pas savoir s'ils seront encore sur l'unité au moment de la prochaine rencontre de groupe.

Également, les participants ont des objectifs très variés. Certains ont souhaité être hospitalisés afin de faire un sevrage sécuritaire pour cesser leur consommation et débuter un processus de réadaptation. D'autres n'attendent que le moment où ils seront physiquement capables de retourner à leur mode de vie de consommation. D'autres encore choisissent de demeurer hospitalisés pour répondre à certains besoins qui peuvent avoir été occasionnés par leur consommation, comme d'accéder à un milieu d'hébergement sécuritaire. L'enjeu de la cible commune se présente donc. Qu'est-ce qui relie ces usagers ? Que partagent-ils ?

Enfin, la coanimation des groupes par une ergothérapeute et un travailleur social aurait pu poser des enjeux de collaboration interprofessionnelle. La diversité était aussi présente du côté de l'équipe d'animation. Comment concilier des cadres de référence différents concernant l'intervention de groupe?

En conclusion, bien que nous connaissions l'importance de se donner des conditions gagnantes pour implanter des groupes; au STMU, nous sommes parvenus au constat que l'adoption de plusieurs éléments généralement importants lors de la phase de planification d'un groupe (critères d'inclusion et d'exclusion spécifiques, but et objectifs prédéfinis, durée déterminée, contenu manualisé...) limiteraient la capacité du groupe à s'adapter à son contexte et participerait à l'exclusion de certains participants. Confrontés à des participants et à un contexte improbables, nous avons surpassé les obstacles à la participation, adapté nos interventions pour susciter l'aide mutuelle et priorisé l'émergence des facteurs d'aide.

Surpasser les barrières liées aux participants

Deux défis émergent des barrières cliniques identifiées. Le premier est que chaque usager soit accueilli dans le groupe et puisse en bénéficier, malgré son internalisation des stigmates sociaux, ses limitations fonctionnelles, ses symptômes et inconforts du moment. Le second défi est que la dynamique de groupe puisse émerger malgré l'hétérogénéité du groupe et les particularités de chacun.

Accueillir chaque participant

Une des actions déterminantes de la tenue du groupe a été de n'établir aucun critère d'exclusion. Cette idée fondatrice que « tous sont bienvenus » nous engagent à faire preuve de courage et à être universellement accueillants.

Pour citer Steinberg (2014), c'est en raison du chaos et de l'imprévisibilité des interventions de groupe que les intervenants devront faire preuve de courage. Dès la phase de préparation, alors que nous anticipons les défis liés à la composition du groupe, nous devons nous encourager mutuellement, nous rappeler notre engagement de n'exclure personne. Tout au long du déroulement de la rencontre de groupe, la présence de l'un et de l'autre nous permet de tolérer le chaos décrit par Steinberg et poursuivre l'intervention. Selon notre expérience, le fait de travailler en co-animation augmente les ressources disponibles pour se donner courage.

Afin d'appliquer une approche inclusive, le temps accordé au recrutement et à la préparation des participants est crucial. Chaque rencontre pré-groupe, même si elle est parfois très brève, sera déterminante pour que la personne perçoive le groupe comme un lieu accueillant et utile. Ainsi, nous rencontrons chaque usager à son chevet pour lui présenter le groupe – ayant lieu le jour même – et répondre à ses questions. Nous utilisons l'approche motivationnelle pour surpasser les résistances qui émergent naturellement. En plus, des adaptations ou aménagements sont souvent requis pour favoriser l'inclusion de tous les usagers. Selon les besoins, cela comprend de décortiquer le fonctionnement du groupe pour atténuer le stress, d'adapter l'information verbale aux limitations cognitives, de fournir une aide à la communication, d'assister physiquement les usagers à mobilité réduite, d'adapter la durée du groupe, et bien d'autres.

Nous devons également veiller à ce que chaque usager soit disponible dans le contexte de son horaire de soins, des rencontres avec les spécialistes, de la prise de médication ou de toute autre besoin comme la faim ou l'envie d'uriner. Cette coordination auprès de l'équipe et cette préparation des usagers nécessitent du temps et une attention particulière. Considérant le roulement important des usagers sur l'unité d'hospitalisation, cette phase de planification et de préparation est répétée à chacune des rencontres de groupe.

Faire émerger la dynamique de groupe

Pour Pelech et ses collaborateurs (2016), la pratique de groupe doit nécessairement être inclusive de la diversité. Bien que l'hétérogénéité dans la composition du groupe soit une caractéristique marquante de ce récit, elle est considérée comme normale et donc inhérente à la création d'un groupe. Ces auteurs conçoivent d'ailleurs la diversité comme un concept relationnel. En fait, la diversité n'est pas une caractéristique portée par un participant, elle se manifeste dans la pluralité des perspectives émergeant de l'interaction entre des personnes, en considérant les précédents historiques, le climat politique, les valeurs et croyances personnelles ainsi que la situation et l'environnement immédiats (Pelech et al., 2016; Foronda, 2020). Afin de faire émerger la dynamique de groupe dans ce contexte, nous nous inspirons des bases de l'aide mutuelle (Steinberg, 2014), de la recherche d'une cible commune, de l'approche du groupe inclusif (Pelech et al., 2016; Chesnay, 2020), des écrits sur l'humilité culturelle (Foronda, 2020) et du concept émergeant d'espace de courage (Arao et Clemens, 2013).

Formés en aide mutuelle, nous sommes convaincus que les participants possèdent les forces pour être des ressources les uns pour les autres. Selon ce modèle, le rôle de l'intervenant est de favoriser l'émergence de différentes dynamiques d'aide mutuelle : le soutien émotionnel entre pairs, le partage d'informations, la confrontation des idées, le sentiment d'être tous dans le même bateau, la discussion de sujets tabous, l'aide à la résolution de problèmes, l'expérimentation de nouvelles façons d'être et de faire, les demandes mutuelles ainsi que la force du nombre (Steinberg, 2014). Pour ce faire, l'intervenant veillera à canaliser les forces des participants au profit du groupe, à créer un sentiment de communauté et à inciter les participants à réviser leurs expériences grâce au partage de celles des autres (Steinberg, 2014). Même dans un groupe de très courte durée, il est possible de favoriser une certaine aide mutuelle (Berteau, 2018). Pour ce faire, même s'il ne s'agit que d'une seule rencontre, nous abordons le groupe comme un tout, comme une association de personnes ayant autant besoin les uns des autres que des intervenants. Aussi, nous invitons à la collaboration en encourageant les participants à construire sur les idées des autres.

Tel que mentionné précédemment, les usagers du STMU sont hospitalisés pour des raisons diverses et leurs objectifs diffèrent grandement. Leurs priorités peuvent être de se relocaliser dans un hébergement de longue durée, de compléter leur sevrage de substances, de traiter un problème de santé causé par leur dépendance, pour n'en nommer que quelques-unes. Les rencontres de groupe sont l'occasion de se regrouper autour d'une cible commune, de besoins communs. Déjà, les participants partagent le fait d'être hospitalisés et d'avoir une consommation de substances qui a contribué à leur hospitalisation. Nous partons de ce point de départ pour proposer un thème de discussion grâce auquel les participants pourront se rejoindre et s'exprimer sur leur vécu dans l'ici-et-maintenant.

En parallèle, nous considérons essentiel de souligner l'individualité de chacun ainsi que d'explorer les tabous et les différences. Selon Chesnay (2020), le groupe inclusif propose un lieu de découverte et d'acceptation de la complexité des individus dans lequel il est possible de susciter l'empathie des participants les uns envers les autres. Dans nos rencontres, nous soutenons les participants lorsqu'ils choisissent de s'identifier à des caractéristiques distinctives ou encore lorsqu'ils questionnent leurs pairs sur des différences qui les interpellent. À titre d'illustration, une participante s'est affirmée dans son identité de genre pour la première fois dans le cadre de notre groupe. Un autre exemple inclut tous les moments où des participants interrogent leurs pairs sur les raisons de certains comportements observés dans la vie de l'unité et obtiennent ainsi des réponses qui augmentent leur compréhension à l'égard des autres. Dans l'ensemble, les différences qui sont discutées dans notre groupe sont celles qui sont directement abordées par les participants. En tant qu'animateurs, nous nous défions des amalgames, surtout ceux qui assimilent toutes les personnes présentant une même caractéristique de marginalité.

Dans un même ordre d'idées, l'humilité culturelle (Foronda, 2020) est l'approche que nous adoptons à l'égard des enjeux de diversité. Nous reconnaissons la place du pouvoir et de ses déséquilibres dans les interactions entre les participants du groupe, entre les participants et les intervenants, mais également entre le groupe et le monde extérieur. Nous demeurons flexibles, ouverts, conscients de nous-mêmes et des autres, soutenants. En dehors des rencontres de groupe, nous nous engageons dans une pratique réflexive et critique de notre façon d'intervenir. Nous nous permettons d'adresser également ces enjeux l'un envers l'autre comme co-animateurs.

Pour en revenir au thème du courage, au-delà d'en faire preuve nous-mêmes, nous nous appliquons à créer un espace de courage au sein du groupe. Selon Arao et Clemens (2013), un espace de courage – ou *brave space* en anglais – est un lieu dans lesquels les participants sont invités à s'engager dans un dialogue et des apprentissages sur les enjeux émergents de la diversité et de la justice sociale. Les normes d'un espace de courage font écho aux phénomènes d'aide mutuelle et aux propositions du groupe inclusif, incluant d'explorer les points de vue différents avec civilité et authenticité, d'encourager la vulnérabilité et l'exposition ainsi que d'assumer l'impacts de ses comportements.

Surpasser les barrières organisationnelles et professionnelles

Dans notre carrière, nous avons souvent rencontré des intervenants qui auraient souhaité développer une pratique de groupe mais qui se sont sentis limités par leur contexte organisationnel. Nous souhaitons donc exposer les moyens que nous avons mis en œuvre pour composer avec les obstacles que nous avons rencontrés dans notre contexte improbable. Nous aborderons l'importance de s'allier avec tous les acteurs de l'organisation, de s'enrichir par la collaboration interprofessionnelle et d'adapter notre pratique à des groupes d'une seule rencontre.

S'allier avec les acteurs de l'organisation

La réussite d'un groupe repose sur la capacité des intervenants à s'allier avec tous les acteurs du milieu pouvant avoir une influence sur sa réalisation. Cette conviction nous anime. Dans un contexte hospitalier, plusieurs acteurs peuvent influencer la réussite d'un groupe, tels que les gestionnaires, les médecins, les infirmières, les préposées, les agentes administratives et les collègues psychosociaux.

C'est grâce à un dialogue constant avec tous ces acteurs que nous sommes parvenus à ancrer graduellement la pratique de groupe dans le quotidien de l'unité de soins. Nous tentons de prendre toutes les décisions en collaboration avec l'équipe, afin de déterminer le meilleur horaire, la procédure de désinfection des locaux, le choix de la salle, la disponibilité des usagers, et les sujets pertinents à aborder dans le groupe. En retour, des médecins encouragent les usagers à y participer, des infirmières modifient leur routine de soins pour favoriser l'accès au groupe, un gestionnaire perçoit que le groupe contribue à donner vie à des valeurs importantes du service, une travailleuse sociale réutilise la participation d'un usager pour mieux comprendre son fonctionnement et déterminer son orientation au congé.

S'enrichir par la collaboration interprofessionnelle

L'équipe que nous formons se compose de deux personnes de professions et d'expériences différentes. Nous avons amorcé cette aventure avec des divergences sur notre façon de voir le groupe ainsi que dans nos outils et habiletés pour l'animer. Mus par un intérêt et un but commun, nous avons appris à nous connaître, puis appris l'un de l'autre. Dans les innombrables heures passées à co-construire notre groupe, nous avons partagé des savoirs provenant de nos professions respectives, nous avons confronté des idées, nous avons expérimenté les propositions de l'un et de l'autre. Du travail social de groupe, nous retenons l'importance de mettre les gens en interaction, de croire en l'aide mutuelle qui existe dans les groupes, même ceux de très courte durée. De l'ergothérapie, nous avons mobilisé des outils et moyens pour inclure et favoriser la participation des personnes présentant toutes sortes d'incapacités. Ici, ce qui aurait pu ressembler à une barrière à première vue, s'est révélée être une opportunité d'enrichissement mutuel. Le résultat de notre partenariat est ce groupe de soutien, inclusif, accessible.

Adapter notre pratique à des groupes d'une seule rencontre

Afin de nous adapter à la durée courte et indéterminée du séjour des usagers, nous avons misé sur les savoirs issus des groupes d'une seule rencontre. Bien que certains participants puissent être présents à plus d'une rencontre, notre contexte de pratique rendait impossible le développement de groupes s'appuyant sur une participation continue.

Berteau (2018) soutient que les groupes d'une seule rencontre se trouvent dans des contextes variés et peuvent s'adapter à un large éventail de situations et de problématiques. Ils permettent d'apporter une réponse rapide à des besoins d'information, de prévention et d'ajustement à une nouvelle réalité, en plus de contribuer au repérage des personnes nécessitant une attention plus spécifique. Elle mentionne également que le groupe d'une seule rencontre s'appuie sur la motivation spontanée suscitée par une situation de vie ou un évènement marquant. Les intervenants se doivent, pour canaliser cette motivation initiale, « de croire aux compétences et aux ressources existantes chez les membres et le groupe, favoriser un climat de sécurité et d'harmonie et éveiller aux possibilités d'aide mutuelle de très courte durée » (Berteau, 2018).

C'est donc avec la croyance que même la participation à une seule rencontre de groupe peut apporter des bénéfices que nous avons développé ce service.

Les bénéfices

Au fur et à mesure de cette expérience, ce sont les bénéfices rapportés par les participants qui ont été nos plus grandes sources de motivation pour surpasser les nombreux obstacles. Certains participants ont nommé le caractère unique de cette expérience de groupe et l'aspect humain et accueillant des intervenants. Plusieurs ont souligné le bien-être, l'encouragement et l'espoir générés par le fait de rencontrer et d'être soutenus par leurs pairs. D'autres ont clarifié leurs objectifs et ont ensuite été plus disposés pour les rencontres de planification des services au congé. Souvent, le simple fait de s'être présenté au groupe est un succès en soi, eu égard à toutes les barrières personnelles que les usagers expérimentent.

En outre, sans que cela n'est fait l'objet d'une évaluation approfondie, le groupe semble avoir des bienfaits sur la vie de l'unité. D'abord, la rencontre des usagers entre eux favorisent la compréhension et la tolérance des comportements de chacun en dehors du groupe. Ensuite, en donnant un espace pour s'exprimer sur les insatisfactions liées au séjour hospitalier (un thème récurrent), on peut espérer éviter des épisodes d'irritabilité ou des refus de traitement. Cette forme spontanée de « comité des usagers » donne par ailleurs une voix aux participants dans l'amélioration continue de leurs soins et services. En effet, au-delà d'accompagner les usagers à développer des stratégies pour se maintenir engagés dans leur hospitalisation, nous rapportons les commentaires faits sur l'organisation et la qualité des soins auprès de notre gestionnaire ou de l'équipe interdisciplinaire. Ainsi, la participation au groupe donne lieu à des opportunités réelles de reprise de pouvoir pour les usagers.

En plus des bienfaits pour les participants, il nous apparaît important de souligner ceux que nous vivons comme intervenants. En effet, ce groupe de soutien est un lieu d'entraide, de compassion et d'inclusion dont les effets sur le bien-être sont ressentis par tous les membres, nous incluant. L'animation de ces groupes donnent un sens à notre travail et son implantation a été un processus de réflexion critique et d'apprentissage significatif. Nous en retenons des leçons qui modifient à jamais notre conception de la pratique de groupe, notamment auprès des communautés vulnérables ou marginalisées.

Un dernier mot

En partageant notre récit, nous souhaitons inspirer d'autres intervenants à ne pas céder aux barrières qui apparaissent comme insurmontables et persévérer dans la mise en place de groupes improbables. Nous avons pour notre part été confrontés à suffisamment d'obstacles pour que les groupes n'aient pas lieu, certains se répétant encore et encore. Avec persévérance, courage, humilité et ouverture, nous les surpassons… donnant lieu à des rencontres de groupe avec des usagers qui typiquement n'y auraient pas eu accès, dans un contexte qui ne favorise pourtant pas la pratique de groupe.

Tout bien considéré, nous croyons que toutes les situations peuvent donner lieu à des groupes et espérons que les usagers qui existent en marge des normes sociales y soient inclus.

Références

Arao, B., & Clemens, K. (2013). From safe spaces to brave spaces, a new way to frame dialogue around diversity and social justice. Dans L. M. Landreman (Dir.), *The Art of effective facilitation, reflections from social justice educators.* Stylus Publishing.

Berteau, G., Jalbert, C., & Gascon, E. (2018). Le groupe d'une seule rencontre en travail social de groupe. https://www.iaswg.org/tips-seule

Chesnay, C. (2020). Pour une pratique inclusive de la diversité en travail social de groupe: Repères théoriques et méthodologiques. *Groupwork, 29*(1), 9-23. https://doi.org/10.1921/gpwk.v29i1.1428

Eaton, M. (2017). Come as you are!: Creating community with groups. *Social Work with Groups, 40*(1-2), 85-92. doi:10.1080/01609513.2015.1069129

Foronda, C. (2020). A theory of cultural humility. *Journal of Transcultural Nursing, 31*(1), 7-12. https://doi.org/10.1177%2F1043659619875184

Improbable. (s.d.). Dans *Le Robert dico en ligne.* https://dictionnaire.lerobert.com/definition/improbable

Pelech, W., Basso, R., Lee, C., & Gandarilla, M. (2016). *Inclusive group work.* Oxford University Press.

Steinberg, D. (2014). *A Mutual-aid model for social work with groups* (3e édition). Routledge.

A Human Rights Praxis Approach to Group Work

Christina M. Chiaraelli-Helminiak, and Michele Eggers-Barison

Introduction

Ongoing human rights issues, such as racial violence and the unequal impact of COVID-19, amount to a critical call to action for social work both locally and abroad. Given the magnitude of human rights crises on a global scale, integrating a human rights frame to social group work can be a powerful solution to addressing critical social change within micro to global levels of practice. While conceptualizing a human rights praxis approach to social work is a relatively new endeavor, the literature is even further limited when considering what a human rights praxis approach to group work means. Based on what social work scholars have thus far outlined as different approaches to a human rights-based approach to practice, this article will introduce a human rights praxis approach to group work through Weisman's three group work principles of conscious use of self, relationship, and participatory democracy. The recent events in the United States of anti-Asian violence and murders; police violence toward Black men, women, and trans folx; state sanctioned violence against water protectors; missing and murdered Indigenous women (MMIW); and the separation of Latinx families via imprisonment and abuse in U.S. detention centers along the U.S.-Mexico border – as well as the unequal impact globally of the COVID-19 pandemic, climate change, poverty, war and conflict, forced migration, human trafficking, among other ongoing human rights issues – are a critical call to action for social work locally and abroad.

Social group work is historically rooted in an ideological frame that contextualizes human experience as embedded in broader socio-political constructs in societies (Coyle, 1935). Social group work came out of a movement of "social reform, social responsibility, democratic ideals and social action..." (Andrews, 2001, p. 47). The developing foci of the pioneers of social group work added mutual aid, humanistic values, and resistance to illegitimate authority (Reisch & Andrews, 2001). Given the magnitude of human rights crises on a global scale, integrating a human rights frame to social group work can be a powerful solution to addressing critical social change within micro to global levels of practice.

The recognition of human rights as an integral part of social work practice and education is gaining momentum; yet, how human rights are conceptualized in and applied to group work has not been fully explored. Approaching social work from a human rights-based frame encourages the practitioner to shift their understanding from a charity or needs-based approach to view social issues as rights violations (Berthold, 2015; Gatenio Gabel, 2016; McPherson, 2016; 2018). Gatenio Gabel (2016) outlined the differences and limitations of historically charity-based approaches and contemporary needs-based approaches to social work, while highlighting what a paradigm shift towards a rights-based approach to social work could add to our professional skill set. When group members are viewed as entitled to having their rights protected and met, it changes the social workers' orientation of practice. This article will introduce a human rights praxis approach to group work.

Human Rights

The Universal Declaration of Human Rights (UDHR) was adopted by the United Nations (UN) General Assembly in 1948 in response to the atrocities committed during World War II. The UDHR consists of 30 articles that include the right to the following: to be free from slavery, discrimination, torture and inhuman treatment; to be treated equal before the law; to a fair trial, democracy, social security, an adequate standard of living for the health and wellbeing of individuals and families, as well as the right to education, work, marriage and to have a family. To simplify the 30 articles, Wronka (2008) divided the UDHR into five dimensions: dignity, nondiscrimination, civil and political rights, economic, social, and cultural rights, and solidarity rights.

In addition to the 30 articles in the UDHR, there are nine core international human rights treaties (Office of the United National High Commissioner for Human Rights, n.d.). These include:

1965: International Convention on the Elimination of All Forms of Racial Discrimination (ICERD)
1966: International Covenant on Civil and Political Rights (ICCPR)
1966: International Covenant on Economic, Social, and Cultural Rights (ICESCR)
1979: Convention on the Elimination of Discrimination Against Women (CEDAW)
1984: Convention Against Torture and Other Cruel, Inhuman or Degrading Treatment or Punishment (CAT)
1989: Convention on the Rights of the Child (CRC)
1990: International Convention on the Protection of the Rights of All Migrant Workers and Members of Their Families (CMW)
2006: International Convention for the Protection of All Persons from Enforced Disappearance (CED)
2006: Convention on the Rights of Persons with Disabilities (CRPD).

The UDHR and its accompanying international conventions and treaties provide social group work practitioners with a foundation of human rights literacy, as well as a conceptual framework when working toward positive and transformative social change (Becker et al., 2015; McPherson, 2016).

Classifying human rights can be helpful when applying rights-based concepts and principles to social work practice. One way of doing this is to separate rights into negative rights (protected rights) and positive rights (entitled rights). Negative rights include protections provided by governments and other rights duty-bearers responsible for protecting individuals from harm by ensuring the right to life, bodily integrity, freedom of speech, religion or spiritual practices, and the right to be treated with dignity. Positive rights include entitlements provided by governments and other rights duty-bearers to ensure a person's access to basic needs, such as healthcare, food, and shelter (Frezzo, 2015).

In addition, human rights are often classified within three categories of rights (Frezzo, 2015). The first is civil and political rights, which are part of the International Covenant on Civil and Political Rights (ICCPR) and considered negative rights. The second category is economic, social, and cultural rights, which are considered positive rights and are within the International Covenant on Economic, Social, and Cultural Rights (ICESCR). The third and final category includes solidarity or collective rights, which are rights that belong to a group, community, society, or nation, such as the right to clean air and water (Ife, 2012). In addition, Indigenous rights and sovereignty, immigrant rights, and women's rights along with issues of police violence, mass incarceration, forced migration, and gender violence, in example, are also considered part of collective rights as they impact specific groups disproportionately.

The categorization of rights is problematic if not understood as interdependent and indivisible (Androff, 2016; Frezzo, 2015; Ife, 2012). For example, protection from state sanctioned violence falls under civil and political rights, however specific racialized groups are more impacted by police violence than other groups, which falls under collective rights. Further, lack of access to adequate health, employment, housing, and education are categorized within economic, social, and cultural rights, but often the groups most impacted by police violence also lack access to these basic human rights.

Human rights are conceptualized and purported as inherent to all humans regardless of nationality, citizenship, sex, religion, language, gender, ability, or racial, ethnic, or tribal status, among other social locations (Office of the High Commissioner for Human Rights, n.d.). Although human rights are considered universal in that they apply to all humans equally, this is not always realized in practice. The emergence of human rights were developed in the global north, embedded within colonial and post-colonial realities and practices (Azoulay, 2015). Consequently, this limits the vision, purpose, and functionality of human rights in practice. Thus, understanding why rights are not protected and realized in practice requires a deeper level of analysis of structural oppression (Ife, 2012). Goodhart (2018) suggests not to abandon human rights discourse as human rights are continually being used to advance emancipatory struggles, as well as create connections and develop solidarity with others (p. 408).

Human Rights and Social Work

Human rights are the foundation of the social work profession (Healy, 2008). Although the International Association of Social Work with

Groups (IASWG) is committed to social justice, they do not have a specific statement on promoting human rights in theory or practice. However, other professional social work organizations such as the International Federation of Social Work (IFSW; 1988) state that,

> Social work has, from its conception, been a human rights profession, having as its basic tenet the intrinsic value of every human being and as one of its main aims the promotion of equitable social structures, which can offer people security and development while upholding their dignity. (as cited in UN, 1994, p. 3)

Further, the IFSW (2021) emphasizes the use of human rights in social work globally. In the Global Social Work Statement of Ethical Principles, the IFSW (2018) conceptualizes the principle of promoting human rights as:

> Social workers embrace and promote the fundamental and inalienable rights of all human beings. Social work is based on respect for the inherent worth, dignity of all people and the individual and social/civil rights that follow from this. Social workers often work with people to find an appropriate balance between competing human rights (Principle 2).

The IFSW's ethical principles further specify social workers' responsibilities to promote the right to self-determination and right to participation (Principles 4 and 5). When paired with social work's emphasis on working towards social justice, the realization of human rights is a critical aspect.

The UDHR (1948) provides a list of rights guaranteed to all based on our basic humanness. Androff (2016) proposed a rights-based approach to social work practice as rooted in the human rights principles of human dignity, non-discrimination, participation, transparency, and accountability. Androff and McPherson (2014) suggested that a rights-based approach to social work practice challenges the micro-macro divide, advancing a holistic and interdisciplinary approach that encourages a person-centered approach to practice (Berthold, 2015), while providing an understanding of fundamental rights and creating a larger context in which to understand the human experience (Pyles, 2006).

From a rights-based approach, the social worker views social issues as rights violations (Berthold, 2015; Gatenio Gabel, 2016; McPherson, 2016; 2018). Berthold (2015) outlined the tenets of clinical social work to operate from a holistic and interdisciplinary approach that encourages an intersectional, person-centered rights-based practice. In practice, she emphasized operating from a stance of resilience and cultural humility to foster a trauma-informed therapeutic relationship that reconstructs safety. Berthold endorsed a strengths-based orientation to set the foundation for understanding individual needs as entitlements or rights.

McPherson and Abell's (2012) seminal research established ways to assess human rights engagement and exposure, which led to the conceptualization of three pillars of practice: human rights lens, methods, and goals (McPherson, 2015). Human rights methods include a strengths-perspective, inclusion of participation, non-discrimination, accountability, capacity building, community and interdisciplinary collaboration, micro-macro integration, and activism (Androff, 2016; McPherson, 2015). McPherson (2015) furthered her scholarship to include interventions at the micro, mezzo, macro, and global levels; fostering partnerships, and employing anti-discriminatory, non-pathologizing, and reflective practice that includes an assessment of human rights access, as well as providing human rights education.

While conceptualizing a human rights praxis approach to social work is a relatively new endeavor, the literature is even further limited when considering what a human rights praxis approach to group work means. Based on what social work scholars have thus far outlined as different approaches to a human rights-based approach to practice, we propose the following as a starting point when engaging in a human rights praxis with group work.

A Human Rights Praxis Approach to Group Work

The social work profession has historically engaged in group work to enact social change. Hull House pioneer, Jane Addams, and Black Settlement House founder, Janie Barrett, are just two of the many reformers who approached early social group work initiatives from a human rights perspective. Settlement houses commonly offered recreational and educational opportunities through neighborhood clubs and impacted legislative and political change through social action (Stern & Axinn, 2018). Coyle (1935) reinforced education and social action as integral to group work as an avenue for social change. In 2015, the IASWG recommitted to the core value of "the creation of a socially just society" through "democratic principles" (p. 2).

A human rights praxis approach is at once a return to and extension of the history of group work by advocating for and moving towards the realization of human rights. The social worker has an opportunity to provide education on the UDHR and related international documents that the group can use as tools to influence social action and change. Weisman's (2000) group work principles of conscious use of self, relationship, and participatory democracy will be used to lay the foundation for a human rights praxis approach to group work.

Conscious Use of Self

The personal is political and so too are human rights. Individual experiences, especially when rights are violated, are rooted within systems of power. For example, the first Women's March in 2016 was a global outcry against oppression faced by women both individually, e.g., when a woman experiences abuse, and societally, e.g., when the United States refuses to ratify the CEDAW as a way to acknowledge the collective rights of women. Human rights are also political in that it is the responsibility of the duty-bearers (i.e., governments) to respect, protect, and fulfill human rights, a blatant conflict when the government is the perpetrator of rights violations, e.g., systemic police brutality.

The social worker is considered one of the most dynamic of practice tools when working with groups. Conscious use of self relates to the National Association of Social Workers (NASW; 2017) core values of integrity and competence. In addition, the Council on Social Work Education (2015) requires accredited undergraduate and graduate social work programs to teach use of self through reflection of personal experiences and relationships (Liechty, 2018). McPherson (2016) provides an insightful reflection on how reading the UDHR shifted her awareness of self in relation to human rights in her social work practice. She demonstrates the process of internalizing and integrating a rights-based lens in practice. The use of self suggests reflection and critical thinking are a means for the worker to move past themselves in order to work objectively with the group (Liechty, 2018; Weisman, 2000).

Use of self in group work practice requires critical self-reflection through an intersectionality lens. The group worker often holds multiple social identities, their own experiences with oppression, as well as access to resources which provide a degree of power and privilege (Mehrotha, 2010). A human rights praxis requires an understanding of the worker's own positionality, in addition to the social worker reflecting upon and challenging any assumptions they may have regarding group members' social identities and lived experience.

Use of self also relates to an awareness of the potential impact practice can have on the social worker. While approaching group work from a rights-based perspective may empower the worker through the use of human rights language and international documents, they may also be particularly vulnerable to burnout, secondary traumatic stress, compassion fatigue, and/or vicarious trauma as a result of continual exposure to traumas and systemic injustices (Berthold, 2015; Reynolds, 2011). While burnout can be experienced in any workplace, compassion fatigue and vicarious trauma are common when individuals and communities have experienced rights violations, whereas with vicarious trauma, the worker's own history of personal trauma is a factor (Newell & MacNeil, 2010). The use of supervision and mentorship are effective means to reflect upon and receive feedback on group work practice and play an important role in buffering the negative impacts of working with those who have experienced rights violations (Berthold, 2015; IASWG, 2015; Maslach et al., 2001). Ignoring the personal impact on the worker increases the likelihood of experiencing one of these conditions; therefore, it is important for supervisors and mentors to be aware of any signs that the group worker is in need of additional support or referral for services. Berthold (2015) relates this to the social worker's use of self and self-care, in addition to ensuring the worker's rights are realized in practice.

In sum, a conscious use of self is an integral part of a human rights praxis approach to group work. Use of self includes an intersectional lens that acknowledges the political nature of self and human rights, active reflection, including the support of supervisors and mentors, and critical thinking. Use of self also relates to the importance of relationships.

Relationships

The core of group work is about relationships. Weisman (2000) stated that it is "basic to the establishment of a helping relationship that does not denote power differentiation, but rather suggests a togetherness in solving problems…" (p. 6). Further, a core special area of knowledge presented in the IASWG (2015) standards states that "The worker understands that the group consists of multiple helping relationships, so that members can help one another to achieve individual goals and pursue group goals. This is often referred to as mutual aid" (p. 4).

Thus, the importance of relationships cannot be overemphasized in a human rights-based approach to group work practice. Relatedly, relationships are built on the respect of the inherent dignity of a person, a central principle of the UDHR (United Nations, 1948). Yet, as Goodhart (2018) stated "power and politics shape human dignity in practice" (p. 404) and it is the group practitioner's responsibility to nurture the relationships both with and among group participants.

The process of relationship building includes the sharing of lived experience among group members. Within a human rights frame, storytelling or giving testimony is a vital component of legitimizing voices and experiences of people of color and others who are marginalized by dominant spaces, constructing a counter-narrative to dominant discourses (Carroll & Minkler, 2000; Razak & Jeffery, 2002). Group workers play a critical role in bridging shared narratives and identifying common struggles among group members (Brysk & Wehrenfennig, 2010; Hays et al., 2010). Brysk and Wehrenfennig (2010) shared that "The creation and communication of appropriate bridging narratives of human rights seems to be the definitive element that transforms this potential alliance into solidarity" (p. 15). Solidarity is defined as a feeling of unity, especially among individuals with similar interests and/or shared experiences (Breton, 2011). As group members begin to develop a feeling of solidarity, this results in empowerment via group cohesion and a sense of belonging.

With strengthened solidarity, group work is a powerful space for increased critical consciousness (Hays et al., 2010). The process of critical consciousness can be facilitated by the group worker via the frame of the personal is political (Ratts, et al., 2010). Helping group members understand that their lived experience is embedded within social, economic, political, and cultural contexts. When group members begin to understand that the context of their lives is embedded within larger systems of inequity and the issues they experience are determined by broader forces outside of themselves, this is the process of conscientization or critical consciousness (Freire, 1989).

Thus, critical consciousness is achieved through the critical reflection of lived experience among group members, leading to an increased sense of personal and collective power to reclaim their rights (Carroll & Minkler, 2000; Freire, 1989). Goodhart (2018) suggested that "Alongside the instrumental rationality of rights-claiming, there is an expressive dimension of human rights praxis through which values and identities are constituted and self-respect affirmed" (p. 409).

Participatory Democracy

Participation is one of the key tenets of a human rights-based approach to social work group practice. The United Nations (1948) highlights participation as a central right throughout the UDHR and other key conventions and treaties. Article 21 of the UDHR specifies the right to participation in the governing of one's country, including the right to vote. Human rights scholars emphasize participation as central to a rights-based practice (Androff, 2016; Berthold, 2015; Maschi, 2016; McPherson, 2018).

Participatory democracy has been a long-standing principle of group work (Weismann, 2000). In 1948, the Committee on Function of the Social Group Workers outline:

> Through [their] participation the group worker aims to affect the group process so that decisions come about as a result of knowledge and a sharing and integration of ideas, experiences and knowledge rather than as a result of domination from within or without the group. Through experience [they] aim to produce those relations with other groups and the wider community which contribute to responsible citizenship, mutual understandings between cultural, religious, economic or social groupings in the community and a participation in the constant improvement of our society toward democratic goals (as cited in Wilson, 1956, para. 17).

While participatory democracy has a place within the group, the social worker works in solidarity to impact broader social change outside the group.

The resurgence of social justice movements, including Black Lives Matter and the Women's March, in addition to increased diversity among political candidates in the United States highlights the demand for a more participatory democracy. A more inclusive democracy will result in the realization of rights for more diverse individuals, groups, and communities, regardless of formal citizenship. In line with rights-based praxis, Boje (2017) stresses that "a meaningful democratic system is a system involving all groups of citizens in a continuous debate and decision-making process concerning the economic, social, and cultural conditions for their living" (p. 349).

The social worker can foster the group's participation in decision-making. For example, historically and systemically marginalized and oppressed communities frequently experience barriers to participate in elections. A human rights praxis approach to group work promotes the realization of the right to vote through voter registration, education, and mobilization campaigns. Nonpartisan resources, such as the National Social Work Voter Mobilization Campaign, have proliferated in recent years[1]. We must embrace social work as a political profession; the increased knowledge and resources in this area will result in the empowerment of the very people and communities in which we work. A more active voter citizenry will result in a redistribution of power and resources, ultimately resulting in progressive civil, political, economic, social and cultural change (Boje, 2017).

Engaging in participatory democracy together, especially social justice advocacy, is a means of self-care for many group workers and members. Domestic violence agencies have a longstanding tradition of engaging workers, those impacted by violence, and allies in Congressional advocacy to reauthorize the Violence Against Women Act, a major funding source for victims services, every 10 years. Self-care through advocacy comes through the satisfaction one gets from seeing societal change when you see the fruits of your labor, which in turn, keeps the worker engaged (Reynolds, 2011).

Political interest groups illustrate a specific modality of group practice from a right-based approach. In today's global political environment, social workers are reviving their ethical obligation to participate in and raise their voices to promote social justice and human rights alongside individuals and communities in which they work. Additionally, social workers are becoming more deliberate about defining the mission and goals of contemporary political interest groups[2].

Participatory democracy combined with emancipatory practice may be the future to achieve a more inclusive society. Sewpaul and colleagues (2015) suggest emancipatory social work will enable us to "free ourselves from the constraints of society, develop moral courage to confront and challenge social injustices and human rights violations, and we develop greater belief in ourselves" especially within communities that have experienced long-term exclusion and oppression (p. 55). Central to emancipatory practice is empowerment to consider one's own role in perpetuating bias that results in critical consciousness that provides more agency, responsibility, liberation, and change. These micro level changes contribute to macro level changes in line with a human rights praxis approach to group work.

In sum, participatory democracy requires engagement in the decision-making process and critical observation of the systems and advocacy to advance human rights. Working in solidarity with the group, the worker can engage in the electoral process and social justice advocacy.

Limitations and Further Considerations

A human rights praxis is by no means a panacea for social issues and outcomes, but it has the potential of leading to better group work practice and social change. Mann and colleagues (2016) acknowledge that mental health can be improved just by respecting human rights. While group work practice primarily occurs at the community level, bureaucracy continues to drive some practice. A human rights practice requires creativity and courage to change the corporatized systems that drive practice. For example, currently most groups are conducted in office settings, or during the global pandemic on-line; while a human rights praxis approach would allow social work to occur within the group's environment, such as a community park.

One critique of social work education is the continual decline of group work as a specialization and requirement of a group work course in all graduate level programs. Another issue of concern is Gatenio Gabel and Mapp's (2019) finding that human rights is not included in 12 percent of social work programs' curriculum and an additional 23 percent simply paired human rights to social justice within further exposition. Teaching group work courses from a human rights praxis approach provides meaningful ways to engage in rights-based practice in the classroom and field. As social workers in the Academy, we must teach by example and advocate for the continual inclusion of group work methods and a more in-depth human rights education. Moving to a human rights praxis approach to group work begins with students' education, for they are the future of the profession.

It is not enough to teach about human rights, social work educators must also approach teaching through a human rights lens. Linde and Arthur (2015) suggested a critical approach to teaching human rights, including taking into account students' histories of oppression connected to the local context and developing relationships, not only with students, but ones that give access to speak truth to power within academic institutions. Quzack et al. (2021) provided an example of a curricular redesign that resulted in a graduate social work specialization grounded in social justice and human rights. Johnson and Chiarelli-Helminiak (in press) presented an elective course focused on human rights within the context of the campus location. Sewpaul and colleagues (2015) highlighted an example of emancipatory social work education. Robinson and colleagues (2016) and Liechty (2018) contributed in class activities to impart on students the applications of intersectionality and use of self, respectively. These examples in the literature and this manuscript are another step towards addressing what Chiarelli-Helminiak, Eggers-Barison, and Libal (2018) found as a barrier to infusing human rights across the social work curriculum: a lack of opportunity for educators' professional development.

Conclusion

This manuscript adds to the growing body of literature that a human rights praxis approach to social work is necessary from micro to global levels of social work practice if we are to achieve our profession's social justice and human rights mandates. Specifically, we extend the literature to group work in line with the method's historical contextualization of the human experience embedded within broader socio-political constructs. The principles of conscious use of self, relationship, and participatory democracy provide a foundation for a human rights praxis approach to group work. This approach is outlined as a powerful solution to addressing critical social change.

Ongoing systemic oppression and recent events in the United States and globally highlight the ongoing critical need for the social work profession to uphold its social justice and human rights mandates. Group work is an ideal venue to be in solidarity with individuals and communities to advocate for social change through public awareness of inequities and injustices. While commonly seen as radical, social workers who embrace the profession's social justice values through an activist orientation paired with a critical analysis of systems, even the ones they are part of, should be the norm. We propose a human rights praxis approach to group work as a way to encourage a culture of human rights as the new norm.

Notes

1.. See https://votingissocialwork.org/ for additional resources
2. See for example the recently launched Core Values PAC: https://www. corevaluespac.org/

References

Andrews, J. (2001). Group work's place in social work: A historical analysis. *Journal of   Sociology and Social Welfare, 28*(4), 45-65.

Androff, D. (2016). *Practicing rights: Human rights-based approaches to social work practice.* Routledge.

Androff, D., & McPherson, J. (2014). Can human-rights-based social work practice bridge the micro/macro divide? In K. Libal, M. Berthold, R. L. Thomas, & L. Healy (Eds.), *Advancing human rights in social work education* (pp. 39-56). CSWE Press.

Azoulay, A. (2015). What are human rights? *Comparative Studies South Asia, Africa and the Middle East, 31*(1), 8-20.

Becker, A., de Wet, A., van Vollenhoven, W. (2015). Human rights literacy: Moving towards rights-based education and transformative action through understandings of dignity, equality, and freedom. *South African Journal of Education, 35*(2), 1-12. https://doi:10.15700/saje.v35n2a1044

Berthold, S. M. (2015). *Human rights-based approaches to clinical social work practice.* Springer.

Boje, T. P. (2017). Concluding essay: Social activism against austerity - the conditions for participatory and deliberative forms of democracy. *Journal of Civil Society, 13*(3), 349-356. https://doi.org/10.1080/17448689.2017.1 362100

Breton, M. (2011). Citizenship consciousness, nonbounded solidarity, and social justice. *Social Work with Groups, 34*, 35-50.

Brysk, A. & Wehrenfennig, D. (2010). My brother's keeper? Inter-ethnic solidarity and human rights. *Studies in Ethnicity and Nationalism, 10*(1), 1-18. https://doi-org/10.1111/j.1754-9469.2010.01067.x

Carroll, J. & Minkler, M. (2000). Freire's message for social workers: Looking back, looking ahead. *Journal of Community Practice, 8*(1), 21-36. https://doi-org /10.1300/J125v08n01_02

Chiarelli-Helminiak, C. M., Eggers-Barison, M., Libal, K. R. (2018). The integration of human rights in US social work education: Insights from a qualitative study. Journal of Human Rights and Social Work, 3(2), 99-107. https://doi-org/10.1007/s41134-018-0050-y

Council on Social Work Education. (2015). *Educational policy and accreditation standards.* https://www.cswe.org/getattachment/ Accreditation/Accreditation-Process/2015-EPAS/2015EPAS_Web_ FINAL.pdf.aspx

Coyle, G. L. (1935). Group work and social change. *Social Welfare History Project.* https://socialwelfare.library.vcu.edu/social-work/social-group-work-and-change-1935/

Freire, P. (1989). *Pedagogy of the oppressed.* The Continuum Publishing Company.

Frezzo, (2015). *The sociology of human rights: An introduction.* Polity Press.

Gatenio Gabel, S. (2016). *Understanding a rights-based approach to social analysis.* Springer International Publishing.

Gatenio Gabel, S., & Mapp, S. (2019). Teaching human rights and social justice in social work education. *Journal of Social Work Education.* Advance online publication. https://doi.org/10.1080/10437797.2019.1656581

Goodhart, M. (2018). Constructing dignity: Human rights as a praxis of egalitarian freedom. *Journal of Human Rights, 17*(4), 403-417. https://doi-org./10.1080/14754835.2018.1450738

Hays, D. G., Arrendondo, P., Gladding, S. T., & Toporek, R. L. (2010).

Integrating social
justice in group work: The next decade. *Journal for Specialists in Group Work, 35*(2), 177-206. https://doi-org/10.1080/01933921003706022

Ife, J. (2012). *Human rights and social work: Towards rights-based practice.* Cambridge University Press.

International Association for Social Work with Groups. (2015). *Standards for social work practice with groups* (2nd ed.). https://www.iaswg.org/standards

International Federation of Social Workers. (2018). *Global social work statement of ethical principles.* https://www.ifsw.org/global-social-work-statement-of-ethical-principles/

International Federation of Social Workers. (2021). https://www.ifsw.org/

Johnson, K. L., & Chiarelli-Helminiak, C. M. (in press). Human rights in Philadelphia. *Urban Social Work, 3*

Leichty, J. (2018). Exploring use of self: Moving beyond definitional challenges. *Journal of Social Work Education, 58*(1), 148-162. https://doi-org/10.1080/10437797.2017.1314836

Linde, R., & Arthur, M. (2015). Teaching progress: A critique of the grand narrative of human rights as pedagogy for marginalized students. *Radical Teacher, 103*, 26-37. https://doi.org/10.5195/rt.2015.227

Mann, S. P., Bradley, V. J., & Sahakian, B. J. (2016) Human rights-based approaches to mental health: A review of programs. *Health and Human Rights Journal, 18*(1), 263-276.

Maslach, C., Schaufeli, W. B., & Leiter, M. P. (2001). Job burnout. *Annual Review of Psychology, 52*, 397-422. doi:10.1146/annurev.psych.52.1.397

Mehrotra, G. (2010). Toward a continuum of intersectionality theorizing for feminist social work scholarship. *Affilia, 25*, 417–430. doi:10.1177/0886109910384190

McPherson, J. (2015). Human rights practice in social work: a rights-based framework & two new measures (Doctoral dissertation). *ProQuest Dissertations and Theses* (Accession Order No. AAT 3705877).

McPherson, J. (2016). Article 25 changed my life: How the Universal Declaration of Human Rights reframed my social work practice. *Reflections: Narratives of Professional Helping, 22*(2), 23-27.

McPherson, J. (2018). Exceptional and necessary: Practicing rights-based social work in the United States. *Journal of Human Rights and Social Work, 3*(2), 89-98. doi:10.1007/s41134-018-0051-x

McPherson, J. & Abell, N. (2012). Human rights engagement and exposure in social work: New
scales to challenge social work education. Research in Social Work Practice, 22, 704-713. doi:10.1177/1049731512454196

National Association of Social Workers. (2017). *Code of ethics.* https://www.socialworkers.org/About/Ethics/Code-of-Ethics/Code-of-Ethics-English

Newell, J. M., & MacNeil, G. A. (2010). Professional burnout, vicarious trauma, secondary traumatic stress, and compassion fatigue: A review of theoretical terms, risk factors, and preventive methods for clinicians and researchers. *Best Practice in Mental Health, 6*(2), 57-68.

Office of the United National High Commissioner for Human Rights (n.d.). The core international human rights instruments and their monitoring bodies. https://www.ohchr.org/en/professionalinterest/pages/coreinstruments.aspx

Pyles, L. (2006). Toward a post-Katrina framework: Social work as human rights and capabilities. *Journal of Comparative Social Welfare, 22,* 79-88. doi: 10.1080/17486830500523086

Quzack, L.E., Picard, G., Metz, S. M., & Chiarelli-Helminiak, C. M. (2021). A social work education grounded in human rights. *Journal of Human Rights and Social Work, 6*(1), 32-40. doi: 10.1007/s41134-020-00159-5

Ratts, M. J., Anthony, L., & Santos, K. N. T. (2010). The dimensions of social justice model: Transforming traditional group work into a socially just frame. *Journal for Specialists in Group Work, 35*(2), 160-168. https://doi-org/10.1080/01933921003705974

Razak, N. & Jeffery, D. (2002). Critical race discourse and tenets for social work. *Canadian Social Work Review, 19*(2), 257-271.

Reisch, M. & Andrews, J. (2001). *The road not taken: A history of radical social work in the United States.* Brunner-Routledge.

Reynolds, V. (2011). Resisting burnout with justice-doing. *International Journal of Narrative Therapy and Community Work, 4,* 27-45.

Robinson, M. A., Cross-Denny, B., Lee, K., K., Werkmeister Rozas, L. M., & Yamada, A. (2016). Teaching note - Teaching intersectionality: Transforming cultural competence content in social work education. *Journal of Social Work Education, 52,*(4), 509-517. doi: 10.1080/10437797.2016.1198297

Sewpaul, V., Ntini, T., Mkhize, Z, & Zandamela, S. (2015). Emancipatory social work education and community empowerment. *International Journal of Social Work and Human Services Practice, 3*(2), 55-62.

Stern, M. J., & Axinn, J. (2018). *Social welfare: A history of the American response to need.* (9th ed.). Pearson.

United Nations (1948). *Universal declaration of human rights.* https://www.un.org/en/about-us/universal-declaration-of-human-rights

United Nations (1994). Human Rights and Social Work: A Manual for Schools of Social Work and the Social Work Profession [Professional Training

Series No. 1]. Retrieved from https://www.ohchr.org/Documents/Publications/training1en.pdf

Weisman, C. B. (2000). A reminiscence: Group work principles withstanding time–from the Settlement House to the United Nations. *Social Work with Groups, 23*(3), 5-18. doi: 10.1300/J009v23n03_02

Wilson, G. (1956). Social group work theory and practice. *Social Welfare History Project.* https://socialwelfare.library.vcu.edu/social-work/social-group-work-theory-and-practice/

Wronka, J. (2008). *Human rights and social justice: Social action and service for the helping and health professionals.* Sage Publications, Inc.

Identifying and Preventing Burnout among Asian Bilingual Social Workers

Sangeun Lee

Social Workers and Burnout

Social workers have previously been identified as being at risk of experiencing burnout (Schwartz et al., 2007), and at often higher rates (75%) than other health and social service provider groups (39%) (Siebert, 2005). Burnout can be defined as a state of emotional and physical exhaustion resulting from an ongoing imbalance of stress and coping resources especially when related to work (Leiter & Maslach, 1988). Social workers' high burnout is related to their working conditions, which are often arduous, emotionally draining, and requiring excessive multitasking—all with limited resources and relatively low pay considering their educational attainment (Lloyd et al., 2002). Burnout among social workers has the potential to lead to serious consequences not only for themselves but for their clients, other social workers in their organizations, and eventually the organizations they are working for, because workers who experience burnout are more likely to be absent from work and to have a higher turnover. Turnover creates problems for social work administrators and organizations because it impacts negatively on the morale of the remaining workers and on clients' trust in the organizations (Geurts et al., 1998). Turnover also affects consistent and stable service delivery to clients (Mor Barak et al., 2001). Subsequently, turnover makes negative impacts on clients' trust in the organizations, and in the long run, it creates financial problems for organizations (Geurts et al., 1998).

Job Demands and Resources (JD-R) Model

In light of the implications of burnout, the Job Demands and Resources (JD-R) model, a conceptual framework, explains burnout as the result of job demands and resources (Wu et al., 2019). "Job demands" refers to those physical, social, or organizational aspects of the job that require sustained physical or mental effort or skill (De Jonge & Dormann, 2006). In contrast, "job resources" refers to those physical, psychological, social, or organizational aspects of the job that are functional in achieving work goals and reducing work demands (De Jonge & Dormann, 2006). Job demands are related to certain physiological and psychological costs such as role stress (Demerouti et al., 2001). Job resources are related to certain job engagements such as social support and job autonomy (Wu et al., 2019). Previous research on burnout confirmed that job demands are positively associated with burnout, while job resources are negatively associated with it (De Jonge & Dormann, 2006).

The strength of the JD-R model is its flexibility to adapt working environments or job characteristics into the model for the specific occupation under consideration. The most important job demands are role stress and workload among human service providers, including social workers (Lee & Ashforth, 1996). Role stress is often characterized by a worker's high role conflict, role ambiguity, and role overload (Kim and Stoner, 2008). Among these, role overload is not studied as frequently as the first two because it overlaps with work overload and job conflict (Kim et al., 2009). Job stress is proved to have direct impacts on workers' emotional exhaustion and depersonalization (Kim et al., 2009). High workload is directly connected to heavy load of work and time pressure for workers, and it also has direct impacts on workers' emotional exhaustion and depersonalization. Social support is the most well-known variable under the job resources category. Social support is supportive interaction or exchange of resources between people in both formal and informal relationships and in the context of job settings (Tack, 1991). It is negatively related to workers' burnout (House, 1981; Karasek & Theorell, 1990). Job autonomy, which is defined as the degree of control a worker has over his or her scheduling and tasks, also has a negative relationship with burnout (Liu et al., 2005). Depending on the working environment or job characteristics of the workers, the JD-R model has been successfully adopted to capture both risk and protective factors for burnout among various professions.

Asian Communities in the United States

Asians are one of the fastest-growing populations in the United States, and they are expected to remain so in the future. The Asian population is around six percent of the national population, according to the latest United States Census (USA FACTS, 2021), yet their growth was about 72 percent (from 11.9 million to 20.4 million) between 2000 and 2015. The population is expected to be around 41 million by 2050 (Pew Research Center [PRC], 2017), or about 10 percent of the United States population. This minority population is divided into more than seven distinctive ethnic origins: China, Philippines, Japan, Korea, Vietnam, India, and others (Wendell, 2015). The Asian immigrant population is one of the minority groups having the highest language barriers, with 35 percent speaking English "less than very well," after the Hispanic or Latino population (United States Census Bureau, 2019; Ramakrishnan & Wong, 2010). For example, according to the latest report on older Asian adults in New York, their limited English proficiency (LEP) rates are much higher than that of any other groups (Center for an Urban Future, 2013). The impacts of LEP on the Asian communities are evident. Older Asian adults, especially those who are foreign-born, are more likely to receive many fewer Social Security benefits because they tend to earn less because of their LEP (Tran, 2017). The largest impacts of LEP on the Asian communities, however, are found in their access to health services.

It is repeatedly found that Asians do not utilize mental health services as much as other racial groups. This situation is due to lack of information on mental health services and lack of culturally and linguistically appropriate service delivery (Lee, 2020; Lee & Rose, 2021; Sue et al., 2012). In light of COVID-19, it is confirmed that minority communities are unevenly impacted in terms of their mortality and comorbidity rates. To make matters worse, Asians are facing a new form of racism, which is labelled as "COVID-19 racism" (Lee, 2020). Asians in the United States and around the world have been physically and verbally attacked and blamed for the pandemic. The long-term effects of their exposure to COVID-19 racism for impacted individuals, as well as among Asian groups, are still poorly understood. The Atlanta shooting targeting Asian women in April 2020 confirmed heightened racism against Asians during the pandemic. Nonetheless, Chen (2020) described the pandemic-driven rise in anti-Asian racism as a "secondary contagion" threatening this population beyond the COVID-19 pandemic phase.

Culturally and Linguistically Appropriate Services (CLAS)

Federal recognition of the importance of providing culturally and linguistically appropriate services (CLAS) for the minority population has been made by the United States Department of The Office of Minority Health (HHS OMH). They have advocated more extensive CLAS in the health and social service fields for the past two decades (Lee, 2021). Even under these changing climates for considering the LEP population and their service provision, the Asian population, especially those with LEP, have been relying on receiving services from bicultural and bilingual professional groups, including social workers in their community Human Service Organizations (HSOs) (Lee, 2020; Weng, 2014). Those bilingual professionals acknowledge that Asians have insufficient access to needed health and social services, and other appropriate benefits, due to cultural and linguistic differences (Lee, 2020; Weng, 2014). Even far before the pandemic, it was repeatedly reported that there were not enough Asian bilingual social workers who could provide needed services for their Asian clients with LEP (Lee, 2020; Lee & Ryan, 2021). The small number of bilingual Asian social workers becomes even more concerning when considering the aforementioned needs of Asian communities during COVID-19. At this moment of the pandemic, there are still not enough Asian bilingual social workers to help the need of this growing population.

Asian social workers represent 3.57 percent of the social work professional group, who are identified with a social work degree in higher education (United States Department of Labor, 2018). This percentage is far smaller than the current United States Asian population of about 6 percent. This finding is backed up by the survey results of social work professional demographic growth. While the number of recent graduates of Masters' of Social Work (MSW) and Bachelor's in Social Work (BSW) programs in the United States has steadily increased for the past decades, Asian graduates were not a part of this trend (2018). They compose only around 3 percent for the past five years, according to the 2019 report on the social work graduates from the Council on Social Work Education (CSWE, 2019).

Language is the strongest vehicle for expressing culture and ideas. A person's cultural beliefs and outlook on the world is generally revealed by the idioms and subtleties of one's language. Hiring Asian bilingual social workers has benefits in delivering culturally and linguistically tailored health and social services for the Asian populations, but there has been little research conducted with them to date. In general, social workers who are working with immigrant populations with LEP are reported to have a higher burnout due to additional jobs they carry in being a cultural bridge between the host and native countries and balancing expectations of two different cultures (Engstrom & Min, 2004). They often find that clients with LEP need more time compared to non-LEP counterparts for follow-up services (Engstrom et al., 2009a; Engstrom & Min, 2004). It is no different for Asian bilingual social workers. So far, hiring bilingual professionals in the clinical fields for culturally and linguistically appropriate service-delivery has proved to be the best method for improving health and social services outcomes for minority populations (Garcia et al., 2017; Lee et al., 2010), a conclusion that is aligned with voices from the community leadership (Weng, 2014). In this sense, it is imperative to promote and retain Asian bilingual social workers by recognizing and mitigating their burnout. Unfortunately, limited research has been conducted to include culturally specific risk and protective factors that can promote an understanding of burnout among minority social workers such as bilingual social workers, especially Asian and Asian descendants.

Culturally Specific Risk and Protective Factors

Previous research on burnout under the JD-R model for the human service professionals, including social workers, has included role stress and workload as risk factors under the "job demands" category, while social support and job autonomy has been included under "job resources". In light of Asian bilingual social workers' culturally and linguistically appropriate service delivery, both variables need to be considered in utilizing the JD-R model: linguistic competency and language fatigue. Linguistic competency, which is identified as one of the personal resources among bilingual professionals, has a negative impact on their burnout (Nayernia & Babayan, 2019). Bilingual social workers are reported to experience 'language fatigue,' which is broadly explained to be caused by "switching from one language to another over the course of the day" (Engstrom et al., 2009a; Lee, 2021). It requires great concentration and mental agility, sometimes under stressful circumstances. More than 60 percent of bilingual social work students whose field practicum encompasses immigrant populations with LEP report that they experience 'fatigue' by switching from one language to another constantly (Engstrom et al., 2009b). It is found that there is a high correlation between fatigue, both physical and mental, and burnout among workers (Aaronson et al., 1999). Considering the broad definition of 'fatigue,' previous research indicates that fatigue has a clear implication in the occupational setting. It has negative impacts on workers' mental, physical, and psychological health, which is directly connected to workers' burnout (Sadeghniiat-Haghighi & Yazdi, 2015). If we apply these findings to language fatigue, language fatigue brings similar symptoms of 'fatigue,' such as mental and physical capacities. Considering the similarity between 'language fatigue' and 'fatigue,' it becomes instrumental to include "language fatigue" as a risk factor for burnout among Asian bilingual social workers.

Burnout Studies for the Asian Bilingual Social Workers

Incorporating both linguistic competency and language fatigue as culturally specific variables into the existing JD-R model to understand Asian bilingual workers, linguistic competency could be understood as a protective factor for burnout, while language fatigue is a risk factor for burnout. Understanding Asian bilingual social workers' burnout, especially focusing on cultural and linguistic risk and protective factors for burnout, would only promote more Asian bilingual social worker groups. They are in dire need in the United States, considering the demographic changes in the future and the impact of COVID-19 related racism beyond the pandemic. Thus, proposed ideas on adding culturally specific risk and protective factors for burnout among Asian bilingual social workers could be adopted, similar to those used to understand larger social worker groups, such as Hispanic or Latino bilingual social workers, who are fortunately increasing as their national demographic changes.

Conclusion

This literature review provides a novel framework for integrating culturally nuanced factors into burnout research for Asian bilingual social workers. Social workers are reported to have high burnout, and burnout reflects an increased level of emotional exhaustion, which usually deteriorates the quality of care and services that a worker provides. Burnout makes negative impacts on social workers, coworkers, organizations, as well as clients. Workers who experience burnout are more likely to be absent from work and to have a higher turnover. Their turnover could create problems for social work administrators and organizations because it obstructs the morale of the remaining staff and impacts clients' trust in the organization. Considering all these factors, paying close attention to social workers' burnout is imperative, and the Job Demands and Resources (JD-R) model is a frequently utilized model to capture both risk and protective factors for burnout. However, this JD-R model has not been used to study burnout among Asian bilingual social workers, a highly under-researched area despite the high needs in the community, as Asian Americans are one of the fastest growing populations in the United States and as the major target of COVID-19 related racism during the pandemic. They are expected to compose 10 percent of the national demographics by 2050 (USA FACTS, 2021). Their racially motivated hate crime in 2020 has increased more than 150 percent in the major cities of the United States (Yam, 2021). Social work professionals are growing in number over the last decade, yet Asian social workers, regardless of their bilingual capacity, are not following this trend. Rather, they are decreasing, which does not align with Asian demographics. Asian communities, especially with language barriers, face difficulties in making access to health and social services. Yet, there are not enough Asian bilingual social workers to help them. The COVID-19 pandemic has imposed another challenge on the Asian population: COVID-19 related racism. The long-term impacts of this heightened racism have not been identified. Thus, understanding Asian bilingual social workers, who are able to provide culturally and linguistically appropriate services for Asian communities with limited English proficiency, is crucial to promote them in the future. Incorporating linguistic competency as a protective factor and language fatigue as a risk factor for their burnout using the JD-R model could benefit future research and practice in the field since they are culturally-specific variables which would help us understand the needs of Asian bilingual workers. Furthermore, potential findings may be transferable to other populations, such as Hispanic or Latino bilingual social workers, whose target populations also have a large number of LEP clients.

References

Aaronson, L. S., Teel, C. S., Cassmeyer, V., Neuberger, G. B., Pallikkathayil, L., Perice, J., Press, A. N., Williams, P. D., & Wingate, A. (1999). Defining and measuring fatigue. *Journal of Nursing Scholarship. 31*(1), 45-50.

Center for an Urban Future (2013) The New Face of New York's Seniors. *Center for an Urban Future.* Retrieved from https://nycfuture.org/pdf/ The-New-Face-of-New-Yorks Seniors.pdf.

Chen, J. (2020) During pandemic, racism puts additional stress on Asian Americans. *Massachusetts General Hospital,* Press Release. https://www. massgeneral.org/news/press-release/During pandemic-racism-puts-additional-stress-on-asian americans

Council on Social Work Education. (2019). From social work education to social work practice results of the survey of 2018: social work graduates. https://www.socialworkers.org/LinkClick.aspx?fileticket=eLsquD1s2qI %3d&portalid=0

De Jonge J., & Dormann C. (2006). Stressors, resources, and strain at work: A longitudinal test of the triple-match principle. *Journal of Applied Psychology. 91*,1359. doi: 10.1037/0021-9010.91.5.1359.

Demerouti, E., Bakker, A. B., Nachreiner, F., & Schaufeli, W. B. (2001). The job demands-resources model of burnout. *Journal of Applied Psychology, 86*(3), 499.

Engstrom, D., & Min, J. W. (2004). Perspectives of Bilingual Social Workers: "You Just Have to Do a Lot More for Them". *Journal of Ethnic and Cultural Diversity in Social Work, 13*(1), 59-82.

Engstrom, D. W., Min, J. W., & Gamble, L. (2009a). Field practicum experiences of bilingual social work students working with limited English proficiency clients. *Journal of Social Work Education, 45*(2), 209-224.

Engstrom, D. W., Piedra, L. M., & Min, J. W. (2009b). Bilingual social workers: Language and service complexities. *Administration in Social Work, 33*(2),

167-185.

Garcia, M. E., Ochoa-Frongia, L., Moise, N., Aguilera, A., & Fernandez, A. (2017). Collaborative care for depression among patients with limited English proficiency: A systematic review. *Society of General Internal Medicine. 33*(3). p 347–57. Retrieved from DOI: 10.1007/s11606-017-4242-4.

Geurts, S. Schaufeli, W., & De Jonge, J. (1998). Burnout and intention to leave among mental health-care professionals: A social psychological approach. *Journal of Social and Clinical Psychology, 17*(3), 341–362.

House, J. S. (1981). Work stress and social support, *Reading*, MA: Addison-Wesley.

Karasek, R. & Theorell, T. (1990). *Healthy work*. New York: Basic Books.

Kim, B. P., Murrmann, S. K., & Lee, G. (2009). Moderating effects of gender and organizational level between role stress and job satisfaction among hotel employees. *International Journal of Hospitality Management, 28*(4), 612-619.

Kim, H., & Stoner, M. (2008). Burnout and turnover intention among social workers: Effects of role stress, job autonomy and social support. *Administration in Social Work, 32*(3), 5-25.

Lee, R. T., & Ashforth, B. E. (1996). A meta-analytic examination of the correlates of the three dimensions of job burnout. *Journal of Applied Psychology, 81*(2), 123.

Lee, S. (2020). Expanding Bilingual Social Workers for the East Asian Older Adults beyond the "COVID-19 Racism". *Journal of Gerontological Social Work, 63*(6-7), 589-591.

Lee, S. (2021). Evaluation of the National CLAS Standards: Tips and Resources. *Journal of Gerontological Social Work*, 1-4.

Lee, S., Kim, E., and Chen W. (2010). Research strategies: Lessons learned from the studies of Chinese Americans and Korean Americans. *Journal of Transcultural Nursing. 21*(3). P 265-270

Lee, S., & Rose, R. (2021). Unexpected benefits: New resilience among intergenerational Asian-Americans during the Covid-19 pandemic. *Social Work with Groups*, 1-7.

Leiter, M. P., & Maslach, C. (1988). The impact of interpersonal environment on burnout and organizational commitment. *Journal of Organizational Behavior, 9*(4), 297–308. doi:10.1002/(ISSN)1099-1379

Liu, C., E Spector, P., & M Jex, S. (2005). The relation of job control with job strains: A comparison of multiple data sources. *Journal of Occupational and Organizational Psychology, 78*(3), 325-336.

Lloyd, C., King, R., & Chenoweth, L. (2002). Social work, stress and burnout: A review. *Journal of Mental Health, 11*(3), 255–265.

doi:10.1080/09638230020023642

Mor Barak, M.E., Nissly, J.A., & Levin, A. (2001). Antecedents to retention and turnover among child welfare, social work, and other human service employees: What can we learn from past research? A review and meta-analysis. *Social Service Review, 75*(4), 625–662.

Nayernia, A., & Babayan, Z. (2019). EFL teacher burnout and self-assessed language proficiency: Exploring possible relationships. *Language Testing in Asia, 9*(1), 1-16.

Pew Research Center. (2017). Key facts about Asian Americans, a diverse and growing population. https://www.pewresearch.org/fact tank/2017/09/08/key-facts-about-asian-americans/

Ramakrishnan, K., & Wong. J. (January 29, 2010). Census 2020 has a big Asian American problem. *AAPI Data.* https://aapidata.com/blog/census2020-asian-am-problem/

Sadeghniiat-Haghighi, K., & Yazdi, Z. (2015). Fatigue management in the workplace. *Industrial Psychiatry Journal, 24*(1), 12.

Schwartz, R. H., Tiamiyu, M. F., & Dwyer, D. J. (2007). Social worker hope and perceived burnout: The effects of age, years in practice, and setting. *Administration in Social Work, 31*(4), 103–119. doi:10.1300/J147v31n04_08

Siebert, D. C. (2005). Personal and occupational factors in burnout among practicing social workers: Implications for researchers, practitioners, and managers. *Journal of Social Service Research, 32*(2), 25-44.

Sue, S., Cheng, J. K. Y., Saad, C. S., & Chu, J. P. (2012). Asian American mental health: A call to action. *American Psychologist, 67*(7), 532.

Tack, B. (1991). Dimensions and correlates of fatigue in older adults with rheumatoid arthritis. *Unpublished doctoral dissertation.* University of California, San Francisco, CA.

Tran, V. (2017) Asian American seniors are often left out of the national conversation on poverty. *The Urban Institute.* https://www.urban.org/urban-wire/asian american-seniors-are-often-left-out-national conversation-poverty (Accessed: 30 July 2020).

United States Census Bureau (2019) 2020 Census barriers, attitudes, and motivators study survey report. *U.S. Department of Commerce.* https://www2.census.gov/programs surveys/decennial/2020/program-management/final analysis-reports/2020-report-cbams-study-survey.pdf.

United States Department of Labor. (2018). *Social Workers.* O*NET online. https://datausa.io/profile/soc/social-workers#about

USA FACTS. (2021, May 17). The diverse demographics of Asian Americans. https://usafacts.org/articles/the-diverse-demographics-of-asian-americans/?utm_source=bing&utm_medium=cpc&utm_campaign=ND-Race&msclkid=133eabdacae71471b766ca857be507ff

Wendell, C. (2015, January 12). Asians: America's fastest growing minority. *New Geography*. Retrieved from http://www.newgeography.com/content/004825-asians-americas-fastest-growing-minority.

Weng, S.S. (2014) Founding of ethnic programs and agencies for Asian Americans: An exploration of strategies and challenges. *Human Service Organizations: Management, Leadership and Governance, 38*(1), pp. 55-73.

Wu, G., Hu, Z., & Zheng, J. (2019). Role stress, job burnout, and job performance in construction project managers: the moderating role of career calling. *International journal of environmental research and public health, 16*(13), 2394. doi.org/10.3390/ijerph16132394

Yam, K. (2021, March 9). Anti-Asian hate crimes increased by nearly 150% in 2020, mostly in N.Y. and L.A., new report says. NBC News. https://www.nbcnews.com/news/asian-america/anti-asian-hate-crimes-increased-nearly-150-2020-mostly-n-n1260264

Domestic Violence against Men: A Case Study of Ondo-State, Nigeria

Alkauthar seun Enakele

Introduction

Domestic Violence (DV) is a global problem affecting people of different social-cultural, educational and religious backgrounds in developing and developed countries (UNPF, 2005). For example, in the United States of America (USA), more than one million domestic violence cases are reported to police each year (Silverman et al., 2010). According to the National Violence Against Women Survey in 2000, approximately 4.8 million intimate partner rapes and physical assaults were perpetrated against U.S. women, and 2.9 million intimate partner physical assaults were committed against U.S. men annually (Tjaden & Thoennes, 2000). The National Coalition Against Domestic Violence says that, on average, ten women die at the hands of intimate partners each day (Wood, 2001). In Canada, there were 28,000 incidents of spousal violence reported to the police in 2004, of which 84% involved female victims and 16% affected male victims. However, only 28% of spousal abuse victims report incidents to the police, 36% are female victims and 17% are male victims (Mann, 2008). The World Health Organization defines domestic violence (DV) as "any behaviour within an intimate relationship that causes physical, psychological or sexual harm to those in the relationship" (Krug et al., 2002 p. 1085).

Social work group practitioners have a crucial role in addressing the causes and barriers associated with male victims of domestic violence. The study aims to explore the phenomenon of women's violence toward their male partners, as presented from the lived experiences of male victims of domestic violence.

Domestic Violence Against Men in Nigeria

Nigeria is located in West Africa in the southern hemisphere and is the most populous nation of Africa and bounded by Cameroon, Benin, Niger and Chad (Nwachukwu & Uzoigwe, 2004). Nigeria is a vast country with a total area of 923,768 sq. km. Nigeria is a pluralistic society of over 170 million people with different cultural and ethnic backgrounds, a nation with 36 state governments, one federal capital territory (see Gayawan et al., 2014) and 776 local government areas, a society of heterogeneous cultures and religions (Ugiagbe, 2015). Nigeria is equally multicultural, with over 350 cultures and languages and a religiously volatile population along an ethnoreligious divide (World Bank, 2006).

Domestic violence against men is a sensitive issue in Ondo-State, Nigeria. Domestic violence against men is still a violent family dynamic that is mentally difficult to recognize and understand (Band-Winterstein & Eisikovits, 2009; Koenig et al., 2003; Morrison et al., 2006). In Nigeria, domestic violence against men refers to any abuse committed against a man by his wife or intimate partner (Enakele, 2019). Scholars define domestic violence against men as all acts of violence committed against men by the man's intimate partner (Adebayo 2014; Sugg et al., 1999).

Reports from the Nigerian national population commission estimated women's lifetime exposure to domestic violence from their current husband or partner at 19% for emotional, 14% for physical, and 5% for sexual (NPC, 2014). Previous studies from Nigeria have shown the prevalence of domestic violence among men and women ranges from 31 to 61% for psychological/emotional violence, 20 to 31% for sexual violence, and 7 to 31% for physical violence (Mapayi et al., 2013). Furthermore, studies conducted in different regions in Nigeria have reported prevalence of domestic violence ranging from 42% in the north (Tanimu et al., 2016), 29% in the southwest (Okenwa et al., 2009), 78.8% southeast (NdugasaOkemgboI, 2017), to 41% in the south-south (Dienye et al., 2014).

Cultural Patriarchal Perspective

The patriarchal cultural view of society supports that DV is a gender crime executed by men towards women (Dobash & Dobash, 2004). After all, men are perceived to be physically stronger than women. In this way, the societal notions portray women as helpless against violence perpetrated by an intimate partner. Women are known as the victims of this kind of violence (Dobash & Dobash, 2004). Men are commonly considered victims only in violent cases perpetrated by an outsider or an acquaintance (Adebayo, 2014). The perspective on women as aggressors is opposed because women are perceived as nurturing, feminine, and cannot be violent; this has been the societal norm (Richardson, 2005).

George (2002) stated that men named 'victims', especially on violence in women's hands, have been openly disgraced and chastised. Violence perpetrated by women is frequently observed as less dangerous than that performed by men (Simon et al., 2001). Studies report that women commit violence (both physical and verbal), both in a more extensive setting and within intimate relationships (Richardson, 2005; Steen & Hunskaar, 2004). Nigerian society is highly patriarchal. Men are assumed culturally as the aggressor and perpetrators in abusive relationships, and women remain the victims or blameless in intimate partner violence (Adebayo, 2014). Therefore, the context of violence against men appears directly related to patriarchal cultural structure. The primary reason behind this predicament is the social structures and cultural views associated with gender. In fact, societal norms have contributed to the significant problem that men who suffer DV are hardly given a listening ear in society because they are assumed to be the aggressor, even when they have physical proof of violence. These societal assumptions may result in undetected female domination, discrimination, and abuse against men (Adebayo, 2014). The cultural patriarchy has constructed a notion for male victims in DV to receive far less compassion than female victims (Adebayo, 2014). More so, Carlson and Worden (2005) found that society tends to judge men's violent behaviour as representing DV regardless of the circumstance. Nigerian women are given more support and listening ears than men in DV, while Nigeria men are not believed, and their claims are disregarded in DV (Adebayo, 2014).

There is little knowledge about or understanding of, men's experiences of violence in intimate relationships. The study tends to throw light on how men live with violence and the situations surrounding their experiences in Ondo-State. Ondo-State is a state in Nigeria, created on 3rd February 1976, which has a landmass of about 14,788.723 square kilometers (km²). It geographically lies entirely in the tropical belt, with a population of 3,441,024, comprising 1,761,263 males and 1,679,761 females.

Purpose of the Present Study

The purpose of this qualitative case study was to gain greater insight into men's experiences as victims of domestic violence and to contribute novel knowledge to a research field dominated by women's experiences as victims of violence. Furthermore, the study uses the men's experiences to conceptualize the socio-cultural causes of DV in Ondo-State, Nigeria.

Method

Sample

The study starts with a purposive sampling of cases of men who are recognized as victims of DV. The men were recruited through the physical examination centre of the outpatient department of the General hospital in Akure, Ondo State. Later on, the snowball sampling approach garnered more participants connected to the initial interviewees that have ones treated for wounds sustained from their female partners.

Design

The study was conducted utilizing a phenomenological design to understand men's viewpoints and lived experiences in abusive relationships. Phenomenological research provides the space for individuals to discuss meanings they ascribe to their experiences in their own words (Creswell, 2009; Patton, 2002). The study consists of in-depth interviews with men who were subjected to various forms of violence from their intimate partner or wife. The interviews were conducted face-to-face and via telephone conversation and lasted for 45 to 80 minutes. The discussion was guided by this question: "How do men describe their experiences of being victims of DV in a patriarchal society?" The study followed the ethical guidelines and code of conduct from the Research Ethics of the Masaryk University and Nigeria Association of Social Workers Ethics.

Data Analysis

The study engages the Interpretative Phenomenological Analysis (IPA) that requires a verbatim transcription of the interview. Data were analyzed using IPA which focuses on how individuals portray salient factors of their experience, and make sense of these experiences (Smith & Shinebourne, 2012). Next, the authors clustered common experiences of participants and delineated the essence of these experiences.

Results

The study focused exclusively on ten (10) men who are victims of DV, ages ranged from 32 to 55 years old, and most were married and living with their spouses. The finding aimed to understand the fundamental issues associated with the prevalence of DV in the social settings of Ondo-State, Nigeria and reveal the socio-cultural causes of domestic violence against men.

Unemployment

The study found that unemployment is one of the significant triggers of DV against men in Ondo State. The financial burdens that come with unemployment have resulted in a lower socioeconomic status which increases the risk of women abusing their male partners when men do not complete their responsibilities as expected by the wives. The risk for domestic violence towards men increases when the number of dependants in the household is high. In box 1 of the case study below, the participant demonstrated the assortment of variables that happen to a man to become a victim of DV.

Box 1

I am fifty-two years old, married, with four children (two boys and two girls). We lived together in a four-bedroom rented apartment. I worked with community bank for several years as a cashier until I was sacked from my job due to an economic meltdown. I began to search for a new job, but all efforts to get one proved abortive. Thus, I decided to use my car for commercial transportation as a means of livelihood in other to make provisions for my family and by so doing, I was able to take full responsibility for my family. One fateful day, I was travelling, and I had an accident and the car was damaged beyond repair. I decided to sell the carcass of the car at a giveaway price. I gave the money to my wife, and she invested it into her business to further boost her profit. I started going to the motor park as a motor assistant so that at the end of the day, I could bring home some cash in order to keep my body and soul together. My wife started exhibiting different attitudes towards me immediately after she realized my income had dwindled. She started lambasting me whenever she had the opportunity. She graduated to depriving me of food whenever I returned from the motor park. One day, I came back from where I went to hustle and gave her money to cook food for the family, but instead, she squandered the cash on manicures and pedicures. To my dismay, when I got home on that faithful day, I became so hungry, and I was expecting to be given a delicious meal, but instead, she showed me the jewelry she bought with the money. I was shocked and became so angry and demanded an explanation of why she decided to put on such a nonchalant attitude towards me. I was expecting a reasonable answer from her, but she started flexing muscles at me, which aggravated the matter. She slapped me and tore the shirt I wore at the same time. I was shocked at her bad attitude, and I kept wondering what could have come over her. She started tongue-lashing me and called me all sorts of names. I tried all possible means to ensure she maintained silence to prevent the children and the entire neighbourhood from knowing what was happening by using my hand to cover her mouth. Still, she surprised me with another slap on my face which threw me off balance (SP004).

Power and Control

Domestic violence against men can result from power and control when a woman attains a position of authority/power. When some women are empowered or achieve a higher rank than their spouses, they tend to become abusive in the relationship, leading to violence against their male partners. In box 2, a participant describes his experience as a victim of female perpetrated DV.

Box 2

I am forty-three years old. It all started when my wife got a promotion as the [role of authority], and we both celebrated her promotion. I never knew that was the beginning of my trauma. Her new status changed her character towards me, and she started acting up to me. Anytime I asked her qustions about her movement, she would pick offences. She never remained the faithful, caring and loving wife she used to be. She started accusing me of things I knew nothing about. One day, she came back late from her place of work, which was not supposed to be so, a day that she should have stayed at home and prepared delicious meals for family and friends as usual, but she was nowhere to be found. I dialed her cell phone number on several occasions on that fateful day to know her whereabouts, but she never responded. She returned very late in the night at precisely 1:00 am. I asked her the reason why she refused to honour my call or send a text message, and she said I had no right to ask her to return my calls and this led to a big problem of which made her hit me on the chest and at the same time pressed my throat almost to the point of coma. The children became terrified and started crying and begging her to leave me alone. When I thought she had gotten tired, I tried to move away from her, she dragged me back, pulling my shirt, and as I made to turn to face her, I hit my head on the wall and lost consciousness. Some days later, I was able to recover from being unconscious, and to my dismay, the first person I saw when I became conscious was my wife. She was in a sober mood and pleaded for forgiveness that such an incident would never happen again. I thought she had learnt her lessons, but history repeated itself barely two weeks after I was discharged from the hospital. She came late from work again, and as the head of the family, I asked why she came late, hoping to receive a reasonable explanation in respect of that; instead, she hissed at me and started using all sorts of hurtful words at me and walked out on me. (SP002)

Perceived Infidelity

Perceived infidelity is a primary reason women perpetrate DV in relationships. The study shows that men who are suspected of infidelity by their spouses become potential victims of DV. Infidelity is a matter of lack of trust between partners. Women nursing suspicions of infidelity were more likely to perpetrate DV. In box three of the case study below, a participant demonstrated the assortment of perceived infidelity that happened to him which led to him becoming a victim of female perpetrated DV.

Box 3

I am 38 years old. I was in a relationship with a lady who happened to be my fiancée. The relationship, which was supposed to result in happy matrimony between us, was put to a halt due to her bad temperament. We started planning for our wedding, but fate did not permit us. The problem started two weeks before the date slated for the wedding when we carried out plans to make the day a glorious day. By so doing, my church members were coming to pay me a courtesy visit among a young lady of about 21 years of age. The young lady who was in dire need of a job had submitted her curriculum vitae at my workplace. She made use of that opportunity to make enquiries about her job application, which was forwarded to my office. Immediately the lady left, I discovered that the countenance of my fiancée had changed. As I was trying to ask her why she became moody, she held my tie and asked who the lady was, and I replied that she was one of my sisters in- the -Lord, and we both laughed over it, not knowing that she was not pleased with my response. I discovered she was quiet, and all efforts to start a conversation with her proved abortive. The next step of action she put up was to pack her belongings and wanted to leave. Initially, I thought it was a joke, but suddenly, she started screaming on top of her voice and caused many mayhems. I tried moving closer to her, hoping to calm her down, but she attacked me with a bottle. I tried my best to run away from her, but she wouldn't let go of me. I intensified efforts to break from her grip, but she hit my pelvic region. I pushed her away and ran out of the house in pain. I returned home two hours after, hoping to see a sense of remorse in her, but instead, she didn't give a damn (SP007).

Discussion

This study aimed to explore the experience of domestic violence among male victims in Ondo State, Nigeria. Findings highlight how Nigerian societal norms maintain a culture that is shameful for a man to pronounce abuse perpetrated by a woman. Nigerian men face barriers in pursuing help for their victimization due to shame, embarrassment, denial, fear, and stigmatization associated with the cultural stereotypes of being a victim of DV. This cultural view may lead men to be hesitant in seeking help in the community. They are assumed to be the aggressor even though they have bruises all over their bodies. Nigerian police support female DV victims and their children at all levels, but services for men experiencing DV are not available at the state or national levels. Nigerian societies have been traditionally shaped by a patriarchal belief system where men are generally considered the aggressor. Men are capable of causing more harm than women in relationships. Such a belief system has resulted in communities failing to recognize or accept that female perpetrated violence exists. This lack of public recognition of DV may lead to increased violence against men. Findings from this study reveal opportunities for social group workers to raise awareness of societal barriers and build support for male victims of DV.

Clinical and Cultural Implications

Social group workers in communities have crucial roles to play by breaking down barriers for men who experience domestic violence. They can foster strength for the male victims by creating awareness that will challenge the patriarchal system and inform the societies that such ideology results in people failing to recognize or acknowledge women's perpetrated violence. The group/community practitioners in Ondo State, Nigeria, have engaged in social awareness programs that inform society that women can also perpetrate DV against men. The social awareness programs aimed to sensitize the entire population and were delivered in four ways: school-based, community, media, and government awareness.

School-based awareness is a strategy that attempts to address gender norms and equality among children and youth in their early life before gender stereotypes become deeply ingrained in them. The group/community practitioners aimed to sensitize the youth on the perils of DV and challenge the gender stereotypes and social norms endorsing violence against men with the goals of reducing the rate of DV and improving the level of attention and care towards male victims. When youth are well informed about the consequences of DV in their various schools, it may help them to have a more profound understanding and change their perception of domestic violence against men.

The social work practitioners aim to change the way individuals behave or think and mobilize communities to eradicate violence against men. Their involvement can support women's understanding of their roles as wives, increase their influence in the household decisions, and enhance their abilities to resolve marital conflicts amicably. Also, confronting the patriarchal cultural view of DV and building networks of support and action will give voice to men and potentially reduce all kinds of violence against men. More so, helping to change the community's attitudes and reduce violent behaviour towards their partners.

Media awareness is also a powerful preventive tool that helps to reach across societies. We sometimes use television, radio, newspapers, magazines, posters, handbills, the internet and other printed publication to reach a wide range of people and achieve quick alteration within the society. The group social workers engage in different programs to increase the knowledge of the community about DV. Our involvement aims to create awareness to promote social change to improve men's health and promote men's rights and gender equality in societies.

The government plays a crucial role in addressing the prevalence of DV. The group/community practitioners have advocated for the government to develop laws and policies that promote gender equality and criminalize acts of violations, and implement protection orders for victims and prosecution of offenders. However, the social workers support service aim to improve police and other criminal justice officials' responses to women's violence against men.

Conclusion

Domestic violence against men, like other forms of violent behaviours, can result in significant physical and mental health problems, such as bodily injuries, trauma, stigma, and psychological frustration. The group/community practitioners' interventions will help create awareness across the globe, reduce/eliminate the use of aggression against men, and reduce the incidence or future occurrence of DV in Nigeria and other nations of the world. Social workers can build strength for men by reporting and reducing the effect of DV in society.

References

Adebayo, A. A. (2014). Domestic violence against men: Balancing the gender issues in Nigeria. American Journal of Sociological Research, 4(1), 14-19. https://doi.org/10.5923/j.sociology.20140401.03

Band-Winterstein, T., & Eisikovits, Z. (2009). "Aging out" of violence: The multiple faces of intimate violence over the life span. Qualitative Health Research, 19(2), 164-180. https://doi.org/10.1177/1049732308329305

Carlson, B. E., & Worden, A. P. (2005). Attitudes and beliefs about domestic violence: Results of a public opinion survey: I. Definitions of domestic violence, criminal domestic violence, and prevalence. Journal of Interpersonal Violence, 20(10), 1197-121 https://doi.org/10.1177/0886260505278530

Creswell, J. W. (2009). Research design: Qualitative, quantitative and mixed methods approaches. Sage.

Dienye, P., Gbeneol, P., & Gbeneol, I. K. (2014). Intimate partner violence and associated coping strategies among women in a primary care clinic in Port Harcourt, Nigeria. Journal of Family Medicine and Primary Care, 3(3), 193-198. https://doi.org/10.4103/2249-4863.141601

Dobash, R. P., & Dobash, R. E. (2004). Women's violence to men in intimate relationships: Working on a puzzle. British Journal of Criminology, 44(3), 324-349. https://doi.org/10.1093/bjc/azh026

Enakele, A. S. (2019). Domestic violence against men: Prevalence, implications, and consequences. Social Work, Method and Experience, 24(2),29-43. https://doi.org/10.3238/arztebl.2020.0534

Gayawan, E., Arogundade, E. D., & Adebayo, S. B. (2014). Possible determinants and spatial patterns of anaemia among young children in Nigeria: A Bayesian semi-parametric modelling. International Health, 6(1), 35-45. https://doi.org/10.1093/inthealth/iht034

George, M. J. (2002). Skimmington revisited. The Journal of Men's Studies, 10(2), 111-127. https://doi.org/10.3149/jms.1002.111

Koenig, M. A., Ahmed, S., Hossain, M. B., & Mozumder, A. K. A. (2003). Women's status and domestic violence in rural Bangladesh: Individual- and community-level effects. Demography, 40(2), 269-288. https://doi.org/10.1353/dem.2003.0014

Krug, E. G., Mercy, J. A., Dahlberg, L. L., & Zwi, A. B. (2002). The world report on violence and health. The Lancet, 360(9339), 1083-1088. https://doi.org/10.1016/S0140-6736(02)11133-0

Mann, R. M. (2008). Men's rights and feminist advocacy in Canadian domestic violence policy arenas: Contexts, dynamics, and outcomes of antifeminist backlash. Feminist Criminology, 3(1), 44-75. https://doi.org/10.1177/1557085107311067

Mapayi, B., Makanjuola, R. O. A., Mosaku, S. K., Adewuya, O. A., Afolabi, O., Aloba, O. O., & Akinsulore, A. (2013). Impact of intimate partner violence on anxiety and depression amongst women in Ile-Ife, Nigeria. Archives of Women's Mental Health, 16(1), 11-18. https://doi.org/10.1007/s00737-012-0307-x

Morrison, K. E., Luchok, K. J., Richter, D. L., & Parra-Medina, D. (2006). Factors influencing help-seeking from informal networks among African American victims of intimate partner violence. Journal of Interpersonal

Violence, 21(11), 1493-1511. https://doi.org/10.1177/0886260506293484

NdugasaOkemgboI, C. (2017). Prevalence, patterns and correlates of domestic violence in selected Igbo communities of Imo State, Nigeria. African Journal of Reproductive Health, 6(2). https://doi.org/10.2307/3583136

National Public Commission Federal Republic of Nigeria. (2014). Nigeria Demographic and Health Survey 2013. https://dhsprogram.com/pubs/pdf/fr293/fr293.pdf

Nwachukwu, L. A., & Uzoigwe, G. N. (2004). Troubled journey: Nigeria since Independence.

Okenwa, L. E., Lawoko, S., & Jansson, B. (2009). Exposure to intimate partner violence amongst women of reproductive age in Lagos, Nigeria: Prevalence and predictors. Journal of Family Violence, 24(7), 517-530. https://doi.org/10.1007/s10896-009-9250-7

Patton, M. Q. (2002). Qualitative research and evaluation methods. Sage

Richardson, D. S. (2005). The myth of female passivity: Thirty years of revelations about female aggression. Psychology of Women Quarterly, 29(3), 238-247. https://doi.org/10.1111/j.1471-6402.2005.00218.x

Silverman, J. G., Decker, M. R., McCauley, H. L., Gupta, J., Miller, E., Raj, A., & Goldberg, A. B. (2010). Male perpetration of intimate partner violence and involvement in abortions and abortion-related conflict. American Journal of Public Health, 100(8), 1415-1417 https://dx.doi.org/10.2105%2FAJPH.2009.173393

Smith, J. A., & Shinebourne, P. (2012). Interpretative phenomenological analysis. American Psychological Association.

Steen, K., & Hunskaar, S. (2004). Gender and physical violence. Social Science & Medicine, 59(3), 567-571. https://doi.org/10.1016/j.socscimed.2003.11.024

Sugg, N. K., Thompson, R. S., Thompson, D. C., Maiuro, R., & Rivara, F. P. (1999). Domestic violence and primary care: Attitudes, practices, and beliefs. Archives of Family Medicine, 8(4), 301. https://doi.org/10.1001/archfami.8.4.301

Tanimu, T. S., Yohanna, S., & Omeiza, S. Y. (2016). The pattern and correlates of intimate partner violence among women in Kano, Nigeria. African Journal of Primary Health Care & Family Medicine, 8(1). https://doi.org/10.4102/phcfm.v8i1.1209

Tjaden, P., & Thoennes, N. (2000). Full report of the prevalence, incidence, and consequences of violence against women (NCJ 183781). National Institute of Justice, Office of Justice Programs, Washington, DC. https://www.ojp.gov/pdffiles1/nij/183781.pdf

Ugiagbe, E. O. (2015). Social work is context-bound: The need for indigenization of social work practice in Nigeria. International Social Work, 58(6), 790-801. https://doi.org/10.1177/0020872813515013

United Nations Population Fund. Technical Support Division. (2005). Gender-based Violence in Sierra Leone: A Case Study. UNFPA. https://sierraleone.unfpa.org/en/topics/gender-based-violence-11

Wood, J. T. (2001). The normalization of violence in heterosexual romantic relationships: Women's narratives of love and violence. Journal of Social and Personal Relationships, 18(2), 239-261. https://doi.org/10.1177/0265407501182005

World Bank (2006) 'Pakistani Poverty Alleviation Fund Project'. https://www.worldbank.org.pk/website/exjernal/covenies/southeast/pakist

Applying the Collective-Individualism Framework for the Data Analysis of a Rapid Rural Participatory Research Methodology

Mamadou Seck

Introduction

Following a group work training session, social work students were assigned to various villages to apply their newly acquired knowledge and skills by completing a Rapid Rural Participatory Research Methodology (RPRM) for field practice. They organized focus groups to collect data on women's needs, realities, and aspirations. Then, they analyzed the data and organized their findings in pyramids and Venn diagrams revealing women's needs, social and economic organizations, and their financial and economic networks. The author of the current study selected four of the students' reports to complete a model analysis applying Hofstede's Individualism-Collectivism to analyze the RPRM findings. The results revealed the predominance of collectivistic over individualistic orientations in rural women's needs, organizations, and financial and economic networks. Discussing these findings, the author illustrates the predominance of collectivistic over individualistic orientations and options, despite the constant assaults from the endorsers of individualism in rural communities.

Analyzing and understanding the dynamics of human and social relations in rural areas, as well as the decision-making process and local residents' engagement to sustain particular agreements require that researchers be introduced to the concept of individualism-collectivism. The social, economic, and political realities, that rural populations experience in general, foster collectivism since most decisions are made to benefit the larger community. Hofstede's concept of individualism-collectivism provides a framework to analyze rural realities because of the interdependence between local residents' aspirations and those of the larger community. In fact, Hofstede used this concept to describe the possible forms of relationship between individuals and the group to which they belong (Bochner, 1994). This concept can help understand the dominance and preponderance of the larger community's choices over those of the members, as well as the independence of the residents and their interdependence with regard to the common needs and realities. The complexity of the concept of collectivism-individualism appears in several articles (Baarts, 2009; Schwartz, 1990).

Applied to the realities of social workers, the concept of collectivism-individualism relates to circumstances that these professionals face in many instances when they have to overlook their own personal core values to embrace values that their profession promotes within their code of ethics. Very often, these professionals work with clients and colleagues whose values and beliefs are different from theirs, and with whom they do not share personal experiences. Despite these remarkable antinomic differences, they usually succeed in creating positive working bonds with clients and colleagues; this option enables them to successfully intervene relying on their social work knowledge and skills as they overcome value conflicts experienced during their interactions. This concept of value conflict refers to a major disagreement between someone's individual core belief system and that of another individual, group, organization, or society. For example, social workers would experience value conflicts when required to complete actions that their value system does not condone. So, despite their autonomy and independence in decision-making, they would have to adopt a dependent attitude to meet their profession's expectations since values are assumed to be "embodied and lived out as moral functioning" (Puroila & Haho, 2017, p. 12).

According to Levin et al. (2020), values have a unique position as a unifying mechanism among social workers. Accordingly, it is understandable that, for many social workers, resolving a value conflict is committing a self-sacrifice that enables them to stay on task even when working with other colleagues and clients in certain unfavorable conditions. Through education, they not only gain knowledge of social work values and principles but also learn to apply ethical decision-making skills that enable them to develop and strengthen relationship with other professional partners with whom they do not share the same values. Sustaining this professional relationship requires resolving their personal value conflicts. Literally, this means that, in some circumstances, social workers may have to renounce to their own individual and personal values and beliefs to adhere to the collective values and beliefs that their profession promotes. In other words, social workers may face situations during which they must set aside their own personal values and adhere to principles that the social work profession promotes in order to effectively provide service to their clients. This decision illustrates the concept of collective-individualism which infers that individual choices are sustained only in case they meet collective expectations.

Applied to the current research context, this concept of collective-individualism refers to the process in which individual local residents relinquish their personal interests and adopt what the community favors or what is best for the community. This decision materializes the prioritization of the collective body's goals over those of the individual members. This would be the case for example, when individual residents, who can afford to own a private well in their own yard, not only abstain from digging on their own property, but also decide to join forces with other home owners to drill a deep public well that will provide water to the whole village and facilitate collective access to water.

In this article, the author uses the frame of individualism-collectivism to analyze social work students' findings during a week-long session of Rapid Rural Participatory Research Methodology (RPRM) in four villages located in the district of Thies, around 45 miles from Dakar, the Senegalese capital. This researcher first explores the use of the concept of collective-individualism as documented in the previous literature before presenting the study context and then, addresses the research methodology. After unveiling the findings, they then discuss them before making several suggestions for best practice.

Literature Review

Previous literature has documented definitions, illustrations, and analyses of the concept of individualism-collectivism. It is worth noting that in the literature, as well as in this paper, concepts such as "individualist" and "individualistic" on the one hand, and on the other hand "collectivist" and "collectivistic" are two pairs of synonymous adjectives. Inferences drawn from a separate analysis of the two concepts of individualism and collectivism have uncovered irreconcilable or just opposite realities. Meanwhile, a number of researchers including Baarts (2009) and Schwartz (1990) have studied a combination of the two concepts, to unveil a new notion that introduces a unique reality. In effect, Baarts (2009), has applied the concept of individualism-collectivism to analyze the informal and emergent dynamics of practicing safety in a work environment. This researcher noted that individualist and collectivist preferences have an influence on the amount of risk which each individual worker assumes and exposes workmates. In other words, in the work environment, when one individual makes a decision regarding their own safety, the whole team of workers becomes exposed to the consequences of that decision and may experience the negative outcome of that individual's decision. Further, Baarts (2009) emphasized that an individual's self-regulation, self-confidence, and independence are acceptable values as long as they do not threaten the solidarity of the community and the safety of others. It is important to note that people usually act according to their own dispositions and that these dispositions may be of a strictly personal and individualistic nature. Therefore, based on their own personal rights, they may exercise their responsibilities toward themselves in a different way than with the community. This individualistic attitude may result in unforeseen positive or negative consequences for the community.

Schwartz (1990) wrote extensively on the theme of individualism-collectivism. Analyzing the dichotomy between the two concepts, he first noted that, although there were values that inherently served both individual and collective interests (e.g., wisdom), this dichotomy ignored values that could foster the goals of the collective other than the in-group (e.g., universal values such as social justice). In effect, referring to the value of wisdom, Schwartz (1990) noted that, in most societies, this value was not only an important goal whose pursuit guided behaviors and served the in-group, but attaining it was also in the interest of the individual. Consequently, applying similar values including social justice, preserving the natural environment, and a world at peace, Schwartz (1990) demonstrated that collective and individual values could be strongly aligned and that the dichotomy between them could promote the mistaken assumption that individualistic and collectivist values are in polar opposition.

This mistaken assumption of dichotomy between individualistic and collectivistic values has been made when scrutinizing individual musician's performances during a concert (Angelino, 2020). In effect, when an orchestra generates a musical masterpiece, this product is of a collective value, but at the same time, it materializes the individual performance of each musician. Each one of them has been recruited based on their exceptional personal skills. In order to create that masterpiece, each member of the group has to either relinquish or adjust some elements of their personal skills to make sure that their individual input is in harmony with the other musicians' performance. Therefore, the individual contribution enhances the collective output which is the musical masterpiece. This concept of collective-individualism raises the idea that, in order to successfully produce a collective outcome, individuals may have to damper some of their own personal qualities. This is a perspective that led Angelino (2020) to state that "jazz musicians act together in a very distinctive way, which casts into clear relief the interplay between togetherness and agonism, individual freedom and group commitment, which is contained in every human interaction" (p. 49).

In the context of rural Africa, despite a new popular trend that has emerged in urban metropolitan areas promoting more individualism, the concept of collectivism is still a predominant phenomenon. In effect, the fast-growing phenomenon of migration of rural populations toward large cities, conceptualized as 'rural exodus", reinforces migrants' overwhelming dispositions to adhere to individualistic values which do not reflect those that sustain the lived realities of rural communities. Several not-for- profit organizations aiming at dissuading individuals from moving to towns have initiated several actions to maintain local residents in their villages and reinforce the collective will to support each other. For example, a global network of humanitarian agencies has found that, in Senegal, drought is one of the main factors of rural exodus. Therefore, these organizations "have signed a climate risk insurance policy that will protect up to 160,000 people in Senegal from the effects of drought. One of the first of its kind, the policy will enable aid agencies to offer life-saving support to people in Senegal as soon as a drought is predicted, helping to prevent famine" (ARC-Start Network, 2021, para. 1).

Despite these types of actions, dire living conditions force many residents to decide to move to urban areas. This is an emerging paradigm because, in the 1960s, President Julius Nyerere of Tanzania promoted the concepts of Ujamaa which is a Swahili concept that means "extended family". The concept of Ujamaa illustrates residents' relationships and strong ties that reflect a very close brotherhood and materialize the helping tradition within local communities. President Nyerere brought this concept into the political arena to energize his fellow countrymen involved in community development activities. It is worth noting that this concept of Ujamaa is aligned with the expression "It takes a village to raise a child" which means that, in a village, along with the parents, any resident is expected to help raise children; each villager is responsible for children's education since the child belongs to the whole community not to their birth family only.

This topic of collective-individualism reflects the theme of this International Association for Social Work with Groups (IASWG) 2020 symposium, "Creating connections and restoring hope," since working with groups requires that the interveners connect individual group members' performance with that of the group which is in essence collective. In this article, the author interchangeably uses Hofstede's concept of individualism-collectivism (Schwartz, 1990) and collective-individualism in conformity with the previous literature (Baarts, 2009), collectivism and individualism (Triandis, 1993), and atomistic-holistic (Volkman, 2013).

Purpose of the Present Study

This paper aims to determine the process by which the needs of individual rural Senegalese women, residing in four villages located in the region of Thies, have been integrated to evolve into collective needs that reflect their communities' priorities.

Method

Sample

Several African schools of social work and social development institutions train their students to develop research skills through the implementation of a "Rapid Rural Participatory Research Methodology" (RPRM) in various villages (Seck, 2021). Following the completion of a theoretical introductory group work course, as part of their field intervention practice, students attend a five-day in-school workshop during which they learn about the RPRM tools and strategy, as well as their group's structure, tasks, and activities. Then, during another period of five days, they are assigned to villages where they will apply their group work knowledge and skills assessing the village residents' needs, and local human and natural resources. At the end of the training, each group produces a written report so faculty can assess their completed work. The data used in this study, have been collected from four of those reports.

Data Collection

As a former instructor who has trained social work students to conduct RPRM for field practice, the researcher was authorized to review the eight reports that students submitted after the training session. To determine which community reports to include in the data analysis, he developed the following criteria: standards surrounding the procedures for the focus group sessions, the quality of the questionnaire and sequencing of the questions, and number of participants. Each report had to include a detailed Venn diagram illustrating the connections between organizations within the village and between villages. Reports had to include a clear description of the triangulation process which led to the validation of the findings by the participants. Following the review of the eight reports, four met the inclusion criteria. Data from these reports have been used for this study.

Focus Groups

Students have clearly described how they ran the focus groups to collect data from women in each village where they had been assigned to. They have also noted that, due to the local traditional culture which does not condone male strangers talking directly to married women and to women in general, one female group leader was responsible to lead the interviews and that they asked semi-structured questions such as: What are the most difficult problems you face in this village?

What do you need to overcome these problems? What are your most urgent needs?

When additional information was needed for clarification, the interviewers asked sub-questions to participants so they would elaborate on their responses and provide more specific information.

Venn Diagrams

These are tools that students were required to use to identify all local and external organizations and institutions, public or private, supporting and working with village residents. Their objectives were to empower and help residents bring to reality some of their projects that fell into their areas of competence. The connections or lack of relationship between various communities were illustrated in the Venn diagram that students drew to show the options the villagers made either to keep local resources within their village or to share with other villages. This tool could contribute to the understanding of the desire of local residents to work together to find collective solutions to the problems they faced together.

Data Analysis

For this study, the researcher applied the collective-individualism framework to analyze the data women provided during the focus groups, as well as the data laid out in the Venn diagrams regarding local resources. The researcher verified whether the data collected reflected participants' statements as the students had to use a triangulation strategy to validate their results. This task occurred after the first interview during which students identified and prioritized the needs as provided by the participants who were asked to confirm or refute the order in which their needs had been prioritized. After the first focus groups and following the group gathering to complete the paperwork, a second focus group was held so participants would confirm or reject the findings. This two-step data analysis was designed not only to correct any discrepancy between the information participants provided and the research findings, but also to root out any individualistic choice in the prioritization of the needs; further, it contributed to ensure that the ranking reflected participants' collective agreement on the most urgent needs. Moreover, this two-step analysis process should ultimately determine which needs should be addressed first for the benefit of the whole community.

Results

Women's needs expressed during the focus groups were initially gathered as a list (Figure 1) and then after these findings had been confirmed in a second validation process students presented the results in pyramids (Figure 2). Then, students provided more general needs in Venn diagrams.

Women's Needs

During the first focus group, students established a list of women's needs based on participants ranking in each village (Table 1). Then, after a second focus group aimed at triangulating for validation of the findings, a pyramid was drawn to illustrate these results. There were four pyramids, each one representing women's needs in one village (Figure 1).

Table 1

Step 1- Results of Focus Group 1 in Four Villages: Women's Needs

10	Fence cemetery	Extension of power grid	Kindergarten	Security
09	Funding	Export artistic products	Training	School
08	Koranic school	Well for water	Project	Tar road
07	Funding	Credit union	Food processing	Fishing
06	Women's center	Health center	Threshing machine	Transportation
05	Market	School	Grinder	Market
04	Kindergarten	Electricity	Grain storage	Access to electricity
03	Pharmacy	Women's center	Peeling machine	Access to water
02	Health center	Training	Market	Funding
01	High school	Market	Water grid	Grinder
	Village I	Village II	Village III	Village IV

The results of the focus groups in the four villages revealed similarities and differences in women's needs. For example, in village I, having a high school was the most urgent need when other villages needed a market (village II), water (village III), and a grinder for millet flour (village IV) were the main expressed needs. The prioritization showed that in village I, women considered that it was time to build a high school not only due to the large number of students who had to travel to the city to further their education, but also due to the cost of transportation which required many of their children to have to find hosts in nearby cities during the school year.

In Table 1, step 1, researchers showed that in village I, cognitive needs were predominant since educational institutions (high school and Kindergarten) were in higher demand followed by sanitary and health infrastructures (health center and pharmacy). In the other villages, women's needs were more of a physiological, and safety and security nature since, having a market for food provision (village II), extending the water grid to broaden the availability for drinking water (village III), and having a grinder for millet and corn to make flour for their meals (village IV) were ranked as the highest priorities. Security concerns were illustrated in all villages but mostly in the second and fourth where access to electricity for public lights was listed as the fourth need. In all four villages, the needs for financial or funding institutions were expressed although with different urgency.

In each village, the ranking of women's needs during the first focus groups (Table 1, Step 1), have been confirmed in the second meeting with participants as the researchers completed the triangulation process to validate the findings and draw the final pyramids (Figure 1, Step 2).

Pyramid of Needs

During the second focus group, women were asked to rank-order their needs within their village. Figure 1 portrays the hierarchy of needs within each village.

Fig 1
Pyramid of Women's Needs

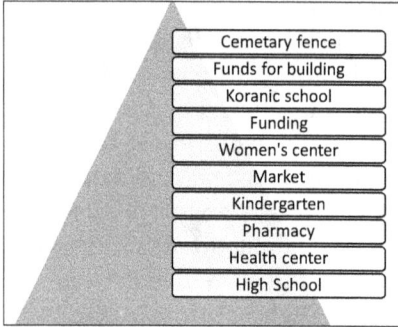

Village 1

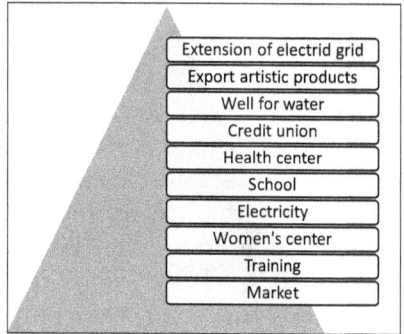

Village 2

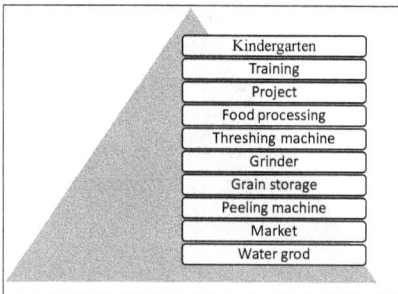

Village 3

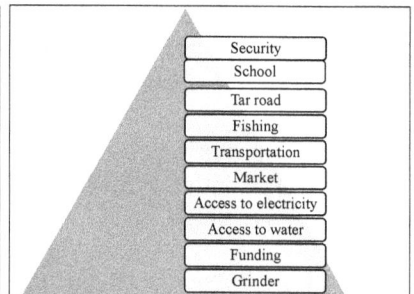

Village 4

Venn Diagram Findings

Venn diagrams provide information on the realities in each village and unveil connections between various local, regional, and national organizations. Images of the Venn diagrams are available from the lead author. Due to the social orientation of the research, organizations and infrastructures that impact the villagers' lives are illustrated. For example, the researchers highlighted local, regional, and national institutions representing public and private organizations, governmental and not for profit entities, etc. The presence of certain institutions in one village reflects the status of the villages. For example, representing City Hall in village 1, illustrates the higher administrative ranking of the village compared to the other villages. Diagrams also display connections between institutions within the village and between local, regional, and national institutions, with a focus on women's organizations' relationships with institutions such as local and regional health, financial, and educational institutions.

The analysis of the data reported in the Venn diagrams revealed that in each village, there were organizations that carried out their members' decisions either to keep their village's resources for their residents only, or to be collectively shared with other villages' residents. Also, the diagrams illustrated the desire of local residents to work together to find collective solutions to the problems they all faced together. The findings revealed that women from villages I and II shared the same health center, but there were two different schedules for patients from the two villages; their medical check-up and treatment were taking place on different days. All villages had local internal and external public and not-for-profit organizations that were autonomous but connected in providing service to women. For example villages II and III shared one public water well that a team including residents from both villages managed. Women in villages II and III shared one financial organization called "Tontine." Leaders weekly collected money from all members and one of them would receive the sum to either start a new business or fund other on-going commercial activities. Many of these women were involved in several economic development initiatives.

Further, the Venn diagrams revealed tensions and conflicts within and between local communities. Students reported conflicts opposing individuals, or individuals and organizations, or communities and organizations. These were conflicts opposing women's groups and other groups within one village (Village II); women had expressed the need to find solutions to conflicts opposing farmers and herders who, almost every year, faced-off following cattle's disappearance or cattle's entry and destruction of family farms (Village II).

Discussion

The Hofstede's concept of individualism-collectivism used as a data analysis framework enabled the author to bring to light the connections between the individual and collective realities and aspirations in rural areas in Africa. The researcher first focused on needs, and then on social and economic networks within and between villages, as well as between local entities and those abroad as revealed by the Venn diagrams. With regard to the women's pyramids of needs, the students' decision to adopt a two-step data analysis strategy was grounded not only in a cultural perspective but also in a desire to root out any individualistic orientation from the final expressed collective needs. In fact, the restitution phase aimed to dispel any choice that would reflect one individual's preference and maintain only expressed needs that reflected collectivist options.

Due to the traditional culture, it is well-known that, in rural areas, local male leaders' influence usually negatively affects the decision-making process particularly when women seek protection or advantages due to their specific needs. In fact, the United Nations (2010) reported that "Women may doubt that certain agencies will support them when they need their support. They may also fear jeopardizing their children's or their own security, if they reported being victimized (UN, 2010, p. 5, para. 4). In addition, the UN noted that "The police, as well as social services and the judiciary may be more difficult to reach by women in rural areas due to lack of transportation and long distance" (UN, 2010, p. 5, para. 4). Consequently, choices made by one individual woman could reflect someone else's ideas. Therefore, it could be presumed that, during the focus groups, some female group leaders could have influenced some participants so their responses to the interview questions would reflect these leaders' needs, choices, and orientations. The two-step process may have successfully eliminated any individualistic request.

A comparison of the four pyramids shows that access to water wells, and markets and educational structures (school, kindergarten, and training centers) were listed among women's needs across-the-board, in all the four villages. These are structures and gathering places for trading, and education and training, that would enable women to access and manage their resources for themselves or their families. These findings illustrate the struggle women face when aiming at autonomy in their quest for independence from their spouses or families in managing their wealth and resources. In effect, the more educated or more trained, the more entrepreneurial women are. These findings align with Fletschner and Kenney (2011) who found that, since rural financial markets are not gender neutral, "family responsibilities and women's access to control over other resources shape their needs for capital and their ability to obtain it" (Fletschner & Kenney, 2011, p. 1). Further, in three villages (I, II, and IV), women requested a connection to the power grid for electricity, a commodity that women explicitly needed to facilitate the use of a number of household equipments they considered as highly necessary including millet grinders, and treshing and peeling machines. These are tools necessary not only to complete farm and kitchen chores but also to reduce the time women were previously obliged to spend in order to complete activities such as pounding grains in a mortar and pestle to make flour. Women would benefit from the use of this earned extra time to get involved in educational and training activities, attend meetings, complete gardening and childcare chores. Consequently, women would become more empowered to have access and control over needed resources. These were conditions that Fletschner and Kenney (2011) viewed as a benefit to women since it "leads to higher investments in human capital and have a stronger impact on children's health, nutrition and education with important long-term implications for families and societies" (p. 1).

The analysis of the Venn diagrams exposed the connections between various women's groups' decisions within one village, but also between villages. The women's social and economic entities and networks, the tensions and conflicts opposing local communities have been explored. In effect the Venn diagrams illustrated women's wishes and their tentative nature in collaborating in various areas of the economy, and education. For example, the creation of a high school in village 1 would not be a reality if youth from other villages were not authorized to attend the institution. So, on the creation of a high school, only a collective agreement could help materialize this need. Unfortunately, this has not been the case when women in village III requested a health center because of the mothers' high number of death during or after child delivery. This request was not materialized due to competing needs expressed by other residents within the village, and the lack of opportunity to reach a collective agreement involving all village III residents. Meanwhile, when women's organizations and authorities reached out to village I authorities, an agreement was found to allow village III women to get consultations and treatment in village I health center. This finding demonstrated that, in rural areas, collectivist orientations were persistent and predominant over individualist options. It illustrated also that women's groups could collaborate to reach an agreement in the area of healthcare. This finding aligns with Fletschner and Kenney's (2011) finding with regard to women's abilities to collaborate when they aim to complete financial activities. In fact, these authors reported that, in rural areas, self-help groups had proven their effectiveness in connecting women with financial institutions as long as these women's groups, operating within one village, required their members to meet regularly and demonstrate their capacity to collect loans; in doing so, they raise the odds that individual women succeed in getting additional capital for their own projects from rural banks. These findings reinforce the idea that the success of collective entities and that of individuals could be intrinsically connected.

Further, the Venn diagrams revealed that, with regard to social and economic networks, these women exhibited a "collective spirit of individualism that redefined community as a horizontal and creative collective necessary to the development of the individual" (Tiampo, 2013, p. 384). In effect, this research's participants put aside their individual needs and aspirations, and adhered not only to the hierarchy of needs that the majority agreed upon, but also to the other groups' choices at the local, regional, and global level as they work with not-for-profit organizations. In each one of the four villages, there were local female residents who were members in several organizations set up for the benefit of various villages.

Tensions and conflicts within and between local communities have been revealed. These conflicts opposed individuals either at the local or the regional, and global level. For example, it was found that there was some tension between village IV residents and a phosphate factory due to the factory's extensive land grab that affected not only women but all residents who lost their land. Another conflict involved farmers and herders who faced-off following a cattle's entry in farms and destroying the harvest. The reported conflicts, due to competing interests, opposed individuals to groups or groups to communities.

Clinical and Research Implications

The concept of collective-individualism analytical framework applies also to group work intervention when individuals co-facilitate group sessions or when making decision as members of task groups. Further, in the context of community development, applying the collective-individualism principle, may not only facilitate discussions on community members' realities, options, and experiences, but also enhance the quality of the decision-making process.

Applying the Hofstede's individualism-collectivism framework when analyzing group work practice phenomena requires that researchers be able to access relevant data on individual members' activities and orientations and those of the group. This limitation stands when researchers consider applying this strategy to analyze data involving only individual members.

Conclusion

As illustrated above, this study's theme aligns with that of the IASWG 2020 symposium, "Creating connections and restoring hope". This study reveals that, when individuals are unable to reach out to the collective entities, the sense of living as a community may be dispelled. In addition, it confirms and reinforces the perspective that rural women are more inclined to pursue the materialization of their collectivistic needs than to hang on individualistic options. In sum, this study's findings demonstrate the persistence of the predominance of collectivistic orientations over individualistic tendencies, despite the constant assaults from endorsers of individualistic inclinations. The satisfaction of women's needs is a pre-requisite to the improvement of their quality of life within the village. It should be noted that, usually, individual participants pursue the satisfaction of their own needs but, because these individualistic needs are interrelated and interdependent with those of other residents, fulfilling them would require a prior satisfaction of the collectivistic needs.

References

ARC Start Network. (2021). *New insurance policy will protect up to 160000 People in Senegal from drought.* https://reliefweb.int/report/senegal/new-insurance-policy-will-protect-160000-people-senegal-drought

Angelino, L. (2020). Collective intentionality and the further challenge of collective free improvisation. *Continental Philosophy Review, 53,* 49–65. https://link.springer.com/article/10.1007/s11007-020-09484-y

Baarts, C. (2009). Collective individualism: The informal and emergent dynamics of practicing safety in a high-risk work environment. *Construction Management and Economics, 27,* 949-957. https://doi.org/10.1080/01446190903147501

Bochner, S. (1994). Cross-cultural differences in the self-concept: A test of Hofstede's individualism/collectivism distinction. *Journal of Cross-Cultural Psychology, 25*(2), 273-283. https://doi.org/10.1177/0022022194252007

Fletschner, D. & Kenney, L. (2011). Rural women's access to financial services: credit, savings and insurance. (ESA Working Paper N 11-07). Agricultural Development Economics Division; The Food and Agriculture Organization of the United Nations. http://www.fao.org/policy-support/tools-and-publications/resources-details/en/c/423752/

Levin, L., Benish-Weisman, M., & Savaya, R. (2020). Value profiles and perceived job performance of social workers in Israel. *British Journal of Social Work, 50,* 348-368. https://doi.org/10.1093/bjsw/bcz150

National Association of Social Work. (2021). Code of ethics. https://www.socialworkers.org/About/Ethics/Code-of-Ethics/Code-of-Ethics-English

Puroila, A.-M., & Haho, A. (2017). Moral functioning: Navigating the messy landscape of values in Finnish preschools. Scandinavian Journal of Educational Research, 61(5), *540–554.* https://doi-org.proxy.ulib.csuohio.edu/10.1080/00313831.2016.1172499

Schwartz, S. H. (1990). Individualism-collectivism, critique and proposed refinement. *Journal of Cross-Cultural Psychology, 21*(2), 139-157. https://doi.org/10.1177/0022022190212001

Seck, M. M. (2021). Methodology for understanding human behaviors in a social environment. In R. Prinsloo, & J. Ananias (Eds.), *Bridging the divide: Group work for social justice* (77-88). Whiting and Birch.

Tiampo, M. (2013). Gutai chain: The collective spirit of individualism. *Positions, 21*(2), 383-415.

Triandis, H. C. (1993). Collectivism and individualism as cultural syndromes. *Cross cultural Research, 27*(3-4), p. 155-180. https://doi.

org/10.1177/106939719302700301

United Nations. (2010). Les femmes Rurales et les objectifs du millénaire pour le développement. https://www.un.org/womenwatch/feature/ruralwomen/documents/Fr-Rural-Women-MDGs-web.pdf

Volkman, R. (2013). Collective intelligence and ethical individualism. *Computers and Society, 43*(1) p. 36-46. https://doi.org/10.1145/2505414.2505418

Community-Academic Partnership: A Successful Inter-Organizational Group Effort to Improve the Delivery of Government Social Services

Elisa D Giffords, John E. Imhof,
and Jaclyn McCarthy

This chapter examines an inter-organizational collaboration among members from the public and private sectors on a project aimed to assess and improve service delivery systems and client satisfaction at a Department of Social Services (DSS) located in a suburban area of New York State. This project began with a small group of nonprofit service providers, public administrators, advocates, researchers, and consumers that sought to examine clients' perceptions of the ease or challenges they experienced while seeking income support programs to help meet their basic needs. Similar to what Perrault et al., (2011) described, this inter-organizational community collaboration is comprised of government and nonprofit service providers (the community-based and the academic partners) who in this instance came together to address a perceived problem with service delivery. The article identifies how the working group initially came together to launch this research initiative. It continues by discussing each community partner's experience, identifies their group roles, describes how they developed a survey instrument, shares their data collection plan, evaluation results, and plans for improvement. Finally, the article reveals authors' individual reflections including barriers related to their experiences throughout the collaboration.

According to Knight and Gitterman (2018), "Group work is ideally suited to promote client empowerment and community change" (p.14). Groups of people will have a higher success rate of making substantial change within the community than if they worked alone (Breton, 2012; Knight & Gitterman, 2018; Staples, 2012). Group work is essential to promoting and initiating social justice and empowering communities and individuals (Hays et al., 2010; Knight & Gitterman, 2018; Ratts, et al., 2010; Staples, 2012). This working group collaborated to develop a plan to address concerns raised by clients. Analogous to Bronstein (2003), the authors view interdisciplinary or interprofessional collaboration as a process that best enables inter-organizational group members to effectively contribute or pool their own resources to achieve collective goals.

The target system in this instance was the local Department of Social Services (DSS). In this regard, the community partner is the entity that first called attention to the difficulties that the organization's clients experienced. Below readers will find a discussion of the roles relevant to each community partner within the context of this collaboration.

Public-private partnerships are not uncommon; however, they are not always meaningful or productive. The partnership or inter-organizational collaboration the authors discuss in this article was extremely rewarding for each member and fits the explanation of Mendel's (2013) depiction of a meaningful partnership, wherein all parties are in agreement that their collective action was transformative and strengthened each team member's ability to meet an identified outcome. In this instance, to (a) collaboratively seek out and complete a small grant proposal to submit to a local funding source; (b) develop a survey; (c) administer it to clients of DSS income support services to assess client satisfaction with the services received; and (d) share what they learned from the data and the experience.

To accomplish these goals the authors agreed to utilize the Participatory Action Research (PAR) model, an approach to investigation, which involves researchers and participants working collaboratively to understand a problematic situation and change it for the better, while simultaneously engaging members of the community in the research project (Kirst-Ashman & Hull, 2018). In this case, the community is comprised of clients from DSS who originally expressed their dissatisfaction with the services for which they sought assistance. For example, clients of the CBO stated their frustrations in not being able to speak directly with their worker and they reported having a difficult time navigating DSS policies and procedures in order to obtain needed services. This group of clients are key stakeholders as Kirst-Ashman and Hull's (2018, p. 439) description of the benefits of involving clients in research via PAR as they "are the ones most acutely aware of and affected by the problem." In keeping with the intent of PAR, the people impacted by the problem (clients of DSS), assisted the partners in the following ways: (a) to examine their complaints (study the issue), (b) to implement a plan to identify areas for improvement, and (c) to take concrete steps to facilitate data collection, and evaluate outcomes.

The Partners

Community Partner

Community-based organizations (CBO) are responsible for the overall welfare of the community and individual clients that seek assistance from them. In this respect, the primary focus of the CBO is to ensure that individuals in the community have access to and understand all of the available resources, and advocate to break down barriers and cut through red tape. Furthermore, CBOs are responsible for being champions of change by listening to the feedback of the community, working to make necessary changes and empower community members (Gitterman & Knight, 2016). The National Association of Social Workers (2017), states that "Social workers should act to expand choice and opportunity for all people, with special regard for vulnerable, disadvantaged, oppressed, and exploited people and groups" (Section 6.04 [b]). One main component of the social work profession and CBO is to enhance the well-being of both individuals and society (Bisman, 2004; Giffords & Calderon, 2015; Gitterman & Knight, 2016; Knight & Gitterman, 2018).

In order to effect change, social workers and CBO's need to embody their mission and values and then act in order to achieve them. The presence of a value or ethical code is an imperative for CBOs and social workers (Bisman, 2004). Lewis (1982) conceptualizes values as, "those enduring beliefs we hold about what is to be preferred as good and right in our conduct and in our existence as human beings" (p.12). These values drive the work of the social worker and CBO. Fleming and Caffarella (2000, Studies in Leadership, para. 2) emphasize that there is, "a focus on moral and ethical leadership, grounded in socially responsible beliefs and values". When the beliefs and values of individual leaders align with the values of the CBO, change can follow.

In fulfillment of its mission statement, when staff from the CBO partner CN Guidance & Counseling Services heard clients of several programs complaining about their difficulty accessing and obtaining services from the local DSS, the CBO took action to facilitate needed change by exploring the experiences of individuals accessing DSS services. In order to explore client satisfaction, the CBO partner reached out to the Commissioner of DSS to inquire about the feasibility of whether inter-organizational collaboration could take place to explore clients' perceived experiences at DSS.

The CBO group member first applied for a grant through the Long Island Community Foundation (LICF) to obtain needed financial resources to conduct a survey to assess the level of satisfaction of consumers to obtain services through DSS. The CBO also arranged for individuals with direct experience applying for services at DSS, referred to as "peers," to participate in the efforts to assess client satisfaction for which they received remuneration of $8.75 per hour for their work from the grant. The CBO group member was also a Co-chair for one of the subcommittees on the DSS Advisory Council. Through this role, the CBO group member had direct contact with the DSS Commissioner and the Chair of the DSS Advisory Council, who was the academic partner. The CBO partner presented this idea and potential to obtain grant funding to the DSS Commissioner who later brought in the academic group member, creating an inter-organizational collaboration to study this reported concern and seek necessary social changes.

The Department of Social Services Partner

New York Codes, Rules and Regulations of the State of New York ([NYRR], Section 18, 341.1 1976) states that each social services district shall establish an advisory council. All of the membership are appointed by the social services commissioner, including but not limited to community and nonprofit organizations, health and human service professionals, consumers, client advocates, members of the general public, and the business and financial community.

While New York State Social Services Law details the legislative origin of the advisory council's structure, function, and membership categories, there is no specific regulation that compels or mandates a DSS commissioner to accept any recommendation of an advisory council. However, to ignore or consistently discount its intentions and recommendations would not only be ill-advised but furthermore is entirely contrary to the spirit and intent of the statute. Therefore, with regard to the extensive groundwork carried out by the CBO and its presentation to the department, the DSS commissioner wholly embraced the CBO's initiative and recommendations that further steps were essential. The DSS commissioner became an integral part of this inter-organizational project and made DSS staff and resources available that would ultimately prove essential in the conduct of the study.

The DSS Commissioner's support of the project described in this article fulfilled the Department's mission statement of "providing quality services and maintaining the dignity and respect of those we serve" (Nassau County DSS, Annual Report, 2018, p. 4). Furthermore, DSS support of and active participation in the CBO's proposal indeed validated the intent and purpose of the legislation that established the creation of the DSS advisory councils. The DSS Commissioner realized that the project proposed by the CBO presented a unique opportunity for an inter-professional and inter-organizational collaboration that could move such a project forward and begin to directly challenge the perception that DSS was unresponsive to the needs of its constituents. Hence, being aware that the Advisory Council Chair was also an academic with extensive experience in research and program analysis, the Commissioner contacted the academic partner to discuss involving her in the project.

Advisory Council / Academic Partner

Benson, et al. assert "respectful collaboration between academics and practitioners" can identify, solve, and ultimately meet the needs of clients irrespective of how big the problem may be such as "poverty, environmental degradation, illiteracy, hunger, poor schooling, and urban crises" (2000, p. 24). Academic-community partnerships enhance research efforts, human services and resources, ultimately benefitting the community (Williamson et al., 2017). This was true for the partnership as well. The academic group member had the dual role of also chairing the DSS Advisory Council, which led to this member undertaking several roles. The most obvious role of the university partner is an analyst/evaluator. In this capacity the faculty member helped the working group to design a survey that enabled the members to collect information by lending expertise necessary to develop a questionnaire, to come up with a sampling plan (e.g., who will collect survey data and complete the questionnaire), and finally, to develop a strategy to analyze the survey data. The latter was accomplished in conjunction with the Director of Quality Management/Planning and Research at DSS. Additionally, the faculty member was able to link the working group with necessary resources such as the university's Human Subjects Committee and to ensure the group adhered to formal research protocols (e.g., Institutional Review Board (IRB] policies). This aligns with the literature that suggests agencies with limited resources may benefit by collaborating with universities because they gain access to those institutions' information, knowledge, skill, and empirical research Giffords & Calderon, 2015; Ostrander & Chapin-Hogue, 2011; Perlman & Bilodeau, 1999).

Method

Instrument

The three inter-organizational partners *CN Guidance and Counseling Services, Long Island University Social Work Program and Nassau County DSS* collaboratively created a 49-item survey to be completed by persons applying for or receiving benefits from DSS. The intent of the items was to identify what clients perceived to be obstacles in accessing social services. Additionally, the purpose was to measure clients' perceptions of the quality of DSS services, workers' attitudes, and clients' satisfaction of their experience with DSS. The work team all agreed that they would use the results to enhance services at DSS, to give a voice to clients and to share any lessons learned with policy makers. Once the group completed the first draft of the survey, they shared it with members of their own organizations. The agency partner shared the survey draft with clients of both the community and public organizations. The academic partner, who also has the dual role of chairing the DSS Advisory Council, shared the draft with members of the Advisory Council, who at the time represented 84 members from 60 agencies. This member also requested feedback from a sub-group of student volunteers. The DSS partner solicited feedback from a core sub-group of agency administrators. The academic and community partners worked together to integrate the feedback into the final survey instrument. Once complete, the community partner asked individuals with lived experience, or peers, who had received or were currently receiving services from DSS to review the items again and to take the survey. Accordingly, consistent with PAR, clients' perspectives and personal experiences are central to this work. Moreover, not only are clients the beneficiaries of this research, their involvement in this project led to increased confidence in their ability to make a meaningful contribution to this work. They expressed feeling empowered by their participation in the process and demonstrated pride when they later shared their perspective with the larger community regarding what it felt like to work with the inter-organizational partnership and to have their voices heard throughout the process.

Data Collection

The work team compiled a robust group of survey administrators that included DSS interns, students from the university and peers from the CBO. The university partner arranged for survey administrators and data entry volunteers to earn an NIH Office of Clinical Research Training and Medical Education certificate in order to protect human subjects. The university partner collected the certificates and sent them to the university IRB secretary. All survey administrators received training by the DSS Director of Quality Management, Research and Planning and were instructed to follow a simple script.

DSS clients were asked to complete the survey as they exited the agency, after they conducted their business. The survey administrators told subjects that their participation was voluntary and that they could withdraw from the study at any time without any negative consequences. Notably, their names were not included nor asked for at the time of administration. They were told, that should they decide to participate, that it would take about 20 minutes to answer the 49-item survey. Additionally, they were informed they would not receive any direct benefits for participating. However, the survey administrators explained that the empirical knowledge gained from the study would contribute to the scientific understanding of the population of people receiving DSS benefits through publications and presentations and used to make recommendations to the Commissioner of DSS. If the consumer said no, they were asked again to participate. If they said no again, they were thanked for their consideration.

The intent of this article is not to provide a rigorous empirical report of the authors' data analysis but rather to discuss their collaborative process. The authors decided it would be prudent however to share some results that provide readers with a context of how the outcome data challenged long-held stereotypes about DSS, including the notion that DSS staff were disrespectful to DSS applicants, that waiting times for service were unnecessarily long and that denials of benefits were subjective and arbitrary. The persistence of these general yet un-proven perceptions of DSS' reputation further spurred and motivated collective actions by the partners, and later in the discussion encouraged individual partner reactions and plans for improvement.

Results

The collaboration yielded nearly 500 surveys. Seven out of 10 visitors (69.3%) were satisfied with their visit to DSS, while 16.3% were dissatisfied, and 14.5% felt neutral. Security screeners (Public Safety officers) received high scores (86.4%) for treating visitors with respect, as did the Welcome Desk staff (82.9%). More than seven out of 10 visitors (72.8%) thought that workers treated them respectfully. Additional analysis demonstrated that although receiving approval does not seem to impact clients' overall satisfaction, accomplishing the purpose of the visit does impact overall satisfaction. Clients' satisfaction seemed to vary by visit purpose. For instance, clients reported above average performance if they went to DSS to recertify, or needed to drop off documents (80% and 83% respectively). If their visit was to get help with an issue such as housing (e.g., eviction, utility or homeless) client satisfaction was low (25%). Clients' satisfaction also varied by program area such as Medicaid (Approximately 84% satisfied; 9% neutral; 7% dissatisfied) or Temporary Assistance (approximately 59% satisfied; 17% neutral; 24% dissatisfied). The overall model used in the analysis reveals that clients' interaction with the worker was critical to driving satisfaction ratings, especially factors such as answering questions and explaining next steps.

Stakeholder Reflections

The opportunity to collaborate and further explore the anecdotal evidence gathered by the CBO yielded useful information that challenged the stereotypes about DSS. This project began when the CBO suggested that clients had a difficult time negotiating DSS policies and procedures to obtain needed services. Through collaboration, the inter-organizational group successfully worked together to design a survey that focused on several aspects of service delivery, including clients' perceptions and potential areas for improvement. They also worked together to analyze the results. There was no evidence found that clients are highly dissatisfied with their experience at DSS. On the contrary, most clients who participated in the survey reported that they were satisfied.

The partnership discussed in this article is notable because it recognizes the strengths of each group member. Allen-Mears (2008) emphasizes that a project of this nature can empower community members by enabling them to share their expertise, participate in setting project goals and objectives, and contribute to the outcomes within the collaborative. In this instance, the CBO's "peers" had the opportunity to share their perceptions of their ability to access and maintain services at DSS. Additionally, they had a role in developing and administering the survey and later shared the results with key stakeholders. Regularly scheduled meetings throughout the project and after its completion enabled the authors to periodically review, reflect upon, and share their experiences.

CBO

One result of this collaboration was sharing the results of the study with the larger agency including the Board of Directors. It demonstrated the ability for inter-organizational collaborations to address the needs of clients and the community. It also brought to light that the overall satisfaction rate of clients obtaining services at DSS was much higher than anticipated. In addition, it provided the ability for the CBO's clients to work, provide input into a large social service system and feel empowered by the ability to make a substantial change for not only themselves, but for their community.

In addition, the CBO was able to inform and educate other community organizations about its ability to replicate the collaborative process in its community, whether it be with DSS or another community provider. Outlining the lessons learned will help lead the way for replication of this process in other areas. The inter-organizational collaboration has continued between the partners. We have been able to present and educate social service agencies throughout our state with the hopes of encouraging them to replicate this process in their counties and shared this experience in professional conference presentations and in the classroom. Lastly, each organization brought its own unique strength and perspective to the relationship and without that, the project would not have been as successful.

The collaboration had overall benefits for each of the organizations involved, but it was not without challenges, in particular reconciling differences among the organizations. Each partner had its focus or area of interest and worked to bring those together to ensure that the process was beneficial to all.

DSS

The cooperative interaction of this community-academic-government alliance yielded many positive outcomes for the DSS partner. As noted in the authors' prior work that detailed the origins of the project, the outcome corroborated "what can happen when agencies decide to step outside of their comfort zones and strive to positively impact the individuals they serve" (Giffords, et al., 2019, p. 5).

Small and Uttal (2005) note that "developing collaborative, productive research relationships between academic and community partners can often be challenging" (pp. 936-937). Despite the challenges, the multi-year existence of the DSS Advisory Council previously revealed the three partners' capacity to discuss and collaborate on a wide variety of social and economic issues. This strengthened their working relationship and over time facilitated the willingness and cooperation of each partner to align itself as facilitators of the project.

Upon the opportunity to collaborate with its community partners, DSS mobilized the full range of its internal resources thereby enabling the project to proceed. With the support and encouragement of its academic and community partners, following the conclusion of the project, DSS initiated internal operational changes to improve its service delivery to clients. Despite its perceived organizational intransigence and complexity, DSS presented itself as a full working partner with its community and academic collaborators.

Advisory Council / Academic Partner

The university partner had dual roles in this project: (1) academic and (2) Chair of the Advisory Council. In this regard, the academic partner was able to help the group articulate a shared vision and to promote partners' agreement on common goals and to foster members – all stakeholders – sense of vested interest in the project. This partner saw the collaboration as an opportunity to work with two organizations to develop a survey, collect, and analyze data. This helped in fulfilling the academic partner's professional mandate to publish and disseminate information and to engage in service to the community. Additionally, this collaboration enabled the CBO and DSS to procure an expert consultant, which helped both agencies to bring their goal of conducting research about clients' satisfaction with DSS service delivery systems to fruition. Still, despite the incentives to collaborate, the initiative was not challenge-free.

Barriers

Several barriers impacted effective collaboration. The three organizations have different purposes and understandings about how to progress to meet project goals. The CBO, for instance, wanted the results quickly to "prove their hypothesis" and ensure that they remained in compliance with the grantor's annual reporting date. The academic partner emphasized the need to be patient with the process of developing the survey and underscored the importance of completing the IRB process. The timeline factor presented an additional challenge to the inter-organizational collaboration as the academic partner worked with the DSS partner to develop a rigorous plan for data analysis. Thus, despite the shared underlying vision of measuring client satisfaction with DSS service delivery, the academic partner believed that better communication about the research process could have assuaged some of the CBO's concerns.

Conclusions

Inter-agency collaborations are beneficial in that meaningful partnerships are possible. Maintaining open communication among government entities, community-based organizations, and universities is at times challenging but focusing on common goals will more likely result in a successful outcome. Professionals can look within their own communities, networks, and alliances to identify potential opportunities that may result in the improvement of services for clients and others in need. This successful collaboration can be replicated once partners establish trust and identify a common problem to address. Group members should establish a common sense of purpose and collectively determine primary goals. This commitment can lead to an evaluation plan that may bring about improved services, planning opportunities and strengthening the group's relationship to pursue further collaborations. The stakeholder groups worked to create a foundation for collaboration that continues to exist. Ongoing meetings through the DSS Advisory Council, which includes the CBO and academic partner, continue. Despite a leadership change within DSS, the partners apprised the new Commissioner about this study and she expressed interest in continuing the collaboration.

References

Allen-Meares, P. (2008). Schools of social work contribution to community partnerships: The renewal of the social compact in higher education. *Journal of Human Behavior in the Social Environment, 18*(2), 79–100. https://doi.org/10.1080/10911350802317194

Benson, L., Harkavy, I., & Puckett, J. (2000). An implementation revolution as a strategy for fulfilling the democratic promise of university-community partnerships: Penn-West Philadelphia as an experiment in progress. *Nonprofit and Voluntary Sector Quarterly, 29*(1), 24–45. https://doi.org/10.1177/0899764000291003

Bisman, C. (2004). Social work values: The moral core of the profession. *British Journal of Social Work, 34*(1), 109-123. https://doi.org/10.1093/bjsw/bch008

Brenton, M. (2012). Small steps toward social justice. *Social Work with Groups,* *35*(3), 205-217. https://doi.org/10.1080/01609513.2011.624369

Bronstein, L.R. (2003). A model for interdisciplinary collaboration. *Social Work, 48*(3), 297-306. https://doi.org/10.1093/sw/48.3.297

C.N. Guidance Center and Counseling Services (2019). *Annual Report.* https://centralnassau.org/wp-content/uploads/2020/12/CN-2019-Annual-Report.pdf

C.N. Guidance Center and Counseling Services (2021). *Mission Statement.* https://centralnassau.org/get-to-know-us/

Fleming, Jean E. A. & Caffarella, Rosemary S. (2000). Leadership for adult and continuing Education, *Adult Education Research Conference.* https://newprairiepress.org/aerc/2000/papers/24

Giffords, E. D. & Calderon, O. (2015). Academic and community collaborations: An exploration of benefits, barriers and successes. *The Human Service Organizations: Leadership, Management and Governance. 39*(4), 397-405. https://doi.org/10.1080/23303131.2015.1034907

Giffords, E.D., McCarthy, J. & Imhof, J. (2019). A social justice narrative detailing university-community-government collaboration: Improving health and human services delivery. *Social Work with Groups.* 43(1-2). https://doi.org/10.1080/01609513.2019.1639017

Gitterman, A., & Knight, C. (2016). Empowering clients to have an impact on their environment: social work practice with groups. *Families in Society: The Journal of Contemporary Social Services, 97*(4), 278-285. https://doi.org/10.1606%2F1044-3894.2016.97.34

Hays, D.G., Arredondo, P., Gladding, S.T., & Toporek, R.L. (2010). Integrating social justice in group work: The next decade. *Journal for Specialists in Group Work, 35*(2), 177-206. https://doi.org/10.1080/01933921003706022

Kirst-Ashman, K., & Hull, G. (2018) *Generalist practice with organizations and communities* (7th Ed.). Brooks/Cole.

Knight, C., & Gitterman, A. (2018). Merging micro and macro intervention: Social work practice with groups in the community. *Journal of Social Work Education, 54*(1), 3–17. https://doi.org/10.1080/10437797.2017.1404521

Lewis, H. (1982). *The intellectual base of social work practice: Tools for thought in a helping profession.* Haworth Press.

Mendel, S. C. (2013). Achieving meaningful partnerships with nonprofit organizations: a view from the field. *Urban Publications, 3*(2) 66-81. https://engagedscholarship.csuohio.edu/urban_facpub/673/

Nassau County Department of Social Services (2018). *Annual Report.* https://www.nassaucountyny.gov/DocumentCenter/View/25386/Annual-Report-2018?bidId=

National Association of Social Workers (NASW) Code of Ethics (2017) https://www.socialworkers.org/About/Ethics/Code-of-Ethics/Code-of-Ethics-English

N. Y. Comp. Codes R. & Regs. (1976) tit. 18, § 341.1, 18 NY ADC 341.1, (NYCRR).

Ostrander, N., & Chapin-Hogue, S. (2011). Learning from our mistakes: An autopsy of an unsuccessful university-community collaboration. *Social Work Education, 30*(4), 454-464. https://doi.org/10.1080/02615479.2010.504768

Pearlman, S.F., & Bilodeau, R. (1999). Academic–community collaboration in teen pregnancy prevention: New roles for professional psychologists. *Professional Psychology: Research and Practice, 30*(1), 92-98. https://doi.org/10.1037/0735-7028.30.1.92

Perrault, E., McClelland, R., Austin, C., & Sieppert, J. (2011). Working together in collaborations: Successful process factors for community collaboration. *Administration* in *Social Work, 35*(3), 282-298. https://doi.org/10.1080/03643107.2011.575343

Ratts, M.J., Anthony, L., & Santos, K.N.T. (2010). The dimensions of social justice model: Transforming traditional group wprl into a socially just framework. *Journal for Specialists in Group Work, 35*(2), 160-168. https://doi.org/10.1080/01933921003705974

Small, S.A., & Uttal, L. (2005). Action-oriented research: strategies for engaged scholarship. *Journal of Marriage and Family, 67*(4), 936-948. https://doi.org/10.1111/j.1741-3737.2005.00185.x

Staples, L. (2012). Community organizing for social justice: Grassroots groups for power. *Social Work With Groups, 35*, 287-296. https://doi.org/.10.1080/01609513.2012.656233

Williamson, H. J., Young, B. R., Murray, N., Burton, D. L., Levin, B. L., Massey, O. T., & Baldwin, J. A. (2016). Community-university partnerships for research and practice: Application of an interactive and contextual model of collaboration. *Journal of Higher Education Outreach and Engagement, 20*(2), 55–84. https://pubmed.ncbi.nlm.nih.gov/28184179/

Working with a Māori Model of Social Work Practice: An Experiential Lens to Support Knowledge Transfer for Students

Donna Guy

Introduction

Experiential group work is a critical component of social work education. Traditional education with its focus on passive lectures, does have a place, but is limited in relation to preparing social work graduates for the reality of social work as a profession (Colby, 2009). Only through the use of experiential group work can students experience, not only the accumulation of knowledge (surface learning approaches), but also the application of theory (deep learning approaches) (Hermida, 2014). Indeed, experiential group work has been replicated and adapted within social work education extensively (Pollio & Macgowan, 2010). The need for experiential group work in social work education is even more urgent for Māori, the indigenous people of Aotearoa New Zealand. Comprising 16.5% of the population, Māori have experienced 180 years of colonization policies, oppression and discrimination leading to an over representation across a range of disparities in social and economic status, education, health and overall wellbeing (Ministry of Health (MOH), 2015; Tertiary Education Commission, 2011). Consequently, Māori form a large client base for social workers; hence the need for qualified Māori practitioners who can work with their people and support the social and emancipatory transformation of their families and wider communities. However, the key to such success lies in the ability of teaching institutions to provide a culturally responsive pedagogy to enhance Māori student success (Bishop et al., 2009). Research clearly demonstrates Māori students require learning environments that are interactive, creative and include the provision of opportunities linking theory to practice (Curtis et al., 2012).

Aligning with this body of literature, new insights from the author's Masters' research highlighted student demand for more opportunities to translate theory learnt in the classroom to the reality of social work practice. Students spoke of the need for more interactive case studies, scenarios, role plays and/or simulations. According to students, such group work interactions were their most powerful and profound learning experiences. Importantly, these meaningful experiential activities increased their understanding and ability to transfer knowledge gained to their future social work practice (Guy, 2019).

To set the context for the workshop, an overview of higher education within Aotearoa New Zealand, particularly in relation to Māori learners will be discussed. A body of literature supporting the development and inclusion of experiential group work to enhance learning transfer for social work students will then be explored. To complete the literature foundation informing the workshop topic, an overview of the holistic model of wellbeing Te Whare Tapa Whā will be shared. The second part of this paper aims to provide a comprehensive overview of the workshop delivered. Step by step instructions, including comprehensive planning, briefing and debriefing components are included in the hope that readers will be positioned to adapt the workshop within their own practice as either a social work educator or practitioner. Finally, implications for future development related to the use of experiential group work in social work education will be presented.

Background

Context of Aotearoa New Zealand

In Aotearoa New Zealand, Māori are the indigenous people of the land (tangata whenua) and represent 16.5% of the population. Akin to other indigenous cultures, Māori have experienced over 180 years of colonization, oppression, discrimination and policies of assimilation (Harris et al., 2012; Masters-Awatere et al., 2019; Pihama et al., 2019).

The consequences of such practices (at an individual, micro and macro level) have left Māori featured within disparities across social and economic status, education, health and general wellbeing (MOH, 2015; Tertiary Education Commission, 2015). For example, it is likely that if you are of Māori descent (male or female) you are more likely to die eight to nine years earlier than non Māori New Zealanders (MOH, 2016).

Higher Education in Aotearoa New Zealand

It is not surprising coming from this place of oppression, Māori learners' experience in higher education is often a difficult journey, indicative of low achievement and completion rates (Arini et al., 2011; Ministry of Education (MOE), 2020). The dominance of western discourse and pedagogy within higher education contributes significantly to disparities in academic achievement. Government policy and education frameworks such as Tertiary Education Strategy, Māori Tertiary Education Framework, and the Ka Hikatia 2013-2017 Framework aim to improve Māori learner engagement, retention and success. (MOE, 2020; Sciascia, 2017). Durie (2009) acknowledges some improvement with this strategic direction, but in reality, delivery is still primarily a mono cultural western education system (Penetito, 2010, as cited in Savage et al., 2011). Sciascia (2017) concurs that there is still a lack of commitment to ensuring that Māori knowledge is as valued as western discourses.

A body of literature by Māori academics purports approaches in teaching and learning need to be embedded within a culturally responsive pedagogy (Sciascia, 2017). Indeed, what really works for Māori learners in the higher education classroom is very clear. According to Curtis et al. (2012), "In order to guarantee Māori student success, it is important for educational institutes to provide non-lecture based teaching and learning contexts for Māori students" (p. 28). Research clearly demonstrates Māori students require learning environments that are interactive, creative and include the provision of opportunities to link theory to practice (Curtis et al., 2012; Greenwood & Te Akia). Arini (2011) affirms interactive approaches can assist Māori student success. Likewise, a study by Apanui and Kirikiri (2015) highlights the need for dynamic, responsive and highly adaptive teaching that is rich in content and context.

Of significance, research confirms the use of such approaches to teaching and learning reduces the gap between high and low achievers, while also raising overall levels of achievement for all learners. In short, a culturally embedded approach promotes improved learning outcomes not only for Māori, but for all students (Berryman & Eley, 2017; Bishop et al., 2009; McNabb, 2019). Clearly traditional and more formal didactic approaches to teaching pose significant issues for Māori learners. Group learning is intrinsic to te ao Māori (Māori worldview) (Durie, 2001). As McNabb (2019) writes, experiential group work provides the ideal framework from which students can explore culturally responsive models of social work practice.

Theories of Learning

Experiential Learning Theory

The groundwork of experiential learning was developed by a number of educational scholars, John Dewey, David Kolb and Paulo Freire to name a few. All support that learning needs to be focused on learning by doing and learning through experience. As Dewey (1916) stated "an ounce of experience is better than a ton of theory simply because it is only in experience that theory has vital and verifiable significance (cited in Southcott, 2004, p. 2). Together, all these theorists offer experiential learning as a foundation for learning that will lead to learning as a lifelong process (Kolb, 2015; Kolb & Kolb 2005).

A body of literature highlights experiential learning as a critical component of social work education (Cheung & Delaega, 2014; Foels & Bethel 2018; Kolb & Kolb 2005; Skolnik 2019; Warkentin 2017). The use of experiential learning informed activities offers a foundation from which students can experiment and reflect on theory more closely aligned to the reality of future practice. As Brame and Biel (2015) state, only through the use of experiential activities can theory in the classroom be translated to future practice (as cited in Calvo-Sastre, 2020).

Kolb's four stage experiential learning cycle provides the framework for the experiential activity. Kolb's cycle comprises a concrete experience, reflective observation, abstract conceptualization and active experimentation. Participation in all four steps ensures students have 'hands on' experiences of engaging in course content and reflecting on the application of said content (Kolb, 1984; Kolb 2015). Put simply, the learner has an experience, reflects on said experience, and by utilizing other perspectives, draws conclusions about these reflections and links these to theories and concepts which in turn leads to experimentation and action (Kolb, 1984; Kolb, 2015; Kolb & Kolb, 2005; Yalom & Leszez, 2005). "This cycle of learning continues as students develop greater mastery of the material through an evolving process of practice and reflection (Kolb 1984, as cited in Humphrey, 2014, p. 63)

Critical Reflection

A key difference between experiential group work and some other forms of class group work relates to the inclusion and focus on reflection. Within the experiential approach, the student is the focus and the experience they encounter provides a basis from which critical reflection can then generate knowledge construction and thus, new learning (Kolb, 1984; Kolb, 2015). As Lombardi (2007) and Lazar (2014) write, requiring learners to engage only in a group experience is not enough, the experience must be processed by means of reflection and debriefing in order to maximize the value of the activity. Lazar (2014) adds it is therefore important that facilitators ensure adequate time for reflection and that substantial processing time is allocated

Learning Transfer

One of the most recognisable and widely proclaimed benefits of experiential group work relates to its ability to increase student opportunities for learning transfer (Furman & Sibthorp, 2013). A number of authors support the view that experiential group work activities and experiences have implications well beyond the classroom environment (Kolb, 2015; Woods et al., 2011). Unlike the more traditional didactic techniques, "experiential learning techniques foster a depth of learning and cognitive recall necessary for transfer" (Furman & Sibthorp, 2013, p. 17).

That most often, it is only through experiential group work activities that students gain a view of theory to practice, the reality of the application of course material to the 'real world'. (Hawtrey 2007; Lumpkin, et al., 2015).

Deep versus Surface Learning

Overall, the literature is clear, social work students require what Rhem (1995) and Biggs (1999) refer to as 'deep' rather than 'surface' learning' experiences. Surface learning approaches are those in which students are required to memorize content in order to be able to regurgitate information for examinations (Hermida, 2014). As Biggs (1999) elaborates, there is little connection of theory to practice as the primary intention of these approaches is to deliver large volumes of knowledge to meet course requirements. Biggs (1999) writes that a deep approach to learning gives students the opportunity to seek further understanding of content delivered and identify possible connections. Cohen et al. (2004) agree that deep learning is promoted through the application of knowledge, rather than just leaving it inert. A study by Kek and Huijser (2011) reinforced this belief when it determined that students who participated in problem based active learning, acquired deep learning rather than surface learning. Furthermore, this 'deeper learning' was statistically significant and had a direct influence on students' readiness for self-directed learning and hence, transfer of learning to their future profession.

According to Rowell and Benshoff (2008) and Bellefeuille (2006) well facilitated group work founded in experiential approaches are more likely to enhance student opportunities to participate in deep rather than surface learning experiences. Thondhlana and Belluigi (2014) along with Watts Garcia-Carbonell and Rising (2011) add that experiential group based activities can contribute significantly to achieving deep learning. Gibbons and Gray (2002) add further, deep learning experiences contribute significantly to optimal transformational learning outcomes for social work students.

Te Whare Tapa Whā A Māori Model of Health and Wellbeing:

Te Whare Tapa Whā is a holistic model of health and wellbeing often used in social work practice in Aotearoa New Zealand. Embedded in the public health system at a policy level, Te Whare Tapa Whā is a culturally responsive model also used across a range of sectors including mental health, education and justice. Initial development was instigated by a research project carried out by the Māori Women's Welfare league in 1982. Results identified the declining status of Māori health and over the following six months, Māori medical professionals, academics and communities sought solutions to the obvious failure of mainstream health services. Dr Mason Durie was tasked with building a holistic framework founded upon a te ao Māori (Māori worldview). Rather than being founded upon the western biomedical model, Te Whare tapa Whā takes into account not only Māori culture, values and beliefs but also the current social position of Māori. Key to the model, was the recognition and inclusion of wairua (spirituality) as the starting point for improving Māori health (Durie, 1985, 1998, 2001).

Durie's (1985) model Te Whare Tapa Whā aligns health (hauora) to the four walls of a house (whare). Each wall represents a specific dimension of wellbeing. Taha Hinengaro represents ones psychological wellbeing. The focus is on cognitive functioning, thoughts and feelings.

The dimension of Taha tinana represents physical wellbeing and refers to one's physical growth, development and wellness. Taha whānau represents family and social wellbeing. Importantly, whānau is the foundation of Māori society. In contrast to western notions of family, Māori Whānau /family extends past the typical nuclear family to comprise extended whanau siblings and grandparents. Of significance, friendship and other relationship groups (for example members of the International Association for Social Work with Groups) are also regarded as whānau. The final dimension represents Taha Wairua. *Wairua* translated literally means ones' soul or spirit and encompasses all aspects of spirituality (Durie, 1994, 2001). According to Durie (1985, 1998, 2001) each of the four dimensions (walls) are considered necessary to ensure strength, symmetry and stability. Only with a balance of all dimensions can optimal health and wellbeing being achieved. As Durie and Kingi (1997) state, if one dimension is deficient this impacts one's overall health.

Te Whare Tapa Whā: Theory to Practice

The section below will provide the reader with a comprehensive overview of the full workshop activity including instructions and debriefing questions.

Learning Objective One

Increase knowledge of an holistic Māori model of well-being often used within social work practice in Aotearoa New Zealand

In alignment with adult learning principles, the first task is to seek participants' thoughts and opinions in relation to each dimension of the physical (taha tinana) mental (taha hinengaro), social (taha whānau), and spiritual (taha wairua) wellbeing.

Instructions to access prior knowledge

Task: The facilitator invites group members to join one of four of the dimensions of holistic wellbeing. They then ask group members to identify key aspects of the dimension they have been assigned. Once discussed, members are asked to note each idea their group comes up with on the paper provided (one idea per piece of paper) and when the facilitator calls time, a group member can post notes/ideas under the appropriate dimension on the white board.

Feedback discussion

Each group then vocalizes their key aspects and the rationale behind their ideas.

Once all groups have finished, there is opportunity for the class as a whole to discuss and determine what each of the four dimensions might mean for them. It is important to note that at this point other participants might add their interpretation and the facilitator can add these additional thoughts on the white board for each specific dimension.

Linking prior knowledge to new knowledge

Once completed, the facilitator adds new knowledge (PowerPoint slides) highlighting key points and beliefs around each of the four dimensions. This again provides the opportunity for more class discussion and clarification. To conclude this section, a visual of the model is presented (see Figure 1). Participants are able to clearly see the four walls with each one being clearly labelled as one of the four dimensions explored.

At this point, discussion expands to the fundamentals of the model and how the four walls need to be symmetrical in order to keep standing. If one wall is unbalanced or leaning in a different direction, the whare (house) will be unstable. In essence, optimal wellbeing requires each wall (dimension) to be strong and well supported.

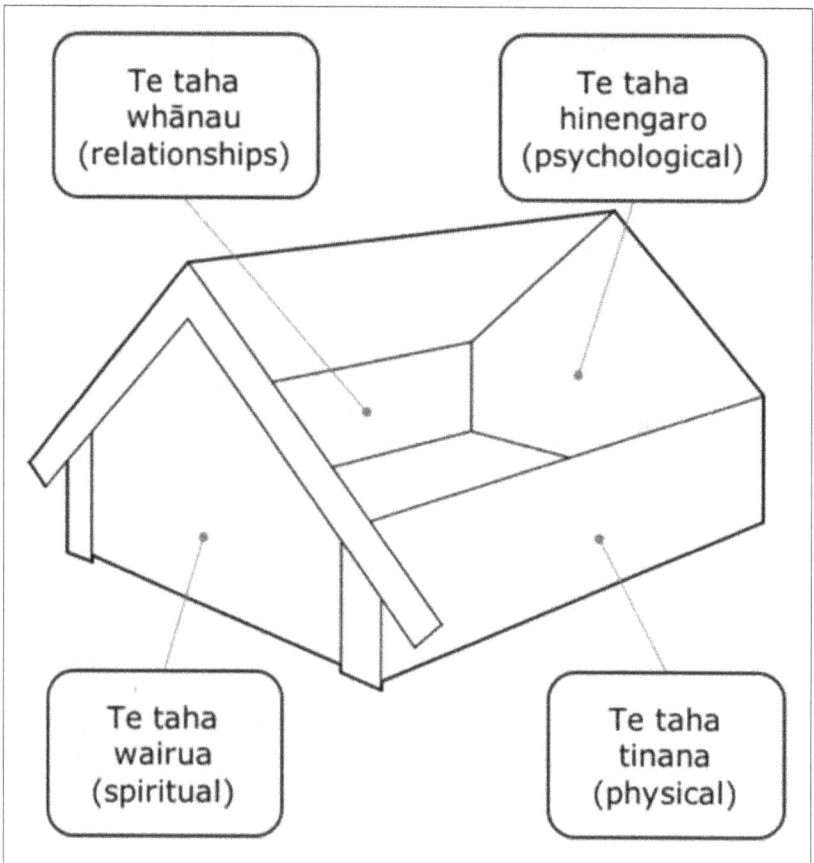

Learning Objective Two

Participants will engage in an experiential activity using a case study to increase understanding of the implementation of the model presented

This part of the experiential process aims to enable participants to gain increased understanding of the model, particularly in experiencing ways in which instability within any of the four dimensions can impact on an individual's well-being. Participants are advised that they will physically (using themselves) to construct a whare which will comprise four walls/dimensions; Taha tinana (physical); Taha hinengaro (mental) Taha whānau (social) and taha wairua (spiritual).

Group formation

Four groups, one for each dimension, will require need a minimum of 12-15 people.

Group membership remains the same as for first activity as participants have already fully explored one dimension.

Group members' roles and responsibilities.

One member from each group will represent a pou (post, support pole). The selected pou has a key leadership role as they will be responsible for holding up their group's wall (dimension). Be sure to select a physically strong representative for this role. The other group members will work together to represent one of the four dimensions (wall). Their role as a collective is to support their selected pou to ensure that dimension (wall/structure) is stable and stands strong. They physically do this by gathering together alongside and/or behind their pou. As the facilitator, advise participants that this involves some close physical contact which includes hands on shoulders/backs or similar.

Client's role and responsibilities

One person will represent the client. It is the facilitator's responsibility to scope class members for a suitable person to take this role. As they will be in a chair and physically lifted, it is useful and appropriate to select a smaller framed individual for this role. In terms of safety and risk management this position is not offered for someone to volunteer, rather the facilitator will ask individual(s) if they would be comfortable taking this role. Once an agreement is reached, the facilitator briefs them individually prior to the rest of the class receiving instructions.

Facilitator's role and responsibilities

Briefing

The facilitators' first job is to clarify roles and responsibilities for the activity.

As the activity involves physical engagement throughout, it is critical for the facilitator to provide clear and concise instructions. Like any experiential activity planning, preparation is key to successful implementation.

Explaining the activity.

After clarifying everyone's roles and responsibilities, the facilitator will then explain how the activity will unfold. The activity will commence with the chair (the client) being lifted in the air to about waist height by the four pou who are in a literal sense holding/supporting the client. Immediately, other members of each groups dimension will step in to physically support their pou.

Note: Other adaptations of activity:

- Sometimes useful to have a selected few to be observers, this helps to ensure people who do not want to engage can still have a role in the activity.
- If a small group, a ball can represent the client and be placed in the chair rather than a person. This can work well with groups of less than 10-12, although the debrief often is not as profound as when there is a person represented.

Ensuring risk/safety management.

Prior to commencing, the facilitator will clarify risk and safety management for engaging in this experiential activity. In the classroom, this is often an extension of the class group contract. Key aspects to be relayed to participants are as follows:

- Emphasis is placed on the need to always support your peers throughout the activity; no dropping people, joking around, pulling out unexpectedly, etc.
- Ensure surrounding environment is clear; remove obstacles that someone may step/trip over while stepping back and/or removing themselves from the whare structure.
- Ensure chair is rigid and stable for holding persons' weight.
- The final step before starting the activity is to allow participants in

each group/dimension to strategize and work out their structure for decision making. They also can practice moving into their position changes.

Facilitator implements the case study

From this starting position, the facilitator will then introduce a prepared case study related to the client (our person in the chair). The most effective approach is for the facilitator to read brief statements related to the client's life situation. Once each statement is read, the facilitator pauses, and members of each of the four dimensions have the opportunity to discuss and come to a consensus as to whether the statement delivered relates to the dimension they collectively represent.

If the statement does not relate to their dimension, no action is required. However, if the group statement does relate to a group's dimension, one member of the group will take a step back. The facilitator continues to relay further statements and the process is repeated. Over time the number of participants in each dimension will decline (NB: group members are able to strategize and move themselves into positions which best support their pou and the safety of the client in the chair). The eventual outcome sees the client being supported by only two or three pou. At this point the facilitator will end the activity.

Once the activity is underway the facilitator must be watchful and constantly gauge the safety of the 'client' in the chair. As the activity progresses, one dimension may find all group members having stepped back, leaving their pou to maintain sole responsibility for their dimension. Again, the facilitator must reassess safety making sure they are not under too much physical pressure. It is recommended that the facilitator check in with each pou intermittently to determine they are comfortable and able to maintain the task of supporting the client. The most significant part of the experiential process is next.

Learning Objective Three

Participants will engage in critical reflection & discussion in relation to clarifying transfer of knowledge learnt to their future social work practice

For the debrief component of this activity, participants form a circle with their chairs.

Timing of the debrief is often around 20-30 minutes depending on the size of the group.

The following are a range of reflective questions the author has developed to guide a comprehensive debriefing process.

Member debriefing

Person in the Chair – The client: (this person goes first).

The following questions are prompts to promote post-activity reflection:

How did you feel at the start of the activity? Secure, scared, safe?
How did you feel as people stepped away?
When less people were supporting you - how did you feel?
Did you feel a lack of stability? If so, what caused this? When?
What was your response to this lack of stability?

Members acting as the pou
- How did you feel at the start of the activity?
- How did you feel being in a more responsible position in the activity?
- How did you feel when group members started moving away?
- How did you feel when you felt your support weakening?
- How did it feel being the last man/women standing?

Members holding up the wall/dimension for the pou

- How did you feel at the start of the activity?
- How did your group come to a consensus when deciding if the statement(s) related to your dimension?
- How did your group manage the take a step back process? Who decided to take the step back?
- How did it feel when the first group member stepped back a little?
- How did it feel when a group member became completely out of the support structure?
- If you were a group member who eventually was no longer part of the support structure, how did you feel?

Knowledge transfer

The next step involves the transition of participants' reflections to the reality of social work practice. The objective here is to provide questions which will lead participants to make connections between what they have experienced and the reality of working with a client in practice. Some questions which have proved successful to enable this transfer of knowledge include:

- How would this activity help you to understand the position of the client in the case study?
- How do you think those family members (mentioned in the case study) are feeling about everything that is happening for the client?
- How do those feel who are located outside the clients' personal life (social worker, therapist).
- Can you transfer this model into your own practice?

Participants' feedback/integration of knowledge

The delivery of the experiential activity represented is one which has now been delivered to the authors BSW year one cohort since 2014. Similar to the author's Masters' research, course evaluations regularly highlight the value of being able to learn about Te Whare Tapa Whā in this way, and ultimately, student opinions that they are better positioned to transfer the model from theory to practice. Kiweewa et al. (2013) support these perceptions, writing that students require numerous opportunities to bring to the forefront the reality of dilemmas associated with social work.

The real learning and integration of knowledge is most often revealed during the debriefing, process. It is important to point out that the most profound learning outcomes correlate strongly to very little, if any input from the facilitator (apart from asking the questions). The power in the activity lies within the design of the reflective questions and the opportunity for students to work their own way through the feelings and emotions generated by participation.

The following are the most common outcomes for students:

Participant outcomes

The client (person in the chair).

Feedback from students in the role of the client is usually carried out first. Students always speak of some anxiety especially when they are dependent on the four groups to keep them safe. They have visibly seen and felt the instability when one dimension or aspect of well-being is removed and/or less stable. Likewise, the student in this role also conveys the physicality of being 'out of balance'. In every instance, students are able to metaphorically connect the client in the chair's feelings of powerlessness to the reality experienced by many social work clients.

The pou

The students who represent the pou often reveal the heaviness (literally) of their role as the leader of their dimension. As the activity progresses and group members leave they are consciously aware of the increasing weight they are carrying.

Group members for each dimension

These feelings of powerlessness are also voiced by students who participate as group members of each dimension. Students speak of their feelings of helplessness when they have to step back and/or are ultimately removed from the support structure; many describe feeling like they are abandoning their pou, and hence their 'client'. Again, being able to visually see the disruption of everyone shifting positions (which impacts on the 'client') tends to increase student's ability to transfer their own feelings and emotional response to the despair of a family/whanau member who may also feel helpless as they watch a loved one struggle with life altering situations.

Others speak of their struggle to make decisions collectively on the spot and knowing such decision making will affect others in their group, the pou and the client. This aspect ultimately leads to students correlating such decisions to the ongoing need to keep strategizing to ensure client safety in their future practice.

Discussion

The Power of Affect

Kiweewa et al. (2013) support such perceptions, stating students require numerous opportunities to bring to the forefront, the reality of dilemmas associated with social work. Interestingly, often the reality of such dilemmas creates not only new learning but often gives rise to emotions that are common place in the social work classroom. The majority of students always indicate the most powerful and positive group work experiences have been those that have evoked emotions.

The role of emotion in adult learning is not a new concept in the literature (Dirkx, 2008). Wolfe (2006) speaks of the benefits for students when learning takes place when the affective and cognitive domains flow into one another.

Yalom (1995) clarifies, only through such involvement can the student "...experience, on an emotional level, what they had learned through didactic training" (as cited in Anderson & Price, 2001, p. 111). Kolb (2015) agrees, for the most part these emotional reactions only occur during group work that is experiential in nature with strong reflective components. Most often students share their surprise of the depth of this emotion and indeed the empathy they feel after participating. Anderson and Price (2001) explain emotions created from such an experience provides the emotional component that encourages the development of insight and empathy in the student. Also of importance, students feel the learning experience is one which has 'stuck' with them ever since.

Increased Ability to Retain Knowledge

This notion that learning 'has stuck' or that affect increases students' ability to retain knowledge is well represented in the literature (Barkley et al., 2014; Wolfe, 2006). Students declare awareness that when emotionally affected by an experience, there is an increased ability to retain new knowledge (Guy, 2019). Dirkx (2008) supports these findings, stating the role of affect and emotions are directly linked to cognition and thus, support the ability to retain knowledge.

Conclusion and Implications

In conclusion, it is the author's view that social work education needs to be 'intentional' in creating rich interactive experiences from which students can identify connections from the classroom to the reality of future practice. The notion that group work provides students with the opportunities to put in practice knowledge accumulated is well represented in the literature. In fact, the opportunity to encapsulate the 'reality' of working collaboratively to implement Te Whare Tapa Whā in this manner always proves to be an emotional and deep learning experience for students. The opportunity to gain awareness in a physical and visual activity has provided students with an increased understanding of how the four dimensions interact and more specifically, the fundamental ideology Mason Durie (1985) proposes - the four dimensions of wellbeing (walls of the whare (house) need to be balanced. When there is instability in one dimension there is an impact across all four dimensions of well-being.

Therefore, it is fair to conclude that the use of experiential group work such as the one delivered in this workshop, offers a foundation from which students can experiment and reflect on theory more closely aligned to the reality of their future practice. As Gitterman (2004) writes, experiential learning is the foundation from which students can reflect on theory in a more real manner. Lazar (2014) concurs, experiential learning experiences are powerful and meaningful.

The development and implementation of experiential group work activities akin to the one featured in this paper are an important component of social work education. The evidence base founded in experiential learning, knowledge transfer, and provision of deep learning experiences is unarguable. Looking forward it is critical for social work educators to always seek to develop, adapt, and/or evolve experiential group activities to support student learning.

Also of significance was the connection made to this indigenous model by primarily all western participants who engaged in this activity. This was unexpected for the author. The holistic dimensions represented in Te Whare Tapa Whā appear to be easily transferred to a western discourse. The key difference, a dimension linked to spirituality, is one which workshop attendees (anecdotally) did not see as problematic. In fact, many stated they already practice in a manner which encompasses all dimensions, and that the experiential activity could easily be adapted regardless of nationality or culture.

As a current educator of social work students, and like other educators throughout *not only* Aotearoa, New Zealand but globally, there is an obligation to ensure graduates leave teaching institutions prepared for the complexities of the social work profession. Working in experiential groups throughout their degree is the optimal tool to increase the likelihood that they have developed the skills transferable to the reality of social work practice.

References

Arini, Curtis, E., Townsend, S., Rakena, T., Brown, D., Sauni, P., Johnson, O. (2011). Teaching for student success: Promising practices in University teaching. *Pacific-Asian Education, 23*(1), 71- 90. http://hdl.handle. net/2292/13472.

Anderson, R. D., & Price, G. E. (2001). Experiential groups in counselor education: Student attitudes and instructor participation. *Counselor Education and Supervision, 41*(2), 111-119. https://doi.org/10.1002/j.1556-6978.2001. tb01275x

Apanui, N., & Kirikiri, T. (2015). *Hei toko I te tukanga: Enabling Māori learners' success. Ako Aotearoa: The National Centre for Tertiary Teaching Excellence.*

Barkley, E. F., Major, C. H., & Major, C. H. (2014). *Collaborative learning techniques: A handbook for college faculty.* Jossey-Bass Publishers.

Bellefeuille, G. (2006). Rethinking reflective practice education in social work education: A blended constructivist and objectivist instructional design strategy for a web-based child welfare practice. *Journal of Social Work Education, 42*(1), 85-103. https://www.jstor.org/stable/23044080

Berryman, M., & Eley, E. (2017). Accelerating success and promoting equity through the Ako: Critical contexts for change. Asian Education Studies, 2(1), 99-112. https://doi.org/10.20849/aes.v2i1.126

Bishop, R., Berryman, M., Cavanagh, T., & Teddy, L. (2009). Te Kotahitanga: Addressing educational disparities facing Māori students in New Zealand. *Teaching and Teacher Education 25*, 734-742. https://doi. org/10.1016/j.tate.2009.01.009

Biggs, J. (1999) What the student does: Teaching for enhanced learning. *Higher Education Research & Development, 18*(1), 57-75. https://doi. org/10.1080/0729436990180105

Calvo-Sastre, A. (2020). Teaching social work with and through groups. *Social Work with Groups, 43*(3), 227-240. https://doi.org/10.1080/01609 513.201.1593918 Cheung, M., & Delavega. (2014). Five-way experiential learning model for social work education. *Social Work Education: The International Journal, 33*(8),1070-1087. https://doi.org/10.1080/0261547 9.2014.925538

Cohen, L., Manion, L., & Morrison, K. (2004). *A guide to teaching practice.* Routledge Taylor Francis Group.

Colby, I. (2009). An overview of social work education in the United States: New directions and new opportunities. *China Journal of Social Work, 2*(2), 119-130. http://dx.doi.org/10.1080/17525090902992339

Curtis, E. T., Wikaire, E., Lualua-Aati, T., Kool, B., Nepia, W., Ruka, M., Honey, M., Kelly, F., & Poole, P. (2012). *Tatou Tatou/success for all: Improving Māori student success.* Ako Aotearoa, National Centre for Tertiary Teaching Excellence.

Dirkx, J. H. (2008). The meaning and role of emotions in adult learning. *New Directions for Adult and Continuing Education, 120,* 7-18 https://doi.org/10.1002/ace.311

Durie, M. H. (1985). A Maori perspective of health. *Social Science & Medicine, 20*(5), 483- 486. https://10.1016/0277-9536(85)90363-6

Durie, M. (1994). *Whaiora-Māori health development.* Oxford University Press.

Durie, M. (1998). *Te mana te kawanatanga: Policies of Māori self-determination.* Oxford University Press.

Durie, M. (2009). *Towards social cohesion: The indigenization of higher education in New Zealand.* [Paper Presentation].Vice Chancellors' forum: How far are universities changing and shaping our world Kuala Lumpur, Malaysia. https://www.universitiesnz.ac.nz/files/aper_for_ACU_Forum_-_Towards_Social_Cohesion.pdf Durie. M. H., & Kingi, K. R. (1997). *A framework for measuring Māori mental health outcomes.* Massey University Department of Māori Studies Te Pūmanawa Hauora. Durie, M. (2001). *Mauri ora: The dynamics of Māori health.* Oxford University Press.

Greenwood, J., & Te Aika, L. H. (2008). *Hei tauria: Teaching and learning for success for Māori in tertiary settings.* Ako Aotearoa. National Centre for Tertiary Teaching Excellence.

Foels, L. E., & Bethel, C. (2018). Revitalizing social work education using the arts. *Social Work with Groups, 41*(1-2), 74-88. https://doi.org/10.1080/01 609513.2016.1258621

Furman, N., & Sibthorp, J. (2013). Leveraging experiential learning techniques for transfer. *New Directions for Adult and Continuing Education, 137,* 17-26. https://doi.org/10.1002/ace.20041.

Gibbons, J., & Gray, M. (2002). An integrated and experience based approach to social work education: The Newcastle model. *Social Work Education, 21*(5), 529-549. https://doi.org/10.1080/0261547022000015221

Gitterman, A. (2004). The mutual aid model. In C. Garvin, L. Guttierez., and M. Galinksy (Eds). *Handbook of social work with groups* (pp. 93-110). Guilford Press.

Guy, D. (2019). Maori student perceptions of group work in their social work degree. *Groupwork,* 28(2), 74-94. https://doi.org/10.1921/gpwk.v28i2.1202

Harris R, Cormack D, Tobias M, Yeh L-C, Talamaivao N, Minster J, Timutimu R (2012) The pervasive effects of racism: Experiences of racial discrimination in New Zealand over time and associations with multiple health domains. *Social Science & Medicine.* 74, 408–415. https://doi.org/10.1016/j.socscimed.2011.11.004

Hawtrey, K. (2007). Using experiential learning techniques. *The Journal of Economic Education, 38*(2), 143-152. https://www.jstor.org/stable/30042762

Hermida, J., (2014). *Facilitating deep learning: Pathways to success for University and college teachers.* CRC Press.

Humphrey, K. R. (2014). Lessons learnt from experiential group work learning. *Social Work with Groups, 37,* 61-72. https://doi.org/10.1080/01609513.2013.816919

Kek, M., Huijser, H. (2011). Exploring the combined relationships of student and teacher factors on learning approaches and self-directed learning readiness at a Malaysian university. *Studies in Higher Education, 36*(2), 185-208. http://dx.doi.org/10.1080/03075070903519210

Kiweewa, J., Gilbride, D., Luke, M., & Seward, D. (2013). Endorsement of growth factors in experiential training groups. *The Journal for Specialists in Group Work, 38*(1), 68-93. https://doi.org/10.1080/01933922.2012.745914

Kolb, D. (1984). *Experiential learning: Experiences as the source of learning and development.* Prentice Hall.

Kolb, D. A. (2015). *Experiential learning: Experience as a source of learning and development* (2nd ed.). Pearson Education.

Kolb, D. A., & Kolb, A. Y. (2005). Learning styles and learning spaces: Enhancing experiential learning in higher education. *Academy of Management Learning and Education, 4*(2), 193-212. https://doi.org/10.5465/amle.2005.17268566

Lombardi, M. M. (2007). Authentic learning for the 21st century: An overview. *EDUCAUSE Learning Initiative, 1,* 1-12. https://www.bemidjistate.edu/academics/distance/edge/wp content/uploads/sites/90/2016/02/AuthenticLearning_for_21_century.pdf

Lazar, A. (2014). Setting the stage: Role playing in the group work classroom. *Social work with Groups, 37*(3), 230-242. https://doi.org/10.1080/01609513.2013.862894

Lumpkin, A., Achen, R. M., & Dodd, R. K. (2015). Student perceptions of active learning. *College Student Journal, 49*(1), 121-133. *http://www.projectinnovation.biz/csj.html*

McNabb, D. (2019). Decolonizing social work education in Aotearoa New Zealand. Advances in Social Work and Welfare Education, 21(1), 35-50. https://www.anzswwer.org/wp-content/uploads/Advances_Vol21_No1_2019_Chapt3.pdf

Masters Awatere, B., Rarere, M., Gilbert, R., Manual, C., & Scott, N. (2019). *He aha te mea nui o te ao? He tāngata (What is the most important thing in the world? It is people). Australian Journal of Primary Health, 25,* 435-442. https://doi.org/10.1071/PY19027

Ministry of Education. (2020). *The statement of National Education and Learning Priorities (NELP) and the Tertiary Education Strategy (TES).* https://www.education.govt.nz/our-work/overall-strategies-and-policies/the-statement-of-national-education-and-learning-priorities-nelp-and-the-tertiary-education-strategy-tes/government-actions-in-tertiary-education/#accordion-18581

Ministry of Health (2015). *Tatau Kahukura: Māori health chart book 2015.* (3rd ed.). MOH.

Ministry of Health (2016). *Whanau hauora: Healthy families,* MOH.

Pihama, L., Reynolds, P., Smith, C., Reid, J., Smith, L.T., & Te Nana, R. (2014). Positioning historical trauma theory within Aotearoa New Zealand. *Alter Native: An International Journal of Indigenous Peoples, 10,* 248–262. https://doi.org/10.1177%2F117718011401000304

Pollio, D. E., & MacGowan. M. J. (2010). The andragogy of evidence based group work: An integrated educational model. *Social Work with Groups, 33,* 195-209. https://doi.org/10.1080/01609510903498617

Rhem, J. (1995). Deep/surface approaches to learning: An introduction. *The National Teaching and Learning Forum, 5*(1), 1-5. https://www.algonquincollege.com/pd/files/2019/04/Rhem-J.-1995.-Deep-and-Surface-Approaches-to-Learning.pdf

Rowell, P. C., & Benshoff, J. M. (2008). Using personal growth groups in multicultural counseling courses to foster students' ethnic identity development. *Counselor Education and Supervision, 48*(1), 2–15. https://doi.org/10.1002/j.1556-6978.2008.tb00058.x

Savage, C., Hindle, R., Meyer, L. H., Hynds, A., Penetito, W., & Sleeter, C. (2011). Culturally responsive pedagogies in the classroom: Indigenous student experience across the curriculum. *Asia-Pacific Journal of Teacher Education, 39*(3), 183-198. https://doi.org/10.1080/135986 6X.2011.588311

Sciascia, A. (2017). *Māori learner success in tertiary education: Highlights from Ako Aotearoa supported research projects.* Ako Aotearoa. https://ako.ac.nz/assets/Reports/Synthesis-reports/SYNTHESIS-REPORT-Maori-learner-success-in-tertiary-education-Highlights-from-Ako-Aotearoa-supported-research-projects.pdf

Skolnik, S. (2019). Coming together: Factors that connect social workers to group work practice. *Social Work with Groups, 42*(1), 2-17. https://doi.org/10.1080/01609513.2017.1384948

Southcott, J. (2004). Seeing the bigger picture: Experiential education in Tertiary music. *Journal of Experiential Education, 27*(1), 1-14. https://doi.org/10.1177/105382590402700102

Tertiary Education Commission. (2015). *Boosting outcomes for Māori learners in tertiary education: 2015 research findings.* Tertiary Education Commission Te Amorangi.Matauranga Matua. https://www.tec.govt.nz/assets/Publications-and-others/251a0f7efb/Boosting-outcomes-for-Maori-learners-in-tertiary-education-2015-research-findings.pdf

Thondhlana, G. & Belluigi. D. Z. (2014). Group work as 'terrains of learning' for students in South African higher education. *Perspectives in Education, 32*(4), 40-55. https://pureadmin.qub.ac.uk/ws/portalfiles/portal/129530806/Thondhlana_Belluigi_Preprint_Terrains_of_learning_Manuscript.pdf

Warkentin, B. (2017). Teaching social work with groups: Integrating didactic, experiential and reflective learning. *Social Work with Groups, 3*(40), 233-243. https://doi.org/10.1080/01609513.2015.1124034

Watts, F., Garcia-Carbonell, A., & Rising, B. (2011). Student perceptions of collaborative work in telematic simulation. *Journal of Simulation/Gaming for Learning and Development, 1*(1), 1-12. https://www.researchgate.net/publication/258098131_Student_perceptions_of_collaborative_work_in_telematic_simulation

Wolfe, P. (2006). The role of meaning and emotion in learning. *New directions for Adult and Continuing Education, 110,* 35-41. https://10.1002/ace.217

Woods, P., Barker, M. & Hibbins, R. (2011). Tapping the benefits of multicultural group work: An exploratory study of postgraduate management students. *International Journal of Management Education, 9*(2), 59-70. https://www.researchgate.net/publication/269536161_Tapping_the_benefits_of_multicultural_group_work_An_exploratory_study_of_postgraduate_management_students

Yalom, I. D. (1995). *The theory and practice of group psychotherapy.* (4th ed.). Basic Books.

Yalom, I. D, & Leszez, M. (2005). *The theory and practice of group psychotherapy.* (5th ed.). Basic Books

Group Work Practicum Education: A Community Based Anti-Bullying 3 D Group Work Programme to Create Hopeful Outcomes in Primary Schools

Elzahne Simeon and Marie Ubbink

Introduction

Social work and social work education are based on an old Chinese proverb "Give a man a fish you feed him for a day. Teach a man to fish and you feed him for a lifetime." The social work profession in South Africa (SA) has a growing demand for well-trained professional effective social workers who offer good programs (i.e., a three-dimensional learners, parents, and teachers anti-bullying social group work project (3 D Bullying Programme) (Nicholas et al., 2010). The practical training of social workers in the group work method is to teach students to do group work with the groups and teach group members skills to function better in communities; thus, demonstrating the second part of the named Chinese proverb.

In accordance to UNESCO (2017) 246 million children each year fall victim to bullying across the world. Bullying has been identified to be a major challenge for schools. There is an interlinked relationship between bullying behaviour and the physical and emotional welfare of learners. School social workers provide services to students to enhance their emotional well-being and improve their academic performance (Openshaw, 2008). Bullying is highly prevalent in SA (Boyes et al., 2014; De Wet, 2016) and according to Statistics South Africa (2015, as cited in Masilo, 2018) 70.3% of female learners and 66.6% of male learners reported being bullied in schools.

Swearer and Hymel (2015) are of opinion that a school's climate determines the frequency of bullying. Factors such as inappropriate educator reactions, dysfunctional educator-learner relationships, and a lack of educator support in school were all linked to higher levels of bullying (Richard et al., 2011). Educators plays an important role in the control of bullying in classrooms and in school environments (Yoon & Bauman, 2014). Studies have shown that educators' increased involvement in anti-bullying behaviour is associated with lower levels of bullying (Haataja et al., 2016) and that is why educators must be included in anti-bullying programs.

Bullying can be caused by factors that are connected to the parenting children are exposed to, like physical punishment and or abuse, alcohol, and or substance abuse (Brown, 2014). Limited research has been conducted into the perspectives of parents on bullying, which may contribute to our understanding of bullying victimization (Roodt & Ubbink, 2021). Parents are role models for children's relationship skills and attitudes for creating positive situations in how children interact others (Pepler & Craig, 2014; Van Niejenhuis et al., 2020). This highlights the importance of including parents in bullying programmes at addressing the bullying phenomenon.

Much has been learned about bully programmes used by schools in different communities (Rigby & Johnson, 2016). The Olweus Bullying Prevention Programme (Norway) – is one of the most successful multi-level programmes. This programme targets individuals, the school, the classroom, and the community (Farrington & Ttofi, 2010). Some of the different types of approaches in bullying programmes are proactive and other, reactive antibullying programmes. According to Farrington and Ttofi (2010) as well as Rigby and Johnson (2016), proactive anti-bullying programmes include: the employment of a whole-school approach, adults modelling positive relationships, curriculum work, cooperative group work, circle time, cyber mentoring, bystander defender training, and parental meetings. Reactive anti-bullying programmes include utilizing direct sanctions, restorative approaches, mediation, and support group methods, and methods of shared concerns.

Masilo (2018) suggested that social group work may be utilized for addressing bullying in schools. Some primary schools are asking social work organisations to help with group work anti-bullying programmes (Roodt & Ubbink, 2021). In the practicum training of students in social group work at the authors' university (North West University (NWU) in South Africa (SA)), an anti-bullying group work programme for primary school for children (learners) had been used in the past.

Toseland and Rivas (2017) named some of key advantages of groups, including mutual aid and the normalization of a problem. In terms of mutual aid, members may be helpful to each other through sharing their experiences, knowledge, and support. These advantages provide justification for using group work for the potential 3D bullying group work programme that will include learners, parents, and educators. This example programme can be used during undergrade students' training at social work organisations who would like to create anti-bullying programmes for primary schools.

In this article, we explore group work practicum education with the focus on how a community based on a potential 3 D Bullying group work program can be support hopeful outcomes in primary schools.

Context of the Social Group Work Education Modules

The aim of the Bachelor of Social Work (BSW) program is to provide students with foundational knowledge of social work (that includes social group work) skills and principles. The BSW program is a 4-year degree that is practice-orientated. Social group work method is one of the three primary methods (case work, group work and community work) in SA social work. At the NWU they have three semester modules in the group work method in the BSW programme. Social Work Group work theory modules are presented in the second year and third year for the undergraduates and during the final practicum of group work at social work organisations within the third year. According to Toseland and Rivas (2017) group work includes goal-directed meetings with treatment groups to meet members' socio-emotional needs. Activities in the meetings are directed to individual members and to the group with or to a larger community. Treatment groups, a type of social group, is practiced with persons with who have challenges with psychosocial adjustment and functioning. The group leader as facilitator acts as an enabler; enabling the group members to plan, organise and execute the group programme activities that will help them with their personal development (Ezhumalai et al., 2018).

The first theory group work module is intended to provide learners with a foundation of knowledge of social group work skills and principles. The module serves to introduce students to various aspects of social group work dynamics and processes, including stages of group work theory, decision making, formulation of a group, as well as understanding how group work fits into contemporary social work practice in a SA context (Ubbink et al., 2021)

Further, the second module is a theoretical and practical module covering the knowledge of group work and simulated learning activities. This module will guide the students in applying group work in practice. After the successful completion of the module students will have a greater understanding of the social group method of social work and how to apply it successfully in the profession (Ubbink et al., 2021). Rationale for the second group work module is aimed at equipping the social work student with the professional group work method, knowledge, and skills. To reach this goal, the student must master two basic components of knowledge and the practice of group work, as well as the interaction between the two so that they can apply them within a social work organisation during the third module. While in the second module, they practice the skills through simulated learning. The method of the group work practical's is based on the work-integrated learning (WIL) education model.

The third module includes work-based learning where theory and practice are integrated with the aim of guiding students in the practical application of group work in the community. Students are placed at social work organizations in the community where they lead a group, under the guidance of lecturers. The module consists of both theoretical and practical components and covers knowledge of the role of group work in social work. After the successful completion of the third module, students should have a greater understanding of the function of group work as a method of social work and be able to apply it successfully in their professional life (Ubbink, 2021).

The WIL leads to the placements of students at different social work organizations (i.e., Family South Africa (FAMSA) organization) who use different group work interventions for the different social work organizations group work needs in the community. The FAMSA organization is most approached in the Potchefstroom community to deal with bullying problems in primary schools and currently the bullying program that is only for children is used. The potential three-dimensional bullying group work program will most likely be used by FAMSA by the students placed with them. The practicum aims to acquaint the students with the group work methods specifically applicable to social work. It is expected of students to do the practicum as an important outcome of the group work module. The students then must present eight group sessions (to reach the outcome of the third module) regarding bullying in schools in the community over a period of eight weeks. Figure 1 displays the objectives of the bullying group work intervention that FAMSA now use for primary school learners.

Figure 1

Objectives of the Anti-Bullying Programme for Primary School Learners

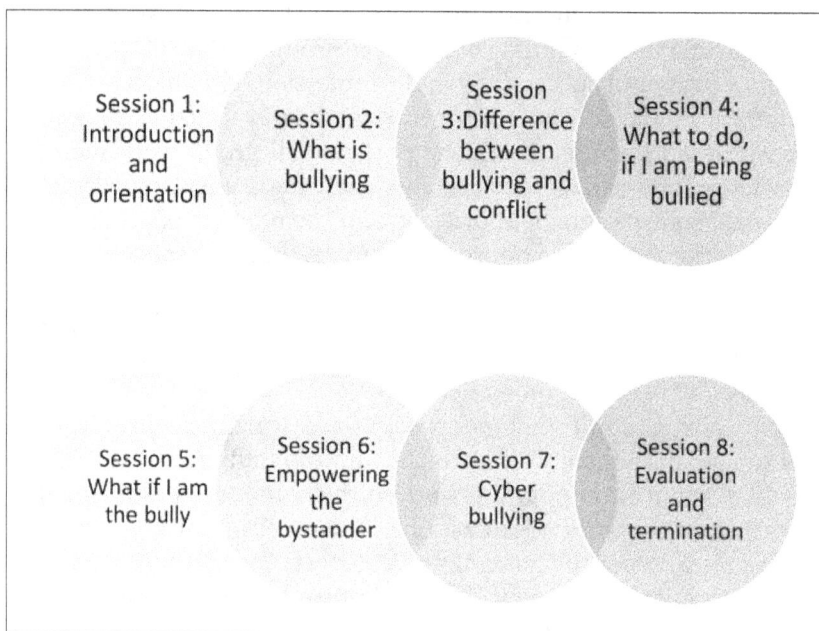

Session 1: Introduction and orientation
Session 2: What is bullying
Session 3:Difference between bullying and conflict
Session 4: What to do, if I am being bullied

Session 5: What if I am the bully
Session 6: Empowering the bystander
Session 7: Cyber bullying
Session 8: Evaluation and termination

(Simeon et al., 2019)

For social work students to comprehend and successfully execute treatment groups in practice, they need exposure to effective group work practices during their undergraduate training (Ubbink & Reitsma, 2021).

3D Bullying Programme

The Family South Africa (FAMSA) organisation where some of the social work students do their practicum, was approached by different primary schools to offer anti-bullying group work programs at the schools. One of the schools wanted a scientifically researched bullying program and not a program set up by social workers. The university took note. Two of the lecturers who guide the group work practicum students was familiar with successful bullying programs that have holistic approach for school settings. They then got the idea of a more comprehensive bullying program that includes the primary role players in the school and in the life of the child. The outcome of the thought process was the idea of the three-dimensional children (learners), parents, and teachers STOP bullying social group work project. The 3D (learners, parents, and educators) bullying group work program is based on the named previous project (the three-dimensional children (leaner), parents, and teachers STOP bullying social group work project) by two lecturers from the {NWU}, Potchefstroom, which received IASWG SPARC funding and endorsement in November 2018 (i.e., the three-dimensional children (learners), parents, and teachers STOP bullying social group work project) (SA), (Roodt & Ubbink, 2021). This social group work initiative comes from a collaboration between the university and a social welfare organisation in SA (FAMSA) to create a rising awareness of the need to eliminate bullying in South African schools. FAMSA, together with schools in the community, identified a need and asked the university if students who are doing their practicum could assist primary schools with group work which focuses on anti-bullying programs.

A need analysis through research can help to compile the 3D bullying group work program as effectively as possible for all the target groups (learners, parents and teachers). Two postgraduate students responded to this request. The research was done with the parents to see what parents preferred to be included in the programme based upon their needs and another student is currently collecting data from educators on their needs (Roodt & Ubbink, 2021).

The 3D Bullying Programme focusses on primary school learners, parents, and educators. Referring to the children, it is the child (learners – children in schools in SA are referred to as learners) who is bullying, and the child being bullied and others who observe the bullying. If we look at the parents, it is the parents of children who are being bullied or parents of children who are bullies and of the bystander child that experiences the bullying by observation. Finally, the educators who observe, with whom children report the bullying and must handle bullying and should try to prevent bullying.

When we look at the components of the 3D Bullying programme we must keep in mind that bullying can be defined as an aggressive behaviour which is repeated or have the potential to repeat itself over time and echoes a discrepancy of power between the victim and aggressor (DeVooght et al., 2015). If the child / learner is considered the first component-- bullying in a child's life can be considered as a harmful external factor that can lay a foundation for permanent damage which may have a negative enduring impact on a child's life, reaching to adulthood (Gibb et al., 2011). Further, if we look at the parent's component of the program, Lombard (2018) believes that parents have a big impact on their children's life. As these findings and Lombard's work demonstrate, providing anti-bullying programs that equip parents with practical information that they can use with their children at home might be a critical component of a 3D Bullying program. The educator's component, according to studies done by Meyer (2009) and Rigby (2014), the educators usually first notice bullying and they don't know how to handle it due to lack of training (Bauman, 2006). According to Sherer and Nickerson (2010), offering adequate training (informative workshops) and boosting adult supervision are the two key techniques to engage school employees in minimizing bullying behaviour.

The 3D Bullying program stems from a request from the community to develop a program to address bullying in primary schools. With minimal awareness of the demands of parents and educators needs for such a group work program, the lecturers, via postgraduate students explored parents 'and educators' perspectives to inform the development of the Three-Dimensional Bullying group work.

As already mentioned, a post graduate student conducted research with parents to determine what needs they would want to see address by the program. Notar and Padgett (2013) stated that adults are the foundation for addressing bullying and that they are instrumental in writing the programme, providing training, enforcing the programme, and reinforcing the anti- bullying attitudes of learners. If parents are included in programmes for addressing bullying, such programmes might be more effective (Pepler & Craig, 2014). However, the effectiveness of these programmes will depend on the extent to which parents are committed to addressing bullying in the school (Juan et al., 2018). The aforementioned post graduate student is now gathering information from educators. This group work research (Roodt & Ubbink, 2021) aligns with the IASWG's mission of "promoting excellence in group work practice, education, field instruction, research, and publication" and the SPARC program's mission of "sparking innovative practice, education, training, and research projects through endorsements and small grants" by contributing to the development of this evidence-based social group work programme for addressing bullying (IASWG, n.d.).

According to Roodt (2021) minimal national and international research studies involve parents for obtaining their insight on content of school bullying prevention programmes. The purpose of Roodt's (2021) research was "... to conduct a needs assessment to obtain parents' preferences in terms of the content that are to be included or addressed in a potential three dimensional-bullying programme (3D-bullying programme) for parents, educators, and learners in a South African context. This research study used a self-developed questionnaire and a cross-sectional survey at five schools in South Africa (SA) with varying socio-economic circumstances. The research methodology included a quantitative-descriptive survey design with the aim of gathering data to inform the development of a three-dimensional social group work school bullying programme to address bullying in primary schools" (Roodt & Ubbink, 2021).

The research of Roodt (2021) identified the following needs of parents to be included in the content of the potential 3D bullying program:

* Preventative measures – how to assess and prevent bullying at school
* Responsive measures – how to report bullying
* Protective factors – how to improve a child's self-esteem
* ^TGeneral guidelines – tips for dealing with the child that bullies, tips for dealing with children being bullied, bullying prevention techniques for parents, tips for bystanders of bullying
* Risk factors – how to model anti-bullying behaviour

As these findings demonstrate, parents seem most interested in general anti-bullying guidelines.

Conclusion

In SA social work education, social group work methods are classified as one of the primary social work methods. The BSW 4-year degree that is practically orientated, and the group work education/training include practicum in simulation and in welfare organisations in the community. Bullying in South African schools is a disturbing reality and the research on this phenomenon in the SA context is limited. The practicum done in the community showed how the partnership between a university and a welfare organisation in the community can be used to address bullying in primary schools. The need for a 3D (anti-) bullying programme for primary schools is clear, where an integrated approach to involve the children/learners, parents and educators can be used for more successful hopeful outcomes.

The potential anti-bullying programs should be an integrated focus on the children (learners), parents, and educators. A needs assessment from the parents and educators in primary schools is necessary before an anti-bullying program can be developed for the primary schools. This needs assessment should be based on the needs of the learners, the parents, and the educators. Prevention of bullying should be part of the primary school's overall behavioural framework and daily operations of schools. More awareness programs to prevent bullying should be developed and made available in communities. Implementation and presentation of the 3D Bullying programme should be sustainable at schools and not just a once off project. After the potential development and the implementation of the 3D bullying program, it is important that the program be scientifically evaluated to see if the program is working, and adjustments made to improve the programme.

Group work education is giving social work students a chance to actively participate in programs to address social issues such as bullying in the community. The potential 3D Bullying programme is comprehensive and can be contributing to the prevention of bullying in schools and helping students to gain the practical real-world experience they need. Students further get the opportunity to interact within their communities.

References

Bauman, S., & Del Rio, A. (2006). Preservice teachers' responses to bullying scenarios: Comparing physical, verbal, and relational bullying. *Journal of Educational Psychology, 98*(1), 219-231. https://doi.org/doi:10.1037/0022-0663.98.1.219

Boyes, M. E., Bowes, L., Cluver, L. D., Ward, C. L., & Badcock, N. A. (2014). Bullying victimisation, internalising symptoms, and conduct problems in South African children and adolescents: A longitudinal investigation. *Journal of Abnormal Child Psychology, 42*(8), 1313–1324. https://doi.org/10.1007/s10802-014-9888-3

Brown, T. (2014). *A review of a decade's trends in bullying in selected academic and media publications* [Unpublished Doctoral dissertation, University of the Witwatersrand].http:// wiredspace.wits.ac.za/ bitstream/handle/10539/18352/FINAL%20Thesis%20Tarryn% 20Brown. pdf?sequence=2&isAllowed=y

DeVooght, K., Daily, S., Darling-Churchill, Temkin, D., Novak, M., & Vanderven, K. (2015). Bullies on the block area: The early childhood origins of "mean" behavior. 1-32. https://www.researchgate.net/ publication/290607321_Bullies_in_the_Block_Area_The_Early_ Childhood_Origins_of_Mean_Behavior

De Wet, C. (2016). The portrayal of bullying in contemporary South African young adult fiction. *Child Abuse Research in South African, 17*(2), 49–63. https://journals-co-za.nwulib. nwu.ac.za/doi/pdf/10.10520/EJC198064

Ezhumalai, S., Muralidhar, D., Dhanasekarapandian, R. & Nikketha, B. S. (2018). Group interventions. *Indian Journal of Psychiatry, 60*(Suppl 4), 514-521, doi:10.4203/psychiatry. Indian Psychiatry_42_18

Farrington, D. P., & Ttofi, M. M. (2010). School-based programs to reduce bullying and victimization. *Campbell Systematic Reviews 6*(6). https:// www.ojp.gov/pdffiles1/nij/grants/ 229377.pdf

Gibb, S. J., Horwood, L. J., &, & Fergusson, D. M. (2011). Bullying victimization/ perpetration in childhood and later adjustment: Findings from a 30-year longitudinal study. *Journal of Aggression, Conflict and Peace Research, 3*(2), 82-88. https://doi.org/https://doi.org/10.1108/17596591111132891

Haataja, A., Sainio, M., Turtonen, M., & Salmivalli, C. (2016). Implementing the KiVa antibullying program: Recognition of stable victims. *Educational Psychology, 36*, 595-611. https://doi.org/doi:10.1080/01443 410.2015.1066758

International Association for Social Work with Groups, Inc (IASWG). (n.d.). *SPARC program.* https://www.iaswg.org/sparc-program

Juan, A., Zuze, L., Hannan, S., Govender, A., & Reddy, V. (2018). Bullies, victims and bully-victims in South African schools: Examining the risk factors. *South African Journal of Education, 38*(1), 1–10. https://doi. org/10.15700/saje.v38ns1a1585

Lombard, L. (2018). Guide against bullying. *Afriforum.* http://afriforum.co.za/ wp-content /uploads/2019/06/Teenboeliegids.pdf

Masilo, D. T. (2018). Social work interventions to address the phenomenon of bullying amongst learners in the school setting: A literature review. *South African Journal of Education, 38*(1), S1–S9. https://doi.org/10.15700/saje. v38ns1a1594

Meyer, E., J. (2009). *Gender, bullying and harassment: Strategies to end sexism and homophobia in schools.* Teachers College Press.

Nicholas, L., Rautenbach, J., & Maistry, M. (2010). *Introduction to social work.* Claremont: Juta & Company Ltd. ISBN 978-0-70217-768-2

Notar, C. E., & Padgett, S. (2013). Adults' role in bullying. *Universal Journal of Educational Research, 1*(4):294-297. doi: 10.13189/ujer.2013.010403

Openshaw, L. (2008). *Social work in schools: Principles and practice.* NY: The Guilford Press.

Pepler, D., & Craig, W. (2014). *Bullying prevention and intervention in the school environment: Factsheets and tools.* Prevnet.

Richard, J. F., Schneider, B. H., & , & Mallet, P. (2011). Revisiting the whole-school approach to bullying: Really looking at the whole school. *School Psychology International, 33*(3), 263-284. https://doi.org/http://dx.doi. org/10.1177/ 0143034311415906

Rigby, K. (2014). How teachers address cases of bullying in schools: A comparison of five reactive approaches. *Educational Psychology in Practice, 30*(4), 409-419. https://doi.org/10.1080/02667363.2014.949629

Rigby, K., & Johnson, K. (2016). *The prevalence and effectiveness of anti-bullying strategies employed in Australian schools.* University of South Australia, School of Education.

Roodt, W. M. (2021). *Parents' preferences on the content of a school bullying programme* [Unpublished mini-dissertation, North-West University].

Roodt, W.M., & Ubbink, M. (2021). Parents' preferences on the content of a 3D-school group work bullying programme: a needs assessment. *Social Work with Groups* https://doi.org/10.1080/01609513.2021.1972717

Sherer, Y. C., & Nickerson, A. (2010). Anti-bullying practices in American schools: Perspectives of school psychologists. *Psychology in the Schools, 47*(3), 217-229. https://doi.org/doi:10.1002/pits.20466

Simeon, E., Ubbink, M., & Mokwele, R. (2019) *The three dimension (children, parents and teachers) Stop Bullying Social Group Work Project, IASWG Symposium presentation.* New York.

Statistics South Africa. (2015). *Gender series Volume 2: Education 2004-2014.* Pretoria: Department of Education

Swaerer, S.M. & Hymel, S. 2015. Understanding the Psychology of bullying: Moving toward a Social Ecological Diathesis-Stress Model. Americam Psychological Association. Vol 70, no 4. 344-353. *http://dx.doi. org/10.1037/a0038929.*

Toseland, R. W., & Rivas, R. F. (2017). *An introduction to group work practice* (8th ed.). Allyn and Bacon.

Ubbink, M., (2021) North-West University West BSWP321 Studyguide: Social work practicum A.

Ubbink, M., Gertse, C., & Ntombela., N. (2021) North-West University West BSWI 313 Studyguide: Social Group work: Theory and Practical B.

Ubbink, M., & Reitsma, G. (2021) Group work education: Teaching through team-based learning to promote social justice in the learning community, IASWG symposium proceedings book: Bridging the Divide: Group work for social justice. Proceedings of the XL International Symposium of the International Association for Social Work with Groups, South Africa Edited by Reineth Prinsloo and Janetta Ananias, ISBN: 978-1-861776-28-0

Ubbink, M., Smith, E. & Gertse, C., (2021) North-West University BSWI 221 Studyguide: Social Group work: Theory and Practical A.

UNESCO. (2017). *School violence and bullying: Global Status Report.* https:// en.unesco.org/news/new-unesco-report-school-violence-and-bullying-be-released-international-symposium-issue

Van Niejenhuis, C., Huitsing, G., & Veenstra, R. (2020). Working with parents to counteract bullying: A randomized controlled trial of an intervention to improve parent-school cooperation. *Scandinavian Journal of Psychology, 61*(1), 117–131. https://doi.org/10.1111/ sjop.12522

Yoon, J., & Bauman, S. (2014). Teachers: A critical but overlooked component of bullying prevention and intervention. *Theory into Practice, 53*, 308-314. https://doi.org/10.1080/00405841.2014.947226

An Inclusive Basketball Club: Eliminating Barriers through Socialization of Individuals with Disabilities in the Community on a College Campus

Samuel Benbow

Introduction

Social inclusion for people with intellectual and developmental disabilities (IDD) continues to be a challenge for both individuals with IDD and community members without a disability (Jones et al., 2016). What makes it particularly difficult to achieve is when there is a lack of opportunities for mutually beneficial interactions that follow a non-hierarchical relationship. Most of the relationships of people with IDD and community members occur in service settings, which model relationships between "professionals" and "clients" thus perpetuating the attitude of "serving the needy" (Smith, 2003). To create more opportunities for non-hierarchical relationships, while bridging the gap between classroom knowledge and real-life experiences outside the post-secondary education classroom (Marra et al., 2018), an initiative on a rural college campus in south central Pennsylvania was created in 2007 entitled the Inclusive Basketball Club. d'Arlarch and colleagues (2009) suggests that there is a need in higher education to continue efforts to develop and nurture partnerships in the communities for which many of the students and employees reside.

Historical Context of the Inclusive Basketball Club

In the spring of 2007 a well-respected, accomplished disability and social justice advocate brought together several community members with IDD, agency employees caring for them, and a few undergraduate social work students interested in playing basketball at an outdoor park one Saturday morning. Playing basketball in this case meant bouncing the ball, passing to one another, shooting the ball close to or in the basket, retrieving the basketball, cheering for one another, engaging in small group conversations throughout the hour-long time together. The purpose of the outing was to provide an opportunity for community members with IDD to meet and socialize with individuals (social work faculty members and college students) outside of the IDD community using basketball play as the common thread. Through the common thread of basketball play, a mutual aid group was formed.

As the Saturday mornings outings continued, group norms were established such as no keeping score, taking turns, include everyone, celebrate success, engage in small group talk, and everyone is treated as an equal(no-hierarchy) member of the group. The group meetings continued several times throughout the late spring into the summer in response to the positive impact on the group. Several of the positive impact expressed were the experience meeting other community members, playing with college students and this author, developing relationships with people outside of the IDD community, and being treated as an equal to everyone else regardless of physical, intellectual and or developmental disabilities. To continue building on the success the Saturday morning basketball group activity was formalized to what has become known as the Inclusive Basketball Club.

Since 2007, the club has expanded to include an increase in the number and type of members with IDDs, student members, parent, family and supportive care givers, identification and inclusion of community partners, club advisors. Facebook has been used as the primary social media platform to communicate club updates, meeting dates for the fall and spring semester and pictures from various events. A more detailed breakdown of members and community partnerships are as follows:

* **club members/students:** These members include undergraduate students majoring in Social Work and Gerontology, Accounting, Business General, Teacher Education, Sociology, Criminal Justice,

Special Education, Psychology, Anthropology Exercise Science, and Communication/Journalism: undergraduate students minoring in Psychology, Criminal Justice, Disabilities Studies, Ethnic Studies, Gerontology, and the Army Reserve Officer Training Corp (R.O.C.T.) program: athletic program members from the Women's Basketball Team, Men's Basketball Team, Women's Softball team, Men & Women Track & Field, and the Cheerleading team. Most students do not identify as having an intellectual and or developmental disability.

- **club members/individuals with IDD**: These individuals have a diversity of intellectual and development disabilities such as traumatic brain injury, muscular dystrophy, visual impairment, paraplegia, multiple sclerosis, arthritis, hearing loss, autism spectrum disorder. They reside in personal care homes, full-care residential programs, in their own homes, and with supportive caregivers such as family members. Additionally, this group consists of family members, supportive caregivers and program employees who transport the individuals (in most cases) and often participate in the various games. Finally, most of the members reside within the local community.

- **club members/parents, family members, supportive caregivers, and agency employees**: These members include
Cerebral Palsy of Central Pennsylvania (*Non-profit organization that provides a variety of services to children and adults with Cerebral Palsy*), Merakey (*Non-profit organization which provides developmental, behavioral health, and education integrated services to individual and communities*), and Aramark Dinning Services (*American food service, facilities, and uniform services provider to clients in areas including education, healthcare, business, prisons, and leisure on the campus*). Aramark also provides a family style holiday meal (Thanksgiving) and food for the end of the spring semester celebration called the Inclusive Party. Finally, all events are held on campus, and are provided to all club members, their parents and supportive care givers at no cost.

- **club advisors:** Advisors consists of the primary faculty member of record (required for university club status through the Student Government Association), supportive and consistently present faculty member (this author), a graduate assistant enrolled in the MSW program, and an undergraduate BSW program student leader. The club advisors coordinate Saturday basketball club meetings via access to the gymnasium, orientation of new members, placement of tables and chairs in the gymnasium, student member sign-in, confidentiality statement and permission to take as well as post photos on Facebook.

* **Philosophy, Application and Case Example** The philosophy of the club is driven by the strength-based approach emerging from the field of social work. Saleebey (2000) stated that "the strengths approach obligates us to understand—to believe—that everybody (no exceptions here) has external and internal assets, competencies, and resources. These may be a realized part of a person's life, or they may be inchoate—unrealized and unused" (p. 27).

* **Inclusive Basketball Club Application:**
  Members Choice of Engagement
  All members chose their level and type of engagement or play throughout the entire time of the event. Their decisions are supported and respected, with encouragement from other members. No pressure is given if a member decides to walk away from play, requires space, shoots the basketball until they make the shot, even if it takes 30 tries to make the basket. Barriers associated with helpers attempting to control decisions and the associated perceptions that members with IDD are incapable of making decisions are eliminated and replaced with empowerment to decide for themselves.

Case Example

John is a tall, slender, gentlemen in his mid- 30s with physical and intellectual disabilities. He resides at home with his parents and participates in a community-social rehabilitation program throughout the week for which he is typically withdrawn from other attendees and the staff members in the program. He attends Inclusive Basketball almost every Saturday with transportation support by his elderly mother. As John enters the gymnasium, he is typically greeted by several members shouting "Hello". John responds by waving hello, with his head down, hurriedly walking towards the farthest basketball court in the gymnasium. His mother stands on the side and provides encouragement.

After a few minutes alone, John is asked if it would be okay to bring someone over to help him retrieve the ball. Sometimes he agrees and other times he doesn't. When he has agreed, we (faculty advisors) observed the tendency of John to be more talkative with female members (students), take turns shooting, and gently bounce pass the basketball. When John by female members about how he is doing, how his week went, and things he likes to do, John provides more in-depth answers than with male members. He also tends to ask similar questions of the female member playing basketball with him. With minimal guidance and direction from the club advisors, members engaging/playing with John have learned to ask general "get to know you" type questions and respect when he decides not to respond.

Increase Client Motivation by Placing a Consistent Emphasis on Client-Defined Strengths

When students and community members first participate in Inclusive Basketball, they are often concerned about their inability to play basketball and working with/ helping members with IDD in fear of physically or emotionally hurting doing something wrong. Great efforts are made to provide an orientation of observing and checking for personal biases before actual engagement. Experienced group members make sure the new members understand supportive language/word choice, culture of the play, and mindfulness of biases associated with members with IDD abilities, intellect, and fragility. Hopefully by initially observing and then interacting with members of the group, member strengths, interests and needs will be revealed versus entering the relationship predetermining what they are. Barriers associated with helpers prejudging, exercising their biases and fear the unknown have been eliminated and replaced with education and hands on application.

Case Example

Tanya was a senior-level Psychology major with a minor in Disabilities

Studies raised in Brooklyn New York. Tanya had past experiences observing and minimally interacting with children with IDD in an elementary school about 15 miles south of the university. Upon entering the gymnasium for the first time, she shared with this author her surprise at the number of people of color participating as she assumed that the only people of color would be she and I. The following are examples of her concerns: "I don't know Dr. Benbow, what if I throw the ball too hard!" "What if I say the wrong thing!" "What if they have a mental issue?" "Is this really safe?".

After Tanya attended eight of the 10 Saturday basketball sessions throughout the fall semester before her graduation, she truly felt like a member of the group/community. She stated "I can't believe the semester went by so fast! I'm really gonna miss my smile buddies Carol, Mike and Rick." When I asked Tanya to share a few take aways from the experience, she stated, "First, we all have strengths regardless of our abilities. Second, communication looks different depending on the person and I need to work on paying more attention to the nonverbals. Third, I need to get my MSW."

Discovering Strengths Requires Cooperative Exploration between Clients and Helpers

Within the Inclusive Basketball experience, members as well as club advisors engage in a number of activities which include warm up exercises for those who wish to participate, a 5–10-minute water breaks mid-way through the session, play within large group consisting of 10-20 members for a full court game, small group play with 2-5 members, and or individual play consisting of 1 player and a supportive club member on the sidelines monitoring, helping out when necessary, and group photos. Through these interactions, group members learn names, learn spatial comfort levels, physical abilities, personalities, sense of humor, concerns, meaningful past and future events (such as birthdays and anniversaries) career interests, and hometowns. Barriers related to assumptions about what a member with IDD are capable of accomplishing has been eliminated by the diversity in the types of play, diversity of members, and the strengths-based approach culture.

Case Example

I serve as one of the club advisors and when I play in the full court games, there are two members with IDD who amongst others attempt to score on me because of the physical size (6 foot 3 inches) and my expressed interest in my hometown professional athletic Philadelphia basketball and football teams. Joel and I are similar in age and therefore share a historical respect for the game of basketball and our two rival teams being the Philadelphia 76ers and the Chicago Bulls. Joel wears Chicago Bulls athletic gear each week and has created opportunities for us to talk about his journey to Pennsylvania, career interests, communication and play style, educational long-term goals, and our love of rhythm and blues (R & B) music of the 1970s and 1980s.

The other member Chris is much younger (early 30s), was raised in the local community, resides with his mother and is a true fan of the Washington football team (formally the Washington Redskins). While playing basketball, he tends to be preoccupied with talking about how good his team is and or how bad my team played in the recent past. This occurs when we are on the same team or on opposite teams. If on the same team, Chris makes his way over to me to say something about my team or his and then follows up with his favorite saying, "In your face". For non-basketball players, the term loosely means that I am going to shoot the ball and make the basket while in your face and your defense couldn't stop it. Joking with Chris and talking with his mother to sometimes seek assistance with understanding some of his phrases (Chris is difficult to understand sometimes, especially when he is excited because his words tend to blend) have been one of the true highlights and memories of Inclusive Basketball.

Focusing on Strengths Turns Practitioners Toward Discovering How Clients Managed to Survive vs. Judging or Blaming.

Throughout basketball play and the associated events of Thanksgiving dinner and the spring party, members develop trust and a level of comfort to share their life experiences with each other, regardless of the various roles within the group. Experience related to or outside of Inclusive Basketball, members with IDD often share them with student members with whom they have built a relationship.

Case Example

Suzy is a member with intellectual developmental delays in processing of certain information and paralysis in her left arm which is permanently bent at the elbow. She has an engaging, energetic personality and is fun to be around. She's under 5 feet tall, runs fast and dribbles just as fast down the court. She has tremendous ball control and usually shoots the ball more than 30 feet away from the basket and makes it! She resides in her own apartment with a great deal of support from family and is often seen walking in town with her significant other. Suzy shared with a student member that she has befriended over the past few years that she was pregnant and wanted to tell everyone but didn't know how or when. The student member double checked with Suzy's mother and the student club advisor (concerned about safety of playing while pregnant) informally to confirm that Suzy was pregnant and that it was okay to share with others. Mom replied, "it's okay, this is her family too."

Towards the end of the session, when we all stopped for a group photo, the student member and Suzy shared the announcement, which was greeted with celebratory cheers and excitement. Suzy felt supported, the student member felt honored and trusted and the club felt a part of the experience. Prior to the COVID-19 pandemic, Suzy returned to Inclusive Basketball with her mother, and newborn daughter. She shared with those who were crowded around, how tough giving birth was and how she was taking a parenting class with her mother to be the best mom she could be. She had the same commitment, energies and excitement that we saw throughout the three years prior to her pregnancy. We were all pleasantly surprised when Suzy stepped back on the court to play. She had the same energy, speed, competitiveness and shooting accuracy as before. During an office visit a few weeks later, the student club advisor shared from a revelation perspective how she unfairly assumed that Suzy would not be able to carry the baby to term, and or take care of the baby because of her disabilities. The student's revelation was that she was unknowingly perpetuating similar biases, stigmas, and stereotypes about people with disabilities as she experiences as a Black woman. She did not recognize this double standard at the time, however when she finally realized, it was equally important that she share this learning experience with me and others. This is another example of how Inclusive Basketball supported breaking done another barrier.

All Environments – Even the Most-Bleak – Contain Resources

Throughout the past 12 years or so of Inclusive basketball, some of the most unpredictable yet impactful resources have come from within the group. Resources such as a friendly smile, a pat on the back, employment possibilities, appreciation for program employees present, gently used maternity clothing, food pantry dates and locations, and school-based counseling support and vocational rehabilitation possibilities. In most cases the sharing of resources occurs in small informal conversations, or in a quick "good shot", "nice pass", "high five" comment from members.

Case Example

Initially parents, family members, supportive caregivers and agency employees would transport the member with IDD to the gymnasium and sit in the vestibule area outside of the gymnasium entrance or remain in their cars. Club advisors observed some nonplaying members completely disconnected from the event and others present. To address this issue, several small adjustments to the program were implemented to encourage active engagement. These included but were not limited to placing chairs and small tables inside the gymnasium (not directly on or near the court), joking with and cheering on members as they played, including everyone in photos (unless requested not to), discussing ways to best meet the needs of a particular member, asking and answering questions about community resources, and sharing of meaningful events in the lives of members such as birthdays, anniversaries, vacations, deaths and health concerns.

Calvin is in his late 30s to early 40s years of age and resides 45 minutes away from the university. He has learning disabilities which over the years have inhibited his ability to accomplish his goal of earning a college degree. He attends Inclusive Basketball with a personal aide that assists him with using appropriate problem-solving techniques, effective management of emotions when things don't go as expected and tempering his intensity when playing basketball. On several occasions we have discussed his interest in taking classes at the university and what it would take to be successful. Through Zoom meetings with Calvin, his mother, and the personal aide, we were able to honestly discuss past academic and behavioral challenges during his time at an educational rehabilitation center.

The center is located several hours south of where Calvin presently resides and is an educational rehabilitation center designed to assist people with intellectual and development disabilities to learn a trade. Calvin was unable to keep up with the educational demands and struggled to recognize boundaries with female students. Additionally, Calvin was living on campus with the much needed social and or emotional support. Once we were able to have genuine conversations with all support systems present, a plan for his success at the local community college was developed. Calvin was able to take one class, access tutorial support, live at home, and still use the support of his personal aide. Year's prior, Calvin's mother made the same recommendations for Calvin to consider community college as an option, however Calvin was not receptive. Based on the trust built over time as members of the Inclusive Basketball club, Calvin and his mother allowed me, as one of his resources, to help develop a realistic plan with a professional academic counselor at the community college to help monitor and guide Calvin towards completion of his goal.

Mechanics: Goal, Structure, Recruitment, Rules of the Game

Program Goals

The four goals of the program are to: 1) provide opportunities for non-hierarchical socialization of community members with IDD within and outside of the IDD community; 2) create opportunities to bridge the gap between classroom knowledge and practical application by using basketball play as the common thread; 3) increase partnerships with community members; and 4) increase the knowledge and experience of student interactions with members of the IDD community to increase awareness of personal biases, thus decreasing stigmas, stereotypes and prejudices towards people who are disabled.

Structure of the Saturday Session

The Inclusive Basketball sessions are held one hour per week for 10 weeks on a Saturday morning beginning at 11:00 am (EST) during the fall and spring semester, for a total of 20 hours per academic year. Student club members have been recruited by word of mouth, e-mail communication with an attached flyer to chairpersons in various academic departments, Facebook postings, posted flyers in key locations where students frequent around the campus, and referrals from other organizational components within and outside the university community.

Recruitment of Members

Recruitment of individuals with IDD, their parents, family members and supportive caregivers are done through word of mouth, e-mails, posted flyers in locations where IDD services are provided, Facebook and community connections of club members. Once recruited each member participates in a brief orientation during their first visit, which includes the club advisor explaining the purpose, philosophy, goals, and culture of the club in addition to the sign-in procedures (for students only). The initial visit for most of the student members tends to be in response to a course-related service-learning requirement.

Rules of the Game

In the beginning phase of this group work experience, the understanding of the purpose of Inclusive Basketball was communicated and then throughout the years, has been restated numerous times specifically for newcomers during their orientation. The members developed the group norms, rules, and expectations for participation, which includes the following:

1. **All who wish to participate can participate:** Participation is encouraged for as long or as short of a time and how much or as

little as the member wishes. Members use the assistance of canes, wheelchairs, safety helmets, and or whatever else they may need to participate.

2. **Participation looks different for every member**: Participation ranges from walking or moving around the gymnasium, cheering, shooting baskets on your own, shooting with two or more members, playing in the large group full court game and /or socializing with others on the side.

3. **Try and keep trying:** Players are encouraged to shoot until they make it, regardless of how many times it takes to make a basket. For several members with IDD, entering and remaining in the gymnasium is a positive stretch towards increasing social engagement in a safe, and meaningful way.

4. **No winners or losers:** We are all winners and although during the full court game where there are two teams, cheers and congratulations are given to everyone who makes a basket, or try, no matter which team you are on and if a member scores or not. For several members, remaining on the court throughout the time is an accomplishment.

5. **Halftime break:** Formal breaks are an integrated into the play time where there is no basketball play for ten minutes or longer as needed per individual choice.

6. **No skills required:** There are different physical and intellectual ability levels, basketball playing experience, motivations for participating amongst the members. It is perfectly okay if a member has never picked up a basketball or require assistance to be directly in front of the rim to shoot the ball. No skills are required, however a willingness to try is expected and reinforced.

7. **Practice respectful behaviors and attitude:** Members encourage and support each other through modeling kindness, encouragement, and celebrations in all types as well as levels of play.

8. **Dress code:** Members participate who are visually impaired, wear protective headgear, have minimal use of limbs or are unable to run. None of which hinders a member's ability to play, however comfortable and safe footwear is a must to help prevent falling.

Program Evaluation: Is the Inclusive Basketball Club Beneficial and Worth the Effort?

On average there have been 120 members participating in the Inclusive Basketball Saturday sessions throughout the academic year, which continued to increase each year from 2007 thru Spring, 2020 when the pandemic forced the closure of the club.

Club Member's/Students' Participation and Feedback

The club has experienced increases in undergraduate student involvement and awareness as evidenced by their reflection on written assignments, research interest, increase in internship requests in the field of disabilities, and increased student interest in pursuing an MSW to continue their practice within disability services.

With regards to mutual aid, students reported having initial fears of what it would be like, and or feel like interacting with someone with a disability. They feared saying the wrong thing, feared that someone (members with disabilities) could get physically hurt during the basketball play, (implying fragility as a primary characteristic of a person with a disabilities), feared the possibility of mental and or behavior outbursts (and how to manage it), and how to "treat" or "socialize" with them. These fears, mindsets and approaches implies that there are separate criterions, rules and guidelines when socially interacting with people with disabilities in comparison to those who present as not having a disability.

Their fear, and lack of understanding were influenced by social media, televisions shows and commercials, word of mouth, past experiences directly or indirectly observing or assisting someone with a disability and the use of case examples from class. Mittelmeier et al., (2017) suggested that one way to overcome cross-cultural group work tensions is to develop social relationships, because they are viewed as a necessary component of cross-cultural collaboration. Although their research focused on relationships between students from different countries, the cross-cultural perspective was clearly expressed in their fears, lack of understanding and preconceived attitudes, behaviors, and assumptions about the needs, wants and interests of those with IDD. The Inclusive Basketball club was able to assist students to reduce in some cases, eliminate their fears through developing social relationships in and between diverse group members in a collaborative, non-threatening way.

Club Members'/Individuals' with IDD Participation and Feedback

The club has experienced an increase in members with IDD participation, which has expanded into another program on campus and housed under the Department of Social Work and Gerontology called People Involved Equally (P.I.E.). P.I.E. provides socialization opportunities for community members with IDD, college students from various majors and or minors, as well as other members with IDD from the local community. Typically, five to seven club members also participate in this program in addition to 5-7 other IDD community members. The meetings are 90 minutes long on a Tuesday evening, 10 times throughout the fall, as well as spring semesters. Activities include salsa dancing, coloring, arts, and crafts, and limited outdoor activities created and decided by the members. Healthy, non-choking snacks and drinks are provided by the university dinning services such as diced up fruit trays, pretzels, diced up vegetables, water, juice and pretzels.

With regards to mutual aid, members have shared time and time again the reason for their continued interests in Inclusive Basketball is the support, relationships, and fun they have socializing with good friends and neighbors. They enjoy the college students, their fellow IDD members and look forward to the return of the program after the pandemic.

Club Members/Parents', Family Members', Supportive Caregivers', and Agency Employees'

The club has experienced an increase in active engagement and support from parents, family members, supportive caregivers, and agency employees. They share when a member is not able to make it, going on vacation and or other challenges that might impact attendance and /or participation. Several also joined in on playing basketball in various forms with members who were not directly connected with them. Their additional activities include helping to design and sizing for club t-shirts, taking pictures and posting to Facebook, pointing out possible play concerns, checking on players who walk out of the gymnasium to use the bathrooms or drink water from the fountains, and helping to decide on the dates as well as activities that will take place at the Thanksgiving and Spring Party.

Community Partners' Participation and Feedback

The Inclusive Basketball Club has expanded its reach to students and families representing three neighboring school districts. In one specific school district, the Special Education Department, Life Skills classroom teacher partnered with the Special Education Department on campus to create a campus-based employment experience on campus for high school and have invited these employees to participate in Inclusive Basketball as well as P.I.E. Also, the various partners previously mentioned have continued to provide transportation, the gymnasium, snacks and meals, activity space (Thanksgiving and Spring Party) at no charge to the club. Advertisements, games, and music for the spring events have been accomplished through support from various student organizations, collaborative sponsorships from various departments and university offices on campus and in the community.

Club Advisors' Participation and Feedback

The Inclusive Basket Club has had a tremendous impact on this author in a way that is unmeasurable. Opportunities were provided to become more mindful of my unconscious and conscious biases specifically towards inclusionary practices for people with IDD, and the ability to develop a non-hierarchical relationship with college students, community members with IDD and their supportive caregivers. Students and community members tend to elevate educators in a way that inadvertently creates a higher status mindset which forms unintentional barriers. With regards to meeting the goals, the club met its goals. Inclusive Basketball is an invaluable resource to the local community, the university, the social work profession and most importantly those of us who are now consider ourselves as members of the IDD community. Since the pandemic safety protocols prevent gatherings such as Inclusive Basketball, it is unclear what the future holds for the club, however our goal is to plan for its return.

Discussion

Feedback from members of the Inclusive Basketball Club demonstrated that students, members with IDD and their supportive care givers all benefitted from the experience. Student benefits were consistent with research showing the positive impact of service learning on college students from various disciplines to include positive changes in attitudes towards people with IDD (Carslon & Witschey, 2018; Kropp & Wolve, 2018; Sullivan & Mendonca, 2017; Santos et al., 2012; Smith, 2003). Members with IDD and their supportive caregivers benefited from an inclusive and equal status environment which fostered opportunities for social collaboration to promote learning (Mercer, 2008). Inclusive in this case refers to the equal opportunity to contribute, equity in the decision-making process, human rights, and democracy (Nilholm, 2006). Also, inclusion from a participation lens, requires respectful, mutual relationships in which the group members actively listen to each other's words, body language and ques throughout play. Shared contacts through meaningful interactions such as Inclusive Basketball, provide opportunities for members to develop cultural competence and shape a vision of inclusive clubs (Jones et al., 2016). Additionally, a 2014 study conducted by two BSW undergraduate social work students on the benefits of the Inclusive Basketball Club for members/participants, showed that what drove student members to continue their participation in the club were the "interactions, which made them close" and "being able to spend time with people and learn from each other" (Koening & Rutter, 2014).

In response to the COVID-19 pandemic, and the recommended social distancing safety protocols, the program has been suspended until such time as it will be safe to gather again. The plans are to continue the Inclusive Basketball Club in the near future.

References

Carlson, W., & Witschey, H. (2018). Undergraduate students' attitudes toward individuals with disabilities: Integrating psychology disability curriculum and service-learning. *Teaching of Psychology, 45*(2), 189–192.

https://doi.org/10.1177%2F0098628318762929

d'Arlarch, L., Sanchez, B., & Feuer, F. (2009). Voice from the community: A case for reciprocity in service-learning. *Michigan Journal of Community Service Learning*, 16, 5–16.

Jones, J. L., Gallus, K. L., & Cothern, A. S. (2016). Breaking down barriers to community inclusion through service-learning: A qualitative exploration. *Inclusion*, 4(4), 215–225. https://doi.org/10.1352/2326-6988-4.4.215

Koening, M., & Rutter, N. (2014). The benefits of Inclusive Basketball. A research paper prepared for the Disability Studies Capstone Seminar.

Kropp, J. J., & Wolfe, B. D. (2018). College students' perceptions on effects of volunteering with adults with developmental disabilities. *Journal of Higher Education Outreach and Engagement*, 22(3), 93–118. http://openjournals.libs.uga.edu/index.php/jheoe

Marra, L. R., Stanton- Nichols, K., Hong, Y., Gottschild, K., Pirzadeh, I., and Stamatis S. (2018). Design thinking as a strategic planning tool for adapted physical activity programs within a university setting. *Palestra*, 32 (4).

Mercer, N. (2008). Talk and development of reasoning and understanding. *Human Development*, 51,

90 –100. https://doi.org/10.1159/000113158

Nilholm, C. (2006). Special education, inclusion, and democracy. *European Journal of Special Needs*

Education, 21, 432-445. https://doi.org/10.1080/08856250600957905

Saleeby, D. (2000). Power in the people: Strength and hope. *Advances in Social Work*, 1 (2) 127-136

https://doi.org/10.18060/18

Santos, R. M., Ruppar, A. L., & Jeans, L. M. (2012). Immersing students in the culture of disability through service learning. *Teacher Education and Special Education*, 35(1), 49–63. https://doi.org/10.1177/0888406411413143

Smith, V. M. (2003). "You have to learn who comes with the disability": Students' reflections on service-learning experiences with peers labeled with disabilities. *Research & Practice for Persons with Severe Disabilities*, 28(2), 79–90. https://doi.org/10.2511/rpsd.28.2.79

Sullivan, A., & Mendonca, R. (2017). Impact of a fieldwork experience on attitudes toward people with intellectual disabilities. *American Journal of Occupational Therapy*, 71(6), 1–8. https://doi.org/10.5014/ajot.2017.025460

Evaluation of Group Work Practice: Status, Need, and Recommendations

Teresa Kilbane and Kristina Lind

Introduction

Social workers, bound by the standards articulated in the profession's Code of Ethics (NASW, 2021), are expected to evaluate their practice and engage in research efforts. Both assist in adopting evidence-based approaches to practice. Standard Five (5), Social Workers' Ethical Responsibilities to the Social Work Profession, Section 5.02 Evaluation and Research, lays bare specific activities which include monitoring and evaluating policies, program implementation, and practice interventions; promoting and facilitating evaluation and research to contribute to knowledge base; and critically examining current and emerging knowledge and fully use evaluation and research evidence in their practice among others (NASW, 2021).

The Council on Social Work Education (CSWE), the accrediting body for education of social workers in the United States, mirrors these expectations for its stakeholders. Of the nine competencies currently undergirding curricular standards, the ninth CSWE Competency states, "social workers understand that evaluation is an ongoing component of the dynamic and interactive process of social work practice". (CSWE, 2015, p.9) This competency presumes social workers "recognize the importance of evaluating processes and outcomes to advance practice" (CSWE, 2015, p.9). As the set of accreditation standards for American undergraduate and graduate social work curriculums, CSWE specifically identifies skill level needs in selecting appropriate quantitative and qualitative methods to evaluate practice outcomes, to conduct critical analysis of outcomes, and to apply findings for the purpose of improving practice effectiveness. Thus, while NASW and CSWE both recognize and expect social workers to pay attention to practice evaluation and research, the latter body spells out the expectation for social workers with more specificity. The directive is to evaluate one's practice, engage in critical analysis, and finally to apply findings to their practice and to the practice of others in the profession.

The International Association for Social Work with Groups (IASWG) also has its own set of standards for social work practice (AASWG, 2013). The standards encourage evaluation of group practice to include observation and measurement of the process, referring to formative evaluations, and on outcomes, referring to summative evaluations (AASWG, 2013). The standards identify the need for an evaluative task being to assess the group's progress towards meeting its goals in the middle stage of group development. Referring to the end stage of the group, the standards mention two important tasks for the group worker: to assess the progress of each individual and the group as a whole and to evaluate the impact of the group experience on the members and the external environment. Given that the evaluation of social work practice is a key requirement set forth by both the NASW Code of Ethics and CSWE, it is a professional activity which needs to be responsibly assumed. IASWG, the international association which serves to promote excellence in group work practice, (AASWG, 2013), speaks directly to social workers facilitating groups. Attention to evaluative processes in group work practice is required in the same way it is required by programs (macro level) and practice with individuals (micro level).

Simon and Kilbane (2014) studied the current status of group work given the changes in focus of group work in graduate social work programs. Their study focused on a survey of all accredited Masters of Social Work (MSW) programs in the United States and their curricular offerings of group work courses. A major shift within CSWE in 1969 was responsible for group work no longer being a stand-alone modality but rather, one adopting a generalist practice approach. Their findings supported others in the field (Goodman & Munoz, 2004; Salmon & Steinberg, 2007) that this pivotal moment marked the beginning of a decline of group work within the social work curriculum. This was also supported by an earlier survey of Birnbaum and Auerbach (1994), which marked a major decline in group work minors and course offerings for which Simon & Kilbane (2014) found continued support in the results of their survey. The goal of group work as a modality within the social work profession requires legitimacy and sustainability. This can only be achieved through the evaluation of group work practice which provides evidence-based support for this social work modality. While the values, expectations, and standards supporting practice research are acknowledged among social work practitioners, with fewer group work course offerings available to students, is equal emphasis provided to group workers on the need for evaluation and research at the mezzo level as is provided to those committed to micro and macro level practice?

This chapter is an appeal to social work professionals, educators, and social work leaders to promote and support evaluation and research activities among social group workers. This appeal is borne out of several questions raised about social work students and professionals who focus their practice at the mezzo level. Some of the questions raised are as follows:

- What is the ability of students, of social group work specifically, to undertake these evaluative and research-based activities?
- Are students attaining these requisite skills in their CSWE accredited programs?
- How do we educate current and future social group workers to ensure that they can uphold this ethical standard as is expected of them?
- What post graduate educational opportunities are necessary to support social group workers in meeting the ethical standard for practice evaluation and research? These supports can only be designed if we accurately identify the challenges social group workers encounter in engaging with any type of practice research.

On a fundamental level, the profession obligates its practitioners to determine whether targeted interventions are effective in promoting positive changes for clients. Evaluation of practice, which is one means of achieving this obligation, serves as an accountability process for agencies. Funders, administrators, and other agency decision-makers rely on evaluation outcomes to determine which programs to keep and which to remove. The quality assurance process in agencies is also aimed at accountability, not only to clients, but to the funders of programs and services within the agency. While the primary intention is the well-being of the client, agency administrators need to ensure that resources are dedicated to the best possible services which achieve the intended benefits.

The obligated assessment of interventions and programs should be achieved through a systematic process applying a basic research design. What follows is a step-by-step model for engaging in evaluative research, recommended for use by social group workers. It is hoped that this brief research design summary can be immediately utilized for group evaluative purposes. However, the questions articulated above persist and thus, the final section of this paper suggests future research to better understand the challenges current and future social group workers encounter relative to engaging in practice evaluation activities. It also recommends that the International Association of Social Work in Groups (IASWG) takes the lead in promoting and supporting the systematic evaluation of group work through sound research methodology.

Status of Social Work Evaluation of Practice

Available literature on social work evaluation offers some consensus on the type and amount of practice evaluation practiced by social workers. Findings suggest social workers are evaluating their practice to a moderate degree (Ventimiglia, et al, 2000). However, the preferred methods of measuring client outcomes tend to include the more pragmatic evaluation methods, such as clinician observation, client satisfaction surveys, and gathering client input (Baker et al, 2010; Kiefer, 2014; Ventimiglia, 2000). While there was mention of practitioners being open to more empirical approaches to evaluation and a sense that they felt prepared to do so by their educational programs (Knight, 2013), a few barriers to using them were mentioned. These include a lack of time and excessive caseloads (Baker et al., 2010; Kiefer, 2014), a lack of confidence, education, training, and supervisory support (Grady, et al, 2017; Kiefer, 2014), and confusion over evidence-based practices (Grady et al, 2017; Knight, 2013). Knight's study (2013) suggested that social workers in her NASW Chapter did not believe the evidence-based practice (EBP) literature was relevant to their practice nor did they understand the implications it raised in the literature. If this is a trend, it is a cause for concern but one which can be ameliorated. Suggestions are included in the section on recommendations.

Interestingly, group workers have a history of engaging in evidence-based practice (EBP) well before it was observed in other social work methods. Robust clinical research on the effectiveness of specific group models has played a central role in social work research (Pollio & Macgowan, 2011, p. ix). Annual meetings focusing on empirical group work have been taking place for almost two decades (p. ix) and well-preceded the current demand for EBP. Leaders within IASWG contributed significantly to group work practice evaluation, which helped to translate evidence-based approaches into the 'real world' of practice and community settings. These writings provide further clarification and development of evidence-based practice (Pollio & Macgowan, 2011). Thus, IASWG seems a natural choice to continue its leadership role in practice evaluation, to revisit the needs of its membership for support in conducting practice evaluations, and in suggesting new and creative ways of offering continuous training in evidence-based activities.

Review of Basic Research Methodology: Steps to Evaluation

To evaluate group practice, the worker must have some familiarity with research design. While workers can focus on a qualitative, quantitative, or mixed methods methodology, for the purposes of this paper, a review of the basic steps in a quantitative research process will be detailed as this is the one shown to cause the most anxiety for social workers. Group workers can use this review, which when followed, can help initiate a process for evaluating their mezzo level practice. This same review can also be used by IASWG to assist its membership in conducting evaluation of their group interventions. The following sections detail the steps involved in group work evaluation.

Developing the Research Question

As any effective group worker knows, one must establish the intention of the group (Rubin & Babbie, 2017). Only when there is an articulated purpose to a group, is one able to measure change against the backdrop of that initial purpose. It is helpful to think of desired outcome. Once the group has disbanded, what should the group be thinking, feeling, doing? Desired outcomes can be divided into categories, such as those behaviors or feelings that involve an increase in behaviors or feelings (i.e., more social connections, higher self-esteem), a decrease in behaviors or feelings (i.e., fewer temper tantrums, less crying), or changes in behaviors or feelings (i.e., changing child disciplining strategies). The research process requires the introduction of the group work intervention, sometimes referred to as the *independent variable*, for the express purpose of changing behavior. In research jargon, the outcome or changed behavior, which has occurred due to the intervention, is referred to as the *dependent variable*.

Once the variables are identified, a clear, simple statement consisting of research question, hypothesis, or purpose is required. This statement assists the researcher in determining the next steps in the research process. These include the research design, the tool selected to measure the intended change, and an approach for the final analysis. An example breaking down the steps in the design might clarify this process. For this example, a social worker is facilitating a group for female high school students who are struggling with low levels of self-esteem. An example of a *research question* for this group might be:

> Will female high school students participating in this group on women's issues (the intervention) experience an increase in feelings of self-esteem (the desired outcome)?

A more rigorous form of research would be to turn the research question into a statement of prediction. This type of evaluation indicates that the researcher has identified a body of research to support their research which allows for a prediction on how the group members will change with a particular intervention. An example of a *hypothesis* is as follows:

> Female high school students participating in a group on women's issues will experience an increase in feelings of self-esteem.

A further variation of the hypothesis is to add a comparison group; a similar group of members who do not participate in the group targeted for the intervention. A comparison group adds more rigor to the research design. More confidence can be achieved in the impact of the intervention if the participating group members change in the desired manner and the comparison group does not simultaneously do so. The hypothesis can be framed as follows:

> Female high school students participating in a group on women's issues will have higher self-esteem levels than similar female high school students who do not participate in the group.

Elements of Research Design

The research design includes the following components:

- *Independent variable,* which is the targeted group work intervention. It is believed to predict the desired outcome.
- *Dependent variable,* which is the outcome. This is the behavior or desired outcome this intervention is trying to impact.
- *Pretest and posttest,* which refers to the measures of the outcome or before and after the group intervention. A pretest determines whether or not the change occurred prior to or after the intervention was introduced.
- *Comparison group,* which can increase the confidence of the impact of the intervention. If the intervention has an impact, change will occur only for group members who participated in the intervention and not for those who did not participate, known as the *comparison group.*

Three Levels of Research Designs

Three levels of research designs are outlined below and each offers increasing degrees of rigor in the design, which in turn, yields increasing confidence to the findings. Regardless of the level of rigor, each level of research will offer some value to the researcher and practitioner. The intention of the researcher is to promote evaluation and sometimes, barriers on what can realistically be accomplished may prevent higher levels of rigor. The point is to evaluate one's practice even at the sacrifice of rigor. One way to increase the confidence in one's findings when rigor is an issue, is in replicating the research over time. This can add to a body of knowledge about the effectiveness of the intervention.

- *Design 1*
  Intervention occurs, measure outcome at the end, *post group design only*. It answers the question, 'what is the members' level of self-esteem at the end of the group'?

- *Design 2*
  Measure the dependent variable (outcome) before the start of the group work intervention, conduct the intervention, measure the dependent variable (outcome) at the conclusion of the intervention – *pretest-posttest one group design*. It answers the question, 'how much have the group members changed as a possible result of the intervention'? For example, how much change occurred in self-esteem levels at the end of the intervention and was the change large enough to conclude it was the result of the intervention.

- *Design 3*
  Measure the dependent variable (outcome) before the start of the group work intervention for both the group members in the intervention and a comparison group of similar members, conduct the intervention only for the intervention group, measure the dependent variable (outcome) at the conclusion of the intervention for both the intervention and comparison groups– *pretest-posttest comparison group design*. It answers the question, how much have the group members changed as a possible result of the intervention compared to a similar group of members who did not? For example, did a large enough change occur in the intervention group and no change in the comparison group allow one to more strongly conclude change was the result of the intervention?

Measurement

A critical element to the evaluation process is in deciding how to measure the outcome variable (Rubin & Babbie, 2017). The measurement tool used must be *valid,* meaning it measures what it is supposed to be measuring. It must also be *reliable*, meaning the tool, when implemented consistently over time, produces similar outcome results. If self-esteem is the target behavior, the research should ensure the actual constructs of self-esteem are being measured (validity). If measuring the target behavior repeatedly to achieve similar results, then reliability is achieved. Identifying or creating a tool to measure the impact of a specific group work intervention is a required component of the research process. The simplest ways of doing so, is in conducting a review of the literature to search for an appropriate tool. If the appropriate measurement tool cannot be located, the practitioner may develop their own, although the validity and/or reliability of that tool might become compromised. Some considerations in the measurement process are listed below:

- The tool needs to be sufficiently sensitive to detect change in the target behavior, i.e., increased knowledge about teen dating violence or decreased feelings of isolation.
- Evaluators need to ensure that the change being measured is reasonable relative to the intervention, its intensity, time interval, and characteristics of the group members.
- Evaluators need to consider the length of time to complete the measurements, its ease to completion, and the match of group member abilities to the demands of the measurement tool (i.e., if a questionnaire is being used as a tool, do all of the group members have the reading and other skills to understand the survey questions?).

There are multiple sources for existing tools. They can be found in journal articles, the internet, published volumes, and through resource web pages of professional associations. One example of a tool measuring self-esteem can be found here: (https://www.tutorialspoint.com/self_esteem/measuring_self_esteem.htm). There is value in using existing tools. Using already published ones is more efficient as additional time is not required for their creation. If the tool is standardized, it then has already been tested for factors of reliability and/or validity. There are some barriers to using existing measures.

At times there may be a lack of congruency of the tool to the target behavior being measured. Some published tools have financial costs associated with them. If some modification of the standardized measure is undertaken, the known reliability and validity factors will be compromised.

Group workers should not be dissuaded from creating their own tools, however. For those practitioners wanting to create their own tools, a few steps should be followed to ease the process. It can begin with referencing a textbook from prior research classes, perusing internet sources on creating survey tools, consulting with colleagues and experts in one's professional network, and/or attending conference presentations. Once the tool has been created, it requires pilot testing with a sample of individuals holding similar characteristics to the group members of the evaluation process. Modifications might be required, based on the feedback from the pilot testing. Experts in the field, colleagues, and consultants can be helpful in providing valuable feedback in the development of an appropriate measurement tool.

If time permits, triangulation in data collection is desirable (Salkind, 2010). Triangulation refers to the use of an additional source of data with which to measure the outcome variable. This serves to confirm or compliment the findings gathered from the primary data collection tool. Two tools resulting in similar findings provide greater confidence in the findings. Adding a qualitative data collection effort can add clarification and/or a deeper understanding of the quantitative findings. One example might be for group members to complete a standardized survey on levels of self-esteem. A way of triangulating this measure using a qualitative means might be to ask group members to keep a 'self-esteem' journal which reflects thoughts and feelings experienced on a day-to-day basis.

Analysis of Data

This stage in the research process is usually the most problematic for the practitioner for several reasons. Lack of knowledge or skill in data analysis, lack of available software options, and anxiety about utilizing appropriate statistical tests all can contribute to data analysis anxiety. Most practitioners will require specific assistance as they begin to evaluate their practice through systematic means. As with most new tasks, the more experience practitioners have in evaluating their practice, the more skilled they become. It becomes incumbent on experts to mentor and aid those who are new to group practice evaluation. There are data analysis software packages available for use by social workers, a popular one being the Statistical Package for the Social Sciences (SPSS). However, such packages may not be available to agencies or individual group work practitioners due to cost and support. Less expensive and more available resources are available (such as https://www.dummies.com/software/microsoft-office/excel/how-to-use-the-t-test-data-analysis-tool-in-excel/). Training might be required in using these resources effectively.

Group Work Practice Evaluation: Recommendations

We know that NASW, CSWE, and IASWG expect social workers to engage in practice evaluation as a regular professional activity. We also know that social group workers do not consistently evaluate their practice (Baker et al., 2010). Thus, it might be helpful to gain a deeper understanding of group workers' motivation, or lack thereof, for this type of activity. A needs assessment administered to practicing group workers could ascertain not only their motivation level but could also determine group workers' skill levels in practice evaluation, the strengths and barriers to engaging in such activity, and could gain a deeper understanding of practitioner perceived needs to engage in the evaluation process.

IASWG is well positioned to provide the necessary education, training, and consultation to those group workers interested in evaluating their practice. The Association is made up of an international cadre of group workers who have many years of expertise in the evaluative process and thus could be tapped to find creative ways of motivating group workers to conduct practice evaluations. There are several existing Association sponsored resources that might be utilized to meet this end. They are as follows:

Annual International Symposium

The Symposium provides an annual setting for possible institutes, presentations, and workshops focusing on evaluation research. Content can range from knowledgebase, skill development, to technical assistance. Sessions can be geared towards group sessions or individual assistance given to members with specific needs regarding their research. While this already occurs, the recommendation is to make this a more highlighted aspect of the annual Symposium.

Continuing Education Workshops

IASWG has experts in evaluation research on their Board of Directors and in the general membership. These experts can be utilized for a series of continuing education workshops on such topics as strengths and barriers within research design, creating a measurement tool, or analyzing and presenting data. IASWG would be providing a valuable service while establishing a revenue source for the Association.

Website Resources

A resource page specific to practice evaluation on the IASWG website can be established to post valuable resources for group work members to assist them in evaluating their practice. Resources could include measurement tools for data collection, affordable data analysis packages, information on how to use online data collection sources such as Survey Monkey or Qualtrics, or posting critiques of evidence-based group work practice articles.

Online Research Support Groups

Members interested in or actively conducting research in their practice could form a support group. The purpose of the group would be to serve as a resource to each other where feedback on current evaluation projects could be offered, and to provide encouragement, support, and assistance to one another. It also might be helpful for group facilitators to experience the realities of being part of a mutual aid group and experience the typical process issues which can emerge in a group.

SPARC

A committee within IASWG, its mission is to "'spark' IASWG members' innovative practice, education, training and research projects through endorsement and small grants to advance the IASWG" (IASWG, 2022). Group workers interested in evaluating their practice may apply for funding for their project through this committee. This would be of value for those projects that might incur costs.

Technical Assistance

IASWG can establish a technical assistance committee using research experts in the organization or seek outside funding. Members, as part of their membership dues, could then reach out to the specialized committee for support and consultation on the evaluation process.

Final Thoughts

Before expectations are placed on group workers to evaluate their practice, they first need to have the means to access the relevant resources and specialized assistance which meet professional, agency, and personal standards. As a profession, legitimacy from the public is necessary as this demonstrates that social work is backed by evidence-based methods to effectively assist their clients. From an agency perspective, group services are obligated to demonstrate to their funding sources that they provide efficient and effective quality services. Group facilitators are committed to providing ethical services which meet the goals of their members. Are group members better off because of participating in these groups? Practitioners need to be able to show that this is, in fact, the case. IASWG has a unique opportunity to be the major resource in assisting group workers to engage in group practice evaluation. At a time when group work is struggling for a place in the social work curriculum, while simultaneously being wildly practiced with or without the necessary background instruction, legitimacy achieved through evaluation of group practice seems essential and timely (Hessenauer & Lind, 2013).

References

Association for the Advancement of Social Work with Groups, Inc. (2013). Standards for social work practice with groups, (2nd ed.), *Social Work with Groups, 36*(2-3), 270-282. https://doi.org/10.1080/01609513.2012.759504

Baker, L., Stephens, F., & Hitchcock, L. (2010). Social work practitioners and practice evaluation: How are we doing? *Journal of Human Behavior in the Social Environment, 20*(8), 963-973. https://doi.org/10.1080/154337 14.2010.498669

Birnbaum, M.L. & Auerbach, C. (1994). Group work in graduate social work education: The price of neglect. *Journal of Social Work Education, 36*(2), 347-356.

Council on Social Work Education (2015). *Educational policy and accreditation standards for baccalaureate and master's social work programs.* https://cswe.org/getattachment/Accreditation/Accreditation-Process/2015-EPAS/2015EPAS_Web_FINAL.pdf.aspx.

Goodman, H. & Munoz, M. (2004). Developing social group work skills for contemporary agency practice. *Social Work with Groups, 27*(1), 17-3. https://doi.org/10.1300/J009v27n01_03

Grady M.D., Wike, T., Putzu C., Field S., Hill j., Bledsoe S.E., Bellamy, J. & Massey, M. (2018). Recent social work practitioners' understanding and use of evidence-based practice and empirically supported treatments. *Journal of Social Work Education, 54*(1), 163-179. https://doi.org/10.1080/10437797.2017.1299063

Hessenauer, S. & Lind, K. (2013). Preparation for group work: Perceptions of bachelor-level social workers. *Journal of Baccalaureate Social Work, 18*, 1-16. https://doi.org/10.18084/basw.18.1.r7x5514345426760

IASWG. (n.d.). SPARC program. https://www.iaswg.org/sparc-program.

Kiefer, L. (2014). How social work practitioners evaluate their practice. https://sophia.stkate.edu/msw_papers/55NASW https://naswor.socialworkers.org/Membership/Resources/Code-of-Ethics" https://naswor.socialworkers.org/Membership/Resources/Code-of-Ethics.

Knight, C. (2013) Social workers› attitudes toward peer-reviewed literature: The evidence base. *Journal of Teaching in Social Work*, 33(2), 177-195. https://doi.org/10.1080/08841233.2013.773955

NASW, 2021. Code of Ethics among National Association of Social Workers, Revised Code of Ethics. https://www.socialworkers.org/About/Ethics/Code-of-Ethics/Code-of-Ethics-English

Nelson, S.L. & Nelson, E.C. (n.d.). *How to use the t-test data analysis tool in Excel.* https://www.dummies.com/software/microsoft-office/excel/how-to-use-the-t-test-data-analysis-tool-in-excel/.

Pollio, D. & Macgowan, M. (Eds.). (2010). Evidence-based group work in community settings. *Social Work with Groups*, 33(2-3), 98-101. https://doi-org.libproxy.plymouth.edu/10.1080/01609510903452994

Rubin, A. & Babbie, E. (2017). *Empowerment series: Research methods for social work* (9th ed.). Cengage Learning.

Salkind, N. J. (2010). Triangulation. In *Encyclopedia of research design* (Vol. 1, pp. 1538-1540). SAGE Publications.

Salmon, R. & Steinberg, D. (2012). Revisiting 'joyful noise': Gateways from Singing the Blues to the Hallelujah Chorus. Talking in the idiom of the other: A necessary skill for responding to the current crisis in social work practice. In G. J. Tully, K. Sweeney, and S. E. Palumbo (Eds.), *Group work: Gateways to growth*. Whiting & Birch, LTD.

Simon. S. & Kilbane, T. (2014). The current state of group work education in U.S. graduate schools of social work. *Social Work with Groups*, *37*(3), 243-256. http://dx.doi.org/10.1080/01609513.2013.840821

TutorialsPoint. (n.d.). *Measuring self-esteem.* https://www.tutorialspoint.com/self_esteem/measuring_self_esteem.htm.

Ventimiglia, J., Marschke, J., Carmichael, P., & Loew. R. (2000). How do clinicians evaluate their practice effectiveness? A survey of clinical social workers. *Smith College Studies in Social Work, 70*(2), 287-306. https://doi.org/10.1080/00377310009517593

Index

Note: Page locators in *italic* refer to figures.

Heise, L. 20, 21, 26
helping others 59, 60
Hessenauer, S. 216
higher education in Aotearoa New Zealand 154–155
human rights 78–80
   categories 79–80
   international treaties 79
   praxis approach to group work 82–83
      amid current events in US 77
      conscious use of self 83–84
      limitations and further considerations 88–89
      participatory democracy 86–88
      relationships 85–86
   and social work 80–82
   Universal Declaration of Human Rights 78, 79, 81, 83, 85, 86
   violations 17, 25, 78, 81, 83, 84, 88
husbands of child brides, engaging with 27–28
hypermasculinity 43
hypotheses 208–209

Iacono, G. 2, 3, 4
independent variables 208, 209
individualism-collectivism *see* collective-individualism
infidelity, perceived, and domestic violence against men 113–114
injunctive norms 21
intellectual and developmental disabilities (IDD), socialization of people
      with *see* basketball club, inclusive
International Association for Social Work with Groups (IASWG) 7, 80–81,
      83, 84
   Annual Symposium 52, 125, 214
   leadership in group work practice evaluation 206, 207, 213
   SPARC 179, 181, 215
   sponsored resources for practice evaluations 213–215
   standards 85, 204
International Covenant on Civil and Political Rights (ICCPR) 79
International Covenant on Economic, Social, and Cultural Rights
      (ICESCR) 79–80
International Federation of Social Workers (IFSW) 81
international human rights treaties 79
interpersonal learning 60
Interpretative Phenomenological Analysis (IPA) 110
invitational practice 39

www.ingramcontent.com/pod-product-compliance
Lightning Source LLC
Chambersburg PA
CBHW050419280326
41932CB00013BA/1925